Norm Kohrer

Saints
in
Sandals

Saints in Sandals

Maude De Joseph West

BAKER BOOK HOUSE • Grand Rapids, Michigan

ISBN: 0-8010-9570-0

Printed in the United States of America

To my mother, Mae Shell West,
and to the memory of my father,
the Reverend Joseph W. West

This book is written with love for all other
completely average saints who need information,
inspiration, and an occasional chuckle.

Maude De Joseph West

Contents

Chapter One	9.	ACTS 1
Chapter Two	19.	ACTS 2
Chapter Three	29.	ACTS 3 and 4
Chapter Four	37.	ACTS 5
Chapter Five	45.	ACTS 6 and 7
Chapter Six	53.	ACTS 8
Chapter Seven	63.	ACTS 9:1-30
Chapter Eight	73.	ACTS 9:31-42
Chapter Nine	79.	ACTS 9:43 – 11:18
Chapter Ten	89.	ACTS 11:19-30
Chapter Eleven	95.	ACTS 12:1-23
Chapter Twelve	105.	ACTS 12:24 – 13:52
Chapter Thirteen	117.	ACTS 14
Chapter Fourteen	127.	ACTS 15:1-35
Chapter Fifteen	135.	ACTS 15:36 – 16:15
Chapter Sixteen	143.	ACTS 16:16-40
Chapter Seventeen	155.	ACTS 17
Chapter Eighteen	165.	ACTS 18
Chapter Nineteen	173.	ACTS 19
Chapter Twenty	185.	ACTS 20
Chapter Twenty-one	195.	ACTS 21
Chapter Twenty-two	205.	ACTS 22:1 – 23:30
Chapter Twenty-three	215.	ACTS 23:31 – 25:12
Chapter Twenty-four	225.	ACTS 25:13 – 26:32
Chapter Twenty-five	233.	ACTS 27
Chapter Twenty-six	243.	ACTS 28

Chapter One

This is a book about a book about people who thrust their feet into sweat-stained sandals and marched out to conquer the world. They had no visible swords, they had no visible shields, they had no visible commander; nonetheless, they marched with matchless unconcern into the gates of prison, through the valley of persecution, and even into the jaws of death. The rhythm of their marching feet echoes down the centuries, a steady throbbing of sound, a background for their battle cry: "Emmanuel! Emmanuel! *God with us!* Man crucified his God and laid His body in a tomb, but He came forth, a victor even over death. He lives forevermore, and we, too, live because we are a part of Him. Emmanuel! Emmanuel! *God with us still!*"

That book was not written as a book, but as a supplemental letter to a man named Theophilus whose identity is not known. *Theophilus* means "friend of God," and in the dim long ago somebody came up with the idea that Theophilus was not a flesh-and-blood man, but a lovely symbol of all "friends of God," i.e., Christian believers of that time. Other scholars hoot politely at that notion, pointing out that the title "most excellent," used in the salutation of the first letter, denoted a personage high in the ranks of government. Theophilus, they insist, was at least a governor of some important province, and for Luke to have identified him more definitely might have cost the man his job, or even his head.

9

Rome, at that time, certainly would have regarded with a jaundiced eye any high official who espoused this new religion.

About Luke himself we know a little more, but even so, he too remains in many respects a man of mystery. For instance, authorities can't even agree as to whether he was a Jew or a Gentile, freeborn or a freed slave. He was a physician. A physician could have been a freed slave? He could. In those days, people with real money went down to the slave market to buy a physician, a philosopher, a teacher, a masseuse, a manicurist, or a team of dancing girls.

Whether Luke had been somebody's "personal physician" in that sense, we do not know, but we do know that he was a free man at the time of his activity as it is recorded in the Bible. Whatever else may be conjectured about the man or his activity, we have abundant proof of one thing: he could *write.* Have you ever encountered anything in the English language more sublime than his account of the nativity, or more pithily concise than his summing up of the history of a man's life in fifteen words in his account of the cripple of Lystra? Like most good biographers and reporters, he seems to have possessed a flair for anonymity. He wrote with remarkable clarity and simplicity about people and events, but used the personal pronoun *I* one time, likewise the word *me* only once.

The former treatise have I made, O Theophilus [he refers to the Gospel which bears his name, of course], of all that Jesus began both to do and teach, until the day in which he was taken up, after that he through the Holy Ghost had given commandments unto the apostles whom he had chosen: to whom also he shewed himself alive after his passion by many infallible proofs, being seen of them forty days, and speaking of the things pertaining to the kingdom of God: And, being assembled together with them, commanded them that they should not depart from Jerusalem, but wait for the promise of the Father, "which" saith he, "ye have heard of me. For John truly baptized with water; but ye shall be baptized with the Holy Ghost not many days hence."

. . . taken up, after that he, through the Holy Ghost had given commandments unto the apostles whom he had chosen.

The risen Lord was still working through the power of the Holy Spirit. Why? Because He had not yet *officially* ascended into heaven to be clothed again with the glory which He had with the Father before the world was.

... **To whom also he shewed himself alive after his passion by many infallible proofs, being seen of them forty days.** ... Those nearest and dearest to Him had, at first, flatly refused to believe that He was alive again. How could they have been so lacking in faith and perception? Hadn't He been telling them all along that He would rise from the dead?

What would your reaction be if you watched a beloved friend die, if you saw him buried, and if you were told three days later by another close friend that she had seen him *alive* in the cemetery, and had talked to him?

His disciples had to be convinced that He was indeed alive again. They touched Him, they talked with Him, they listened to Him, they ate with Him. On one occasion, He even prepared breakfast for some of them by broiling fish over a campfire by the Sea of Galilee. Almost thirty years later, when Paul wrote his first letter to the Corinthians, he told them that the risen Lord had been seen by more than five hundred of the brethren at once, and that the greater part of that number were still living at that time.

The disciples were not easily convinced that their Lord was risen indeed, and alive forever; but once they were convinced, their conviction was utterly unshakable. They held it through brutal persecutions and suffering, and they marched triumphantly into the jaws of death, still proclaiming, "Jesus Christ is risen from the dead, and is alive forever!"

... **And, being assembled together with them, commanded them that they should not depart from Jerusalem, but wait for the promise of the Father, "Which," saith he, "ye have heard of me. For John truly baptized with water; but ye shall be baptized with the Holy Ghost not many days hence."**

Why were they to stay in Jerusalem? Wouldn't they have been safer some place else—say, Galilee, for instance, where the high priest couldn't reach out and grab them? They were to stay in Jerusalem because the Feast of Pentecost was very close at hand, and Jews from all over the world would be there, and would hear of the "wonderful works of God," remember? As for being safe: they were waiting in the wings, so to speak, for their cue to move on stage and begin their part in the drama of the redemption of the world. They were under the special protection of God Almighty, and I am convinced that the high priest couldn't have touched them if they had camped out in the gardens of his palace.

Their part in the drama of man's redemption would begin with baptism—not with water, but with the Holy Ghost. The time was almost upon them: "a few days hence," and so they were to wait.

The former treatise have I made . . . of all that Jesus began both to do and teach, until the day in which he was taken up. . . . And now the man Luke will tell what Jesus *continued* to do through the Holy Spirit whom He sent to permeate with God's awesome fire a group of completely ordinary men that they might become pillars of fire, torches of glory blazing in a dark and melancholy world.

Have you ever wondered about the disciples' state of mind during the period between the Lord's resurrection and His ascension? Joy: He is risen! Awe: *He is God!* Fulfillment: He is our Messiah! But what about His kingdom?

We tend to be smug about this Kingdom question. How, we ask ourselves, could the people who lived and walked and talked with Him during His earthly ministry fail to understand clearly that the Kingdom He spoke of was a thing of the spirit? If we had been waiting for weary centuries for a king to break the oppressor's yoke from our proud necks, we might not be so bright about the matter, either. In fact, from our vantage point on this side of nineteen-odd centuries of the blood of martyrs and the tears of saints, we would be remarkably stupid if we did not understand.

The Kingdom question was yet to be answered in the minds of His disciples. **When they therefore were come together, they asked of him, saying, "Lord, wilt thou at this time restore again the kingdom to Israel?"**

Looking into the eyes of the glorified Christ, were these men ready to start sparring again for positions of power in that Kingdom? The answer, quite likely, is Yes.

And he said unto them, "It is not for you to know the

times or the seasons, which the Father hath put in his own power."

We cannot help wondering if the well-meaning prophets of the last hundred years—the ones who have had our Lord appearing to set up His earthly kingdom at the exact time *they* designated—ever read those simple words: "It is not for you to know." But, ah! What a lovely speculation! What a brilliant ecclesiastical exercise! And so we speculate; we jump through hoops of fire wrought for us by the tongues and pens of students of prophecy. And some poor souls, alas, have landed on the ash heap of disillusionment after the jump.

What then? Are we to be indifferent about our Lord's return? Brace yourself, please. *Who actually wants Him to come now?* How many millions of people pray at least once a week, saying, "Thy kingdom come"? How many of them would collapse from shock if they thought that perfunctory prayer was to be answered before next Sunday? How many of the governments of the world—including our own—would be willing to relinquish their authority to Him? You are so right: None! How many churches would be willing to submit to His direct authority? It may be a fond delusion, but I think mine would. I mean the congregation to which I belong, not the denomination. I could find any number of ecclesiastical stuffed shirts in the hierarchy who would have to be batted into insensibility before God the Son who is "upholding all things by the word of his power" could take over as Supreme Commander.

Again, what then? Dare we pray, "Even so, come, Lord Jesus"? Do we mean it? We shouldn't have to be reminded that it isn't bright to lie to Almighty God.

You love to study prophecy and compare the signs of the times with history, ancient and modern, and perhaps utter now and then a solemn warning? God bless you, beloved; have at it! As for me, that is strictly God's business, and I don't have to worry about it. I am concerned with this terse directive: "Occupy till I come." And if it pleases Him to let me keep mind and hands and voice until He comes, that is what I shall be doing.

And he said unto them. "It is not for you to know the times or the seasons, which the Father hath put in his own

13

power, but ye shall receive power, after that the Holy Ghost is come upon you: and ye shall be witnesses unto me both in Jerusalem, and in all Judaea, and in Samaria, and unto the uttermost part of the earth."

Again, that word—"power." It would be difficult to imagine a group of people less gifted with power than these men who had followed Jesus for three years, from Galilee even to the Garden of Gethsemane. The power that had been theirs through their association with Him had been nailed with Him to the cross, and it had not returned to them with His resurrection. They were confused; they were, perhaps, afraid. From the viewpoint of human logic, they had good reason to be afraid, and to be in hiding. The ruthless hierarchy that had tricked Pontius Pilate into condemning a man whom he knew to be innocent would hardly have hesitated to execute any or all of the less important "troublemakers" who dared to do anything in His name. If they had tried to begin their witnessing before the Holy Ghost came upon them, the temple authorities would in all likelihood have seen to it that there were mob scenes and riots which would have placed eleven more crosses on that grisly eminence outside the city walls.

Power to witness . . . in Jerusalem . . . in all Judea . . . in Samaria [Samaria too, Lord? "For the Jews have no dealings with the Samaritans"] . . . and unto the uttermost part of the earth. This to men who quite probably had never been more than a hundred miles from the place where they were born. A long way indeed would these eleven travel before one of them was fastened to a cross and nine of the other ten were laid in martyrs' graves. And their shed blood hardened into the mighty sinews of the church of Jesus Christ.

And when he had spoken these things, while they beheld, he was taken up; and a cloud received him out of their sight.

Since His resurrection, He had appeared among them many times even though the doors were locked, and had comforted them with His blessed salutation, "Peace be unto you." But each time, they must have wondered afterward, "Will He come again, or has He gone now, finally and forever to be with His Father?" But this time, He did not simply vanish, He was "taken up."

That mighty Force which "brought again from the dead

14

our Lord Jesus" was working before human eyes to lift His glorified body up and up, away from the clinging touch, beyond the reach of upstretched hands. Sunlight glistened on His white garments and shining hair; sunlight etched forever in their memory the livid scars on His hands and feet. But the light on His face was not from the sun which He had made; it was the light of His own Being, the very Light of God.

Against the dazzling blue of the Judean sky, the glistening figure moved up and up and ever up as the people on the hillside watched through the salty curtain of their tears. With hands still uplifted, and still in utter silence, they strained their eyes to watch. And then they saw a billowing white cloud moving majestically to meet their ascending Lord, and their hands clenched to the point of pain as the white figure was enveloped in the white cloud. Wistfully they watched the cloud and saw its serrated edges turn to gold. Would they see Him again? Might He not brush the cloud aside? No. He was gone. He was gone!

Strange voices broke the silence. **"Ye men of Galilee, why stand ye gazing up into heaven? This same Jesus, which is taken up from you into heaven, shall so come in like manner as ye have seen him go into heaven."**

(He will come again! He *will* come again! A cloud will move aside, and we shall see Him. When, Lord, oh, *when?* Will You come back to us as soon as You have sent the Holy Ghost? Will it be before the next great feast? When, O Lord, when? Come quickly, Lord—don't leave us for very long!)

Slowly, their hands relaxed. They looked down and saw **two men . . . in white apparel.** Angels. And with a message: "Be comforted, O men of Galilee. He will come back. He will return with clouds of majesty, and with triumphant feet shall touch and tread upon this holy mountain. Weep not, but go you back unto your place and wait, as He commanded. And when the days have passed, you whose souls were purchased with His holy blood shall be washed through with the fire of His glory." Angels. Messengers from God to comfort men.

The disciples turned their tear-stained faces toward Jerusalem, away from the mount called Olivet, and began to walk the distance of a "sabbath day's journey" back to that arrogant and beautiful city. Back to that city which had mur-

dered its Messiah and was moving now with cynical insouci-
ance toward the day when its streets would be sticky and its
little streams bright with the blood of its own people.

They went back to their "upper room" to wait, and while
they waited, they prayed. A most excellent procedure—try it
sometime. Their concerted and continued prayer produced
remarkable results; yours might do the same thing. You don't
have time to retire to an upper room and pray for days on
end? *Would you take the time if you knew it would save this
doomed generation?* Don't answer that. Just use the time you
do have. Like, for instance, instead of reading trash, or while
you are waiting for a plane, or for a traffic light to change, or
for your absent-minded husband to come to dinner. No, it
doesn't have to be formal; any time you can *think toward
God,* you can pray. You could reform the world. And you
could remodel yourself in the process.

**And in those days Peter stood up in the midst of the
disciples, and said, (the number of names together were
about an hundred and twenty,).** . . . Who were the people in
Peter's audience? The beloved ones we met in the Gospels:
apostles whom our Lord chose and worked with patiently;
the devout women who had followed Him out of Galilee, and
"ministered to him of their substance"; Mary, His mother, a
devout worshiper praying along with the other disciples, very
definitely one of them and one with them as we catch this
last lovely glimpse which Scripture gives of her; her other
sons, the brothers of our Lord. These were all there.

Was anyone missing? One apostle was missing—Judas! Is
it difficult for you to remember that Judas was an apostle? It
is for me. Judas did not betray his Lord in the fury of disillusionment: he sold him out for filthy money. Not, "He is a
fake; come on, I'll lead you to his hide-out"; but, "What will
ye give me, and I will deliver him unto you?" Peter denied
that he even knew his Lord on the night of the betrayal; but
"Peter went out and wept bitterly." Peter was forgiven. The
resurrection angel said to the terrified women, " . . . But go
your way, tell his disciples, *and Peter* that he goeth before
you into Galilee. . . ." Peter was reinstated. The risen Lord
said to him after that memorable breakfast on the beach by

the sea of Tiberias, "Simon, son of Jonas, lovest thou me?" Then, "Feed my sheep. . . . Follow me."

Peter repented; Judas did not. Too late, Judas awoke to the horror of the realization of what he had done, but he went to the wrong place to confess: to the "chief priests and the elders." Those gentlemen were not in the least interested in innocence or guilt, justice or injustice. You can almost see them shrug, almost hear their tones of cynical contempt as they regard the frantic wretch who has brought back their blood money. "What is that to *us?*"

"And he cast down the pieces of silver in the temple, and departed, and went and hanged himself." No, Judas was not with them in the upper room; he was forever gone. And Peter was saying that they must have somebody else to take his place.

Peter did not launch into fiery invective when he mentioned the dead traitor's name. The treachery was the fulfillment of the prophecy which David had written more than a thousand years earlier: "Yea, mine own familiar friend, in whom I trusted, which did eat of my bread, hath lifted up his heel against me." Judas had been with them; he had been one of them, discharging an important task, that of treasurer; he had traveled with them, he had eaten with them, and with them he had listened to the teachings of the Lord and had witnessed His miracles.

Peter continues: **"Now this man purchased a field with the reward of iniquity; and falling headlong, he burst asunder in the midst, and all his bowels gushed out. . . ."** Terse, matter-of-fact summary of the history of Judas at its conclusion.

"Purchased a field with the reward of iniquity." Now Judas, mind you, did not put the thirty pieces of silver in escrow, nor haggle with the real estate man—Judas was already dead. Devil-ridden, he had fled from the eyes of man and hanged himself with his own girdle (according to tradition), and that strip of fabric had either broken or come loose from the tree branch to which it was knotted. Some sources say the tree was one that grew in a crevice of the almost solid rock of a high cliff. Hence, **"and falling headlong, he burst asunder in the midst, and all his bowels gushed**

out." If you can analyze that carefully without turning a little sick, you're less squeamish than I!

The chief priests and the elders were in a bit of a dither. They had money on their hands which the owner was obviously not going to reclaim. Now, it was against the law to put blood money into the temple treasury, and these gentlemen were law-abiding officers. It was they, of course, who had made it blood money, but that was quite beside the point. By the letter of the law, the money still belonged to Judas, so, in his name, so to speak, the chief priests bought the "potter's field" for a cemetery for strangers. And that was how Judas purchased a field with the reward of iniquity.

Peter goes on, **"For it is written in the book of Psalms, 'Let his habitation be desolate, and let no man dwell therein: and his bishopric let another take.' Wherefore, of these men which have companied with us all the time that the Lord Jesus went in and out among us . . . must one be ordained to be a witness with us of his resurrection."**

So, they "appointed" two men for candidates—we would probably say "nominated." Then they turned the matter of actual selection over to the Lord, because they prayed, **"Thou, Lord, which knowest the hearts of all men, shew whether of these two thou hast chosen. . . ."**

The men were Barsabas and Matthias. **And they gave forth their lots; and the lot fell upon Matthias; and he was numbered with the eleven apostles.**

Matthias is not mentioned again in the Bible. Was he actually chosen of our Lord? If so, what about Paul? We know that the Lord chose him. Did the disciples "run ahead of the Lord" in choosing an apostle to take the place of Judas? If they did, the Lord in loving indulgence allowed it. Then, too, the Spirit did not come until they had chosen "another to take his [Judas's] bishopric."

In the event that the disciples could have been over-eager, let us consider this: The Lord had chosen twelve, and His own were completely determined to have things exactly the way He wanted them. When we reach the point where we are that anxious to please our Lord—well, among other things, we'll be so changed that nobody but the Lord will recognize us!

18

Chapter Two

And when the day of Pentecost was fully come, they were all with one accord in one place.

As a child, I thought that Day of Pentecost was the original and only one, so I used to wonder vaguely how the hundred and twenty disciples knew when the "day of Pentecost was fully come." Also, if your thought processes and patterns are at all like mine, you have difficulty trying to picture the events of that mighty day which marked the birth of the Christian church. I find it helpful to transpose the event to a modern setting, like this:

Let's suppose it's a holiday, and that your city is host to a convention that has as many foreign delegates as the United Nations (**And there were dwelling in Jerusalem Jews, devout men, out of every nation under heaven**). Not far from your house is a sort of lodge hall that would accommodate maybe a hundred and seventy-five people, and it's been used a lot lately by a group of farm laborers who seem to have a lot of prayer meetings. (Farm laborers to be compared with the saints who were present at the descent of the Spirit? Please don't be scandalized; the first Christians were not garnered from Jerusalem's social register, you know!)

Let us also suppose that you have a fourteen-year-old son who carries a morning paper route and, like most adolescents, communicates with his elders in grunts or monosyllables. But on this particular morning the boy dashes in from his paper route, pale, wild-eyed, and actually trying terribly hard to talk to you. But his vocal cords seem completely frozen, and you watch helplessly, scared half out of your wits. Eventually he gains control over lips and larynx, and words pour out in a rush of chopped consonants and half-chewed vowels. You learn that as he was riding by the shabby lodge hall shortly after sunrise he heard a noise like the wind blowing up a storm in mountain pine trees. The wind was *inside the building:* outside, there wasn't so much as a leaf quivering.

With the very natural curiosity of a boy he got off his bike, went to the building, and opened the front door. The place was maybe three-fourths full of people. They looked like farm workers in their Sunday clothes. They also looked like they were in a trance, all of them. They just sat there staring at the ceiling, and their eyes were sort of glazed. He thought maybe they'd been hypnotized. The sound like the big wind was still there, and he had a feeling there was enough power in it to blow down every house in town, but it wasn't so much as lifting a lock of their hair out of place. He was scared. This didn't make sense. Something was wrong with those people. He wanted to close the door and run, but he couldn't move; it was like being in a bad dream.

And then, all at once, out of the middle of the big wind, fire! He knew he ought to rush down to the corner where there was an alarm box and turn in an alarm, but he still couldn't move. These poor dopes would be burned to a cinder before they could come out of that trance! He tried to scream a warning to them, but his throat seemed paralyzed. As he watched helplessly, the great blaze began to break itself into small flames which traveled eerily around the room and settled like darting blue-white tongues upon the heads of the hypnotized people.

The flames did not set the people on fire, but made their faces glow as if the flesh were transparent and stretched over a very powerful light. When this unearthly glow lighted their faces they rose from their seats as though they were being lifted. They were still evidently hypnotized, and the spell was not broken, but their silence was, for group by small group they began talking. *But they were not speaking in English!*

One group was talking in Spanish, and the boy had had enough of First Year Spanish to make out part of what they were saying. They were saying mostly "God" and "Jesus," but they were talking so fast he didn't know just what they were trying to get across. He'd heard enough German to know that one small group was talking in that language, and he'd picked up one or two phrases in French, and a bit of Portuguese, some Italian, and some Armenian from the kids in school. Those languages were all being used, and he heard something that sounded like the Russian language he had heard over TV from the U.N.

This didn't make a bit of sense; not one of those people looked foreign. He finally found that he could move, and he backed out, closed the door carefully, and tore out of there. He saw a couple of cops going by in a prowl car, stopped them, and told them something crazy was going on in the old lodge hall, and maybe they'd like to look into it. They said it was just some sort of wild-eyed cult, and as long as no neighbors complained, the wild-eyed ones were enjoying their rights under the Constitution, and that was that.

You find yourself with coat and hat on, and the boy is beside you as you back the car out and start to the old lodge hall. When you get two blocks from the place you decide to park, for the area is full of cars and people—people walking, people running, and all toward the old lodge hall. They are foreign people. You don't know where they're from, but they look foreign and they sound foreign as they babble excitedly all around you.

You and the boy melt into the excited crowd and flow along with it toward the old building. You can barely get close enough to see that the front door is wide open, and the grounds completely clogged with people. There is a most extraordinary babble of sound. Your son clings to your hand like a frightened little boy, and the two of you edge closer.

Finally, you can see the people who have been inside. It wouldn't be hard to distinguish them from other people, even if they didn't look sunburned and shaggy: their faces are still glowing as if there were lights inside them, and above the head of every one of them darting tongues of blue-white flame burn brightly. Feeding on nothing, resting on nothing, held in place by nothing! The flames hover like awesome halos over the men who are speaking to separate groups of people whose color runs from blond-white to sallow white to pale-gold and on through ebony.

It is obvious from their expressions that the separate groups of people know precisely what is being said to them, but you can't understand a word of it, and you are seized with frustration mixed with that spine-tingling fear which comes from contact with the supernatural. You know that the chances are about one in ten thousand that a single one of these migrant farm workers is a linguist—they probably don't even do very well by their mother tongue—but there they are all around you speaking in Spanish and French and Italian and Portuguese and Armenian and German and Greek and Japanese and Russian, and other languages you can't identify because you've never heard or read a word of them.

And then you see edging away from the Japanese group the young student who is financing his university degree by doing garden work for you and a few other people fortunate enough to get him. "Ahito!" you find yourself screaming his name. He finally hears, and makes his way toward you. His face is sober, thoughtful, but he smiles at you with his unfailing politeness.

"What are they saying?" you ask wildly.

His face turns somber. "They are saying that the only Son of the only God came to earth in the form of a man to save other men from their sins and make them fit to live with God forever. They are saying that the church and the government murdered Him—had Him executed as if He had been a common criminal—but that on the third day after His burial, He came out of the tomb *alive.* That they themselves saw Him and talked with Him and even ate with Him after He came forth from the tomb. . . ."

"Ha!" A young man with a camera explodes shrilly, "You don't believe that eyewash, do you? I tell you these jerks are a bunch of winos on a great big binge!"

As if answering him, a huge man with shaggy gray hair moves to the top step of the building, and lifts his hands. The instant and absolute silence that greets this gesture is almost as frightening as the phenomena of fire and strange languages. "Hear me, all of you," the big man's voice, resonant and clear, carries a very long way, "These men are *not* drunk, because they never touch liquor. The meaning of these strange things is this. . . ."

But Peter, standing with the eleven, lifted up his voice and said unto them, "Ye men of Judaea, and all ye that dwell at Jerusalem, be this known unto you, and hearken to my words: For these are not drunken, as ye suppose. . . ."

Did Peter speak in an unknown language then, and have an interpreter? No. Did he speak in Greek, which was then the universal language of educated people? No. He spoke in good old understandable Aramaic, quite possibly with a Galilean accent. He wanted to be sure they *all* heard and understood.

"For these are not drunken, as ye suppose, seeing it is but the third hour of the day. . . ." Nine o'clock in the morning, the hour of morning prayer for the Jews. And no Jew, good, bad, or indifferent, ever ate before that time. And since all concerned were Jews, it was reasonably evident, therefore, that they could not be drunk.

Did they drink at all? Of course they did! We whose hackles raise at the very odor of alcohol (and there are a few of us left in this bleary-eyed world!) should be careful to see to it that we do not condemn our Lord Himself in our extraordinary zeal. Jesus said, "John the Baptist came neither eating bread nor drinking wine; and ye say, 'He hath a devil.' The Son of man is come eating and drinking; and ye say, 'Behold a gluttonous man, and a winebibber, a friend of publicans and sinners!' " People of that time had wine on their tables just as we have coffee and tea on ours, and it is extremely doubtful that the beverage with meals made any of them drunk. I think that we may safely assume that alcoholism was as repugnant to decent people then as it is to decent people now, and that nobody among the early disciples whiled away his time in the Hebrew version (if there was one) of the neighborhood tavern.

Very well; Peter has convinced his hearers in one sentence that he and his fellows are not drunk. Let's see how he tells them what has actually happened.

"But this is that which was spoken by the prophet Joel; 'And it shall come to pass in the last days, saith God, I will pour out of my Spirit upon all flesh. . . !' " Peter didn't need notes. He could quote Scripture because he grew up on it—Jewish boys memorized Old Testament Scriptures in school. If little Peter should memorize Old Testament Scriptures in school now, his teacher might get arrested.

" 'I will pour out of my Spirit upon all flesh.' "

If somebody should suddenly ask you, "What *is* the Holy Spirit?" how would you answer? (I hope you would gently set him straight, in that his question should read, "*Who* is the Holy Spirit"!) The Holy Spirit is a person, and He is God. He is the third person of the Holy Trinity: Father, Son, and Holy Ghost.

Peter had one advantage that you wouldn't have: His audience knew what he was talking about.

It probably would be an oversimplification to say that the Holy Spirit is God in action. But that's a good place to start. The Holy Spirit is the power of God, shattering primordial darkness and replacing the fragments with everlasting light; entering into ordinary men of old and touching mind and muscle to transform them into mighty deliverers of God's people; touching a virgin's womb with that holy impulse which gave human form to the Son of God; living in ancient prophets that the pure Word might come through so that the awareness of God Almighty might not be blotted out of the mind of man; and finally, on this great Day of Pentecost, coming into the world to *live* (even as God the Son had lived here). Heretofore, the Holy Spirit had lived in certain chosen persons for a certain chosen purpose, but now, "I will pour out of my Spirit upon *all flesh.*"

Where is your mind when you rise to repeat the Apostles' Creed and recite the words, "I believe in the Holy Ghost"? Have you any idea what you're talking about?

Suppose some dewy-eyed cultist crawls out from under his flat rock and challenges you to defend your belief in the Holy Spirit—what will you say? (Oh, yes they do; it's happened to me!) If your Bible doesn't have a good concordance, you'd best get one that does, and get busy. Note all the references to the Holy Spirit, and start copying them. If you read something, and copy it, you'll find it's hard *not* to learn what you're copying. By the time you've finished with your checking and copying, the chances are that that part of the Creed won't bounce off your sleeping mind as it somnambulates gently toward home and what's for lunch! Certainly it will take time, and certainly it will be work. That's why so many of us are ineffectual Christians: If knowledge of God isn't dished out as painlessly as vitamin pills, we simply can't be bothered. Of course, we can always blame our spiritual lethargy and our sterile lives on the pastor. He's used to that; but frankly, I doubt that that alibi will go over so big with God.

The rugged fisherman from Galilee searched the faces of his audience, and his voice rolled out like thunder, his tongue cut their consciences like forked lightning. **"Ye men of Israel, hear these words; Jesus of Nazareth, a man approved of God among you by miracles and wonders and signs, which God did by him in the midst of you, as ye yourselves also know: Him, being delivered by the determinate counsel and foreknowledge of God, ye have taken, and by wicked hands have crucified and slain. . . ."**

"*Ye* have taken, and by wicked hands have crucified and slain"! Listen to this man boldly fling an accusation of murder into the faces of a multitude. Can this be the same man who cowered before the babbling tongue of the high priest's slave girl, denying that he even knew the Lord? Yes. Same man. What changed the cringing coward into a thundering accuser? Remember the great wind and the tongues of flame? Remember the Master's words, **"But ye shall receive power after that the Holy Ghost is come upon you: and ye shall be witnesses unto me. . . ."** The promise is fulfilled. The power is there, and Peter is using it. Surcharged with that mighty Force, Simon Peter has become the sturdy rock; he will never again be the cringing coward.

"Jesus of Nazareth . . . ye have . . . crucified and slain. . . . **This Jesus hath God raised up, whereof we all are witnesses. . . . Therefore let all the house of Israel know assuredly, that God hath made that same Jesus, whom ye have crucified, both Lord and Christ."**

Interspersed with words from the prophecies of David (from whose loins they knew their Messiah-Christ was to come) this Galilean fisherman's unexplained eloquence and irrefutable logic have convinced them that they have indeed murdered their Messiah.

The mockers are either silent or gone. Consciences begin slashing ruthlessly with the sword of remorse: Murderers. Murderers! And the man you made the Romans crucify was God's Messiah! *You* saw Him standing there in Pilate's hall, bruised, battered, bloody from the scourge and the thorns pressed down by heathen soldiers. *You* saw Him standing there, and you lent *your* voice to that cursed chant, "Crucify him, crucify him, crucify him!" *You* stood upon that grisly hill to watch Him die, perchance to gloat self-righteously. But when the earth was choked with sudden darkness that blotted out the noontide sun, *you* fled in guilty terror to your home and cowered there. For how many weary generations have your fathers waited for this Blessed Hope, but *you* have killed Him!

Now when they heard this, they were pricked in their heart, and said unto Peter and to the rest of the apostles, "Men and brethren, what shall we do?"

Then Peter said unto them, "Repent, and be baptized every one of you in the name of Jesus Christ for the remission of sins, and ye shall receive the gift of the Holy Ghost. For the promise is unto you, and to your children, and to all that are afar off, even as many as the Lord our God shall call." Look at that for a little while: it takes in a lot. It is the first time in the newborn church that the way of salvation has been pointed out, and it reaches down through all the centuries and embraces even us. "Even as many as the Lord our God shall call." That includes us. Does that warm your soul a little? It ought to, you know.

And with many other words did he testify and exhort, saying, "Save yourselves from this untoward generation."

Untoward generation. I wonder if all small children get quaint notions like the one I entertained about people in Bible times? I think it was because of the long, flowing robes in which they were pictured that my childish mind decided that all people of that era were sort of hallowed. I was half grown before the idea penetrated that they were more filthily wicked (if possible!) than the "now people."

Then they that gladly received his word were baptized:

and the same day were added unto them about three thousand souls.

Three-thousand-odd new members in one day! I wonder what we would do in a case like that. Some of us would be on our knees praising God. And some of us would stay up all night appointing new committees.

"And ye shall be witnesses unto me," the Lord had told His disciples, "Both in Jerusalem, and in all Judaea, and in Samaria, and unto the uttermost part of the earth." The witnessing in Jerusalem has begun.

Across the centuries we look back wistfully at that new church as it moved into the very first weeks of its existence. At its joy in learning more about its Lord, at its joy in fellowship: And they continued stedfastly in the apostles' doctrine [teaching] and fellowship . . . and all that believed were together, and had all things common; and sold their possessions and goods, and parted them to all men, as every man had need. And they, continuing daily with one accord in the temple, and breaking bread from house to house, did eat their meat with gladness and singleness of heart, praising God, and having favour with all the people.

Particularly, I think, do we look with almost unbelieving awe at people who were willing to give their wealth, sacrificing their luxuries that their brothers in the new faith might have the necessities. A brief glimpse of perfect love working in imperfect people, that the needs of every believer might be met as they made haste to tell Jerusalem about their Lord before the high priest's gilded sandal stamped furiously on Holy Fire to put it out. He merely sent its embers, glowing and very much alive, showering into "all Judaea and Samaria," and thus—oh, matchless irony!—helped to carry out the commandment of the hated young Rabbi from Nazareth.

One wonders how the hierarchy would have reacted had they known that He whom they had crucified was sitting at the right hand of God the Father and watching in serene amusement while they fulfilled His purpose by their very efforts to destroy Him.

Chapter Three

Now Peter and John went up together into the temple at the hour of prayer. Look back carefully over the Gospels, and you may wonder how it was that Peter and John went any place together. There was jealousy there, each apparently being afraid that the other would have a place of higher honor in the Master's kingdom than he himself would enjoy. But here they are, going to the temple together. Why this sudden state of "togetherness" for two men who have been delicately sniping at each other for three years? The answer is quite simple: The baptism of Holy Fire had burned away the dross of jealousy, and welded the souls of these two into that unity of perfect love whose passion was to serve their Lord.

Peter and John were about to go in at the gate called "Beautiful," but beside that gate there was something most unbeautiful which they would have to pass: a crippled beggar. We don't see many crippled beggars in our land, and I wonder if we ever stop to think that this also is from "the grace of our Lord and Saviour, Jesus Christ"? Public care for the needy is an adjunct of Christian civilization and therefore a by-product of Christianity.

A crippled beggar by the gate called "Beautiful." For year upon weary year he had sat there, asking alms from those who were about to go into the temple. Did he size people up as they approached, and cry to some and not others, or did he whine his pitiful supplication to all passers-by? Probably to all, and without even looking at their faces,

29

so it must have been something of a shock when two men stopped in front of him and said, "Look at us." This was something new: maybe this was going to be a really worthwhile gift.

He looked expectantly at the men, and if he let his mind linger on Peter's first words, he surely must have been disillusioned: "**Silver and gold have I none.**" "Ah," the beggar no doubt thought petulantly, "if he's broke, why did he bother to stop?" But the rugged stranger continued without pause, "**But such as I have give I thee: In the name of Jesus Christ of Nazareth rise up and walk.**" And he took him by the right hand, and lifted him up, and immediately his feet and ankle bones received strength. And he leaping up stood, and walked, and entered with them into the temple, walking, and leaping, and praising God.

The people in the temple heard the commotion, and turned to see what caused it. They saw a man running and jumping, shouting praises to God, and then turning and running back to two other men whom he embraced in ecstasy. The people looked again—that man's face was familiar. And then they recognized him! The lame man, the one who had never taken a step in his life, the one who was a familiar figure at the temple gate—the very same man they had passed by and tossed coins to for years. What had happened? The people pressed closer. Somebody said that the two men had performed this miracle. The word spread, and others joined the throng until an astonished multitude crowded around Peter and John and looked at them with awe. Miracle workers! The evidence was there before their very eyes.

Peter looked into their awe-struck faces, and instantly began his second sermon: "Men of Israel, you are asking among yourselves, 'Who healed this man? Who is it that has made him completely whole?' I did not do it. He," gesturing toward John, "did not do it. Who, then, healed this man? *Jesus Christ, God's holy Son, whom you forced Pilate to crucify!* You forced Pilate to release a murderer to you and kill the very Author of Life. But God raised Him from the dead and we are witnesses to that fact.

"The very name of Jesus Christ, with the faith of this man in that name, has made him perfectly sound.

"Do you see now what you have done? But I know, brethren, that you did not realize what you were doing; in fact, in your ignorance you even helped fulfill the words of the prophets that Christ should suffer. Therefore, repent now and be converted, that your sins may be blotted out.

"To you first God has sent His risen Son to bless. . . .' "

And as they spake unto the people, the priests, and the captain of the temple, and the Sadducees, came upon them. . . . Freedom of religious expression for the new church was short-lived; it died right there, in fact. From now on in, the high priest was going to be breathing down their necks through some of his hirelings every time they preached Christ. Five thousand were converted because of that miracle performed in the name of Christ, and because of Peter's sermons—but Peter and John spent the night in jail.

By this time, the high priest had begun to realize that he had not rid himself of the troublesome young Rabbi from Galilee whom he had tricked Pontius Pilate into executing. He began to be dimly aware that he had a perpetual headache. What had happened to these uncouth orators that gave them the boldness to emerge from hiding? They had scattered like a covey of frightened quail the night their leader was arrested, and he had had every right to believe that they had melted forever into the obscurity of some Galilean fishing village. Miracles, he fumed, these fanatics who went about, enthusiastically upsetting the status quo and inflaming the public mind with their miracles! Between the rabble on the one hand, and the Romans on the other, the lot of the high priest was not always a happy one. Not that he had any intention of resigning, though; the pay was excellent, and occasionally he experienced the sheer ecstasy of making the mighty Romans squirm.

As for these two troublemakers, he'd scare the daylights out of them with threats after asking a few questions, and perhaps that would at least keep them quiet for awhile. Accordingly, the next day Peter and John were brought from the jail and "set in the midst" of the assembled hierarchy (augmented by some of the high priest's visiting relatives) and asked a question which was really quite silly: **"By what power, or by what name, have ye done this?"** As if they didn't already know! Did they think these fanatical fishermen, awed and intimidated by all the splendor around them, would deny the name which the high priest wanted blotted from the minds of men?

Again, Peter minced no words. Indeed, it takes little imagination to read a certain polite mockery into his answer: **"If we this day be examined of the good deed done to the impotent man, by what means he is made whole, be it known unto you all, and to all the people of Israel, that by the name of Jesus Christ of Nazareth, whom ye crucified, whom God raised from the dead, even by him doth this man stand here before you whole.**

"This is the stone which was set at nought of you builders, which is become the head of the corner. Neither is there salvation in any other: for there is none other name under heaven given among men, whereby we must be saved."

This clumsy Galilean peasant is standing boldly in their midst, charging them with murder, taunting them with the futility of their crime, even daring to tell them that their own salvation depends upon the name they would erase from the records of time. No wonder they "marvelled"! It would be pretty much the same thing if a backwoods evangelist should stand up and tell the assembled Supreme Court that the Honorable Justices were a bunch of murderers! Only, of course, somebody would probably get around to telling him gently that he was out of his bailiwick, since God has absolutely nothing to do with the government, and vice versa!

And they took knowledge of them, that they had been with Jesus. Why? Among other things, could it have been that a certain lack of reverence for the august assemblage was reminiscent of that young Man whose lashing tongue had cut their cultured skins to the quick and sometimes peeled them back? Anybody who reminded them of the Rabbi of Galilee was not to be regarded with anything but downright hostility, but at the moment, they were not free to activate that hostility.

There was that troublesome matter right before their eyes, the evidence of a miracle: the lame man who had been healed. They dared not do anything drastic to the prisoners for fear of stirring up a mob. A mob could get completely out of hand and be vociferously ugly, as they full well knew, having stirred up a few in their day. A really ugly mob could even bring the Roman legions down on their necks to restore order with the fury of relentless efficiency which marked the Roman mind. And anyway, perhaps they'd better not allow anything to happen right now that would further irritate Pontius Pilate. They had the feeling that ever since they had maneuvered the noble Roman into a corner and forced him to order the execution of Jesus of Nazareth, he would really enjoy seeing their limbs stretched and nailed down in that selfsame fashion.

What should they do, then? Try to overawe the prisoners with their priestly majesty, and scare them into keeping still? That was all they could do at the moment. **And they called them, and commanded them not to speak at all, nor teach in the name of Jesus.**

But Peter and John answered and said unto them, "Whether it be right in the sight of God to hearken unto you more than unto God, judge ye. For we cannot but speak the things which we have seen and heard."

The force of that simple answer should have been sufficient to silence even the high priest and his brethren, but it wasn't, for we read, **So when they had further threatened them, they let them go. And being let go, they went to their own company, and reported all that the chief priests and elders had said unto them.**

For doing a good deed in Christ's name, Peter and John had been thrown in jail; they had been "straitly threatened" by ecclesiastical authorities who were capable of putting them to torture and death, even as they had maligned and murdered the Lord. It was quite all right to heal a lame man, you understand—their mistake was doing it in the name of Jesus Christ. Does that still sound familiar?

Did the disciples wring their hands, and sigh, "Lord, we tried to do what You commanded, but look what happened to us! It was such a lovely Movement while it lasted!"? No. They **lifted up their voice to God with one accord, and said, "Lord, Thou art God which hast made heaven and earth, and the sea, and all that in them is** . . . [and therefore would be reasonably capable of handling even the high priest!] **who by the mouth of thy servant David hast said, 'Why do the heathen rage, and the people imagine vain things? The kings of the earth stood up, and the rulers were gathered together against the Lord, and against his Christ.' For of a truth against thy holy child, Jesus, whom thou hast anointed, both Herod, and Pontius Pilate, with the Gentiles, and the people of Israel were gathered together, for to do whatsoever thy hand and thy counsel determined before to be done. . . ."** Herod . . . Pontius Pilate, with the Gentiles . . . and the people of Israel.

Herod, the sadist whose matter-of-fact cruelty still shocks normal minds; Pontius Pilate, representing the Gentile conqueror, forced by political expediency to execute a man whom he himself declared innocent; people of Israel, the wily high priest and the people turned by his manipulation into a maniacal mob. These, "gathered together for to do whatsoever *thy* hand and *thy* counsel determined before to be done." All these, living their own lives, scheming their own schemes, cruel, wicked, cunning, or weak, completely unaware of God Almighty, were nonetheless working out His perfect and inexorable will!

Let that sink in for a minute. Now, answer, please: Who is running the world? Washington? Moscow? Those United Nations gentlemen whose not-so-remote ancestors ate their enemies for lunch? Oh! Let's turn back to the second Psalm, and pick up a verse the disciples didn't use: "He that sitteth in the heavens shall laugh: the Lord shall have them in derision." The pomposity of swaggering dictators and terribly-terribly important presidents must be amusing to God, at that.

"And now, Lord, behold their threatenings: and grant unto thy servants . . . [Safety? Security? Serenity? No!] that with all boldness they may speak thy word. By stretching forth thine hand to heal; and that signs and wonders may be done by the name of thy holy child Jesus."

What happened? And when they had prayed, the place was shaken where they were assembled together; and they were all filled with the Holy Ghost, and they spake the word of God with boldness. God answered—with an earthquake. God answered—with a further filling of the Holy Spirit (God *in* them) so that they spoke the word of God with boldness. And that was what they had asked for themselves.

Chapter Four

Now comes the record of something we wish had not happened; but it *did* happen, so we might as well examine it: The sin of Ananias and Sapphira. Two people—one sin; but it was quite large enough to destroy both of them. They lied. They lied to God. And God executed judgment upon them in the sight of the congregation by striking them dead. They were the church's original hypocrites. What about modern hypocrites in the church? Are they getting by with it? They are not—their judgment is merely delayed. Don't begin purring, please; I don't mean the people *we* call hypocrites, I mean the ones God calls hypocrites. He knows the difference; we don't.

Ananias and Sapphira owned some land which they sold in order to turn the money over to the apostles for the general fund for those of the disciples who were in need. Other property owners were doing the same thing. One other, in fact, is mentioned by name: **Joses, who by the apostles was surnamed Barnabas, (which is, being interpreted, The son of consolation,). . . .**

Did Ananias and Sapphira hope that the apostles would confer some lovely title upon them for bestowing their goods to feed the poor? Or, in the beginning, did they aim solely to do good? We do not know when Satan found the door to the mind of Ananias slightly ajar, pushed it all the way open, and then went in and made himself quite at home. After that, Ananias and Sapphira decided to make an offering of a part of their land money, and keep the rest for their own use. What was wrong with that? Nothing whatever—except the fact that they *said* they were giving *all* of it.

Ananias took the sum agreed upon and, quite probably with a flourish, laid it down before the apostles. It is likely that he waited for a moment, expecting warm words of approval. How was he to know that Peter, through the power of the Holy Spirit, knew precisely what he and Sapphira had done? If there was a smile of anticipation on his face, it froze with Peter's words: **"Ananias, why hath Satan filled thine heart to lie to the Holy Ghost, and to keep back part of the price of the land? While it remained, was it not thine own? And after it was sold, was it not in thine own power? Why hast thou conceived this thing in thine heart? Thou hast not lied unto men, but unto God."**

Ananias crumpled slowly and fell, and he knew that he was dying. Transfixed with sudden fear, the disciples watched Peter's face as he looked down at the doomed man. Tears slid from under Peter's eyelids and mingled with his graying beard as life shuddered out of Ananias through convulsive finger tips. He lifted his head at length, and looked around him at people who still seemed like figures carved from white marble, and when he finally spoke, his voice sounded very tired. "Come . . . you who were his friends, . . . come forward now, and prepare his body for the burial."

Three hours later when Sapphira came in, she probably wondered why Ananias was nowhere in sight, and why everybody who knew her looked frightened when she entered. She must have been mystified when Peter came over and asked, "Sapphira, was this amount," naming the figure Ananias had mentioned, "what you got for the land you sold?"

Sapphira looked straight into Peter's eyes. "Yes," she said, "that was the amount."

"So you, also, were a part of the lie! How is it that you conspired to tempt the Spirit of the Lord? Listen! That tramping you hear is from the feet of the men who have *just buried your husband, and they will also take you to the burial!"*

Then she fell down straightway at his feet, and yielded up

the ghost: and the young men came in, and found her dead, and carrying her forth, buried her by her husband.

And great fear came upon all the church, and upon as many as heard these things.

And that fear was quite understandable. To the church, the message in fire-wreathed words was: "You do not trifle with the Holy Spirit!" And the exclamation point that ended the sentence was death. The message to outsiders was equally clear: "Be careful what you do to these people; be careful even of your attitude toward them: for they have the power both to heal and to destroy!"

Purged of hypocrites, the infant church continued its miraculous growth. **And by the hands of the apostles were many signs and wonders wrought among the people. . . . Insomuch that they brought forth the sick into the streets, and laid them on beds and couches, that at the least the shadow of Peter passing by might overshadow some of them.**

The "shadow of Peter" meant the sunlight of God's healing power to the sick ones, and they were exposed to it by the faith of those who brought them. How long has it been since you placed the pallet of a sick soul where the "shadow of Peter" could overshadow it? How do you do that? Very simple. If you have a preacher worthy of the name, try bringing the sick soul to church. Some, alas, will have to be trussed in the strait jacket of tragedy before they are willing for the shadow to touch them.

It wasn't only Jerusalem's sick who benefited from God's healing power demonstrated through the apostles: **There came also a multitude out of the cities round about Jerusalem, bringing sick folks, and them that were vexed with unclean spirits: and they were healed every one.**

What about the high priest's response to this miracle of wholesale healing? Was he happy? No. Unhappy; in fact, very nearly hysterical! His threatening had had no effect on the uncouth fisherman from Galilee, nor on any of his fanatical companions. They were still healing in the forbidden name, they were still witnessing to His resurrection (particularly annoying and embarrassing to the Sadducees who did not believe in the resurrection of the dead!), and they were still gathering in believers by the thousands. This whole thing was beginning to assume serious proportions; in short, the situation was getting out of hand. What to do *this* time? Well, it wasn't a very original idea, and it hadn't worked any too well before, but they might as well clamp the leaders in jail again. They were not likely to do any wholesale healing or preaching from behind bars, and that would help a little.

But the angel of the Lord by night opened the prison doors. . . . Look back at the second Psalm again, and check the fourth verse: "He that sitteth in the heavens shall laugh: the Lord shall have them in derision." Listen with me. Can you also hear the faint, silvery cadence of angelic laughter echoing the derision of "Him that sitteth in the heavens"?

But the angel of the Lord by night opened the prison doors, and brought them forth, and said. . . . What did the divine messenger say? "You poor darlings, you've *had* it! Go hide out for awhile, and rest"? He did not. He said, **"Go, stand and speak in the temple to the people all the words of this life."** So, very naturally, they went. **" . . . They entered into the temple early in the morning, and taught."**

That simply was not to be one of the high priest's better days. In fact, before it was over, he probably was in a mood to resign. In the first place he **called the council together, and all the senate of the children of Israel** to have a hearing for these troublemakers, to see what disposition could be made of them. Imagine his chagrin, mixed perhaps with foreboding, when the officers he had sent to fetch the prisoners returned with this report: **"The prison truly found we shut with all safety, and the keepers standing without before the doors: but when we had opened, we found no man within."** Everything in perfect order. Just one small thing wrong: no prisoners!

And before the high priest and the captain of the temple, and the chief priests had recovered from that shock, they had another one in the form of a second report: **"Behold, the men whom ye put in prison are standing in the temple, and teaching the people."**

Did the temple authorities, officially the representatives of God, realize by now that they were fighting against God? Whether they did or not, they had no intention of declaring a truce!

Then went the captain with the officers, and brought
them without violence: For they feared the people, lest they
should be stoned. Again that healthy respect for the potential
fury of a mob. The officers must have had a few justifiable
qualms, at that. Suppose the "troublemakers" refused to co-
operate and go with them? Would they dare lay hands on
these men whose miracles and signs and wonders evoked reverence from the common people? Would they dare drag them
by force from their eager audience? Of course they wouldn't.
But their orders were to bring these men that they might be
"set before the council." They must have breathed a concerted sigh of relief when the apostles went along quietly
with them.

Back to the same place the apostles went, and back to the
same group that had questioned and blustered and bullied
and threatened. They had followed God's specific instructions, and here they were again before the high priest. God
could handle the high priest.

"Did we not straitly command you that ye should not
teach in this name? And behold, ye have filled Jerusalem
with your doctrine, and intend to bring this man's blood
upon us."

"This man's blood upon us." Does that remind you of
anything? It should. In Matthew's account of our Lord's trial
before Pilate, we find this cry, instigated, no doubt, by the
"chief priests and the elders": " 'His blood be on us, and on
our children.' " So soon after judicial murder, were the high
priest and his brethren beginning to squirm under the stain of
that holy blood?

Then Peter and the other apostles answered and said, "We
ought to obey God rather than men."

Why don't *we* obey God as they did? We have a matchless
alibi: We counter with, "How do we know what God wants
us to do? After all, the mighty fire of the Holy Spirit has
faded to a very feeble spark in most of us, and we're two-
thousand-odd years removed from the voice of angels. How
do we know what is or is not God's will?" Well, for one thing
we have an infallible guide which the apostles did not have:
the New Testament Scriptures.

By a little careful reading of those same Scriptures, we

can find enough of the will of God to keep us busy several days! For instance, in Paul's very short letter to the Colossians, this: "But now ye also put off all these; anger, wrath, malice, blasphemy, filthy communication out of your mouth." *That* is part of God's will for us. You've done that? So soon? Then try this: "Put on therefore, as the elect of God, holy and beloved, bowels of mercies, kindness, humbleness of mind, meekness, longsuffering; forbearing one another, and forgiving one another, if any man have a quarrel against any: even as Christ forgave you, so also do ye. And above all these things put on charity, which is the bond of perfectness. . . . And whatsoever ye do, do it heartily, as to the Lord, and not unto men. . . . Let your speech be always with grace, seasoned with salt, that ye may know how ye ought to answer every man."

And from the first letter to the Thessalonians, three pithy directives that very few saints pay any attention to: "Comfort the feeble-minded . . . pray without ceasing . . . abstain from all appearence of evil."

You didn't even know those things were there? That is the secret of your ignorance and mine of the will of God for us: we fail to look in the place where it is clearly set forth. Why? Could it be that we are afraid of what we'll find? That it won't be what *we* want to do? Or is it that we're waiting at the foot of some mystic mountain, looking up and listening raptly for God to speak to us with a voice of thunder? Well, if His patience and His sense of humor are sufficient, He may do just that for His oddly insistent little saints, but it shouldn't be necessary.

This was probably the shortest sermon that Peter ever preached. He could have delivered it almost in one breath: **"We ought to obey God rather than men. The God of our fathers raised up Jesus, whom ye slew and hanged on a tree. Him hath God exalted with his right hand to be a Prince and a Saviour, for to give repentance to Israel, and forgiveness of sins. And we are his witnesses of these things; and so also is the Holy Ghost, whom God hath given to them that obey him."**

A very short sermon indeed, but quite long enough to arouse in his audience the fury of those who know they are in the wrong and intend to alter the situation, not by turning from their evil ways, but by destroying their accusers! Illogical? Certainly—and very human.

When they heard that, they were cut to the heart, and took counsel to slay them. Counsel. This might take considerable planning. They had managed murder once—judicial murder, that is—but that was for only one man. There were twelve of these, and they had done more mighty works in Jerusalem than the One who had been executed. Getting rid of all twelve would be a risky business. They "took counsel."

Then stood there up one in the council, a Pharisee, named Gamaliel, a doctor of the law, had in reputation among all the people. Familiar name? This man was used of God in a way that probably would have made him rend his garments if he had known what was happening! To Gamaliel had been committed the task of training a young pupil sent to him by a devout couple in faraway Tarsus. The pupil's name was Saul.

The council respected Gamaliel. They listened to him. He reminded them of two examples of leaders among the people, troublemakers whose followers scattered after the leaders were destroyed, and whose movements had collapsed of their own weight. By inference, he compared this movement with those two: this leader also had been destroyed, so his advice was, "Refrain from these men, and let them alone: for if this counsel or this work be of men, it will come to nought: But if it be of God, ye cannot overthrow it; lest haply ye be found even to fight against God."

A very good idea, the council agreed. A little patience, a little waiting, and this madness would vanish. Of course it would vanish! Of course they were not fighting against God. They represented God. So they turned the apostles loose. With apologies? Hardly! And when they had called the apostles and beaten them, they commanded that they should not speak in the name of Jesus, and let them go. The first time, they had threatened; this time, they beat and threatened; and the next time? The next time they would stain stones with the blood of Christ's first martyr.

And they departed from the presence of the council, re-

joicing that they were counted worthy to suffer shame for his name. Now, preach yourself a sermon on *that* one.

How long has it been since you heard some sweet-voiced gentleman intimating broadly that when you become a Christian, all your troubles—and especially your financial troubles—will vanish into the rarified air of all-rightness which you will breathe from there on in? Lovely, isn't it? Just one small thing wrong: it isn't true. But even as we do not expect our Christianity to yield us caviar and cadillacs, neither do we expect to "suffer shame for his name." And if we did, would we rejoice? No. If one small persecution were to dethrone us from our comfortable perch in the exact center of the status quo, our cries of anguish would drown the music of heaven's choirs!

And daily in the temple, and in every house, they ceased not to teach and preach Jesus Christ. Sublime stubbornness, magnificent disobedience, matter-of-fact defiance! That comes close to making us "feel" for the high priest. In fact, we almost hope that he had access to the ancient world's equivalent for tranquilizer pills! Along about that time, he must have been Jerusalem's most frustrated citizen.

Chapter Five

Despite the high priest's best efforts, the church was still growing. So many people were being added that a problem arose. The needy disciples were still being cared for from a common fund provided by those who had wealth to contribute, and **there arose a murmuring of the Grecians against the Hebrews, because their widows were neglected in the daily ministration.** Deliberate neglect? No; diversity of language. The "Grecians" were descendants of those exiled Jews who had been in countries whose language was Greek, while the "Hebrews" spoke dialects of the language of Aram— Aramaic. In other words, the person who was doing the distributing quite likely had only a hazy notion of what the "Grecian" widows required.

Up to this point, the twelve apostles had had direct responsibility for the practical benevolence of the church, and apparently this had become a thing which was taking too much of their time and strength, for we read, **Then the twelve called the multitude of the disciples unto them and said, "It is not reason that we should leave the word of God, and serve tables. Wherefore, brethren, look ye out among you seven men of honest report, full of the Holy Ghost and wisdom, whom we may appoint over this business. But we will give ourselves continually to prayer, and to the ministry of the word."**

Today's church could do with a long, hard look at that statement. "It is not reason that we should leave the word of God, and serve tables. . . ."

45

Your pastor doesn't "serve tables"? Well, you might as well tie an organdy apron around his outraged middle and have him help out with the next ladies' luncheon—he probably does everything else! He is the diplomat who tries to keep peace among grown-up saints who don't act like it; he is the after-dinner speaker on tap for every group from men's service clubs to overstuffed women who twitter gently about butterflies, or maybe it's Beethoven; he is the long-suffering counselor for married spoiled brats on the verge of divorce because their mates are monsters. Now, you take it from there, and name a dozen other things, including being a genial and wise "big brother" to your screaming teen-aged young while they are out of your hair at summer camp. (That would make him a sort of glorified baby sitter, wouldn't it?)

Look back at that spoiled brat bit for a minute: Can you tell me why it is that nobody, but *nobody* can figure out his own problems any more? Have we produced a generation of jellyfish that slither helplessly this way and that because they simply can't adjust to life? Maybe the whole problem is that they simply can't make life adjust to *them!* I love those rugged souls who are beautifully shaped, ground down, and polished from adjusting themselves (quite without benefit of counsel) to life's relentless wheel.

"But we will give ourselves continually to prayer, and to the ministry of the word." If your pastor works a ninety-hour week, when does he have time to pray? And are you one of those people who complain because the minister never calls on them? You're not? Good; they are the ones who will spend their first hundred years in heaven hunting for something to gripe about.

Have you ever shed sympathetic tears for pioneer preachers who had to work with their hands to support their families? They probably would not willingly have traded places with their grandsons who stand behind pulpits. A man who walks a furrow can listen to the song of a meadowlark — or the voice of God.

So the church acquired its first board of deacons. There were seven of them, chosen by the people and ordained by the laying on of hands by the apostles. Stephen, Philip, Prochorus, Nicanor, Timon, Parmenas, and Nicolas. Of

Stephen, the whole Christian world has heard, and most people know something about Philip; but the other five remain in the shadow of obscurity. We may safely infer, I think, that they went quietly and efficiently about their business of ministering to the needs of hungry and shivering saints from the day of their ordaining until the time of the "great persecution" when the church was blasted out of Jerusalem to carry out the second phase of the Lord's commission to be His witnesses in "all Judaea, and in Samaria."

And Stephen, full of faith and power, did great wonders and miracles among the people. The cynical might say that if Stephen had quietly "served tables" he wouldn't have gotten into trouble and been haled before the council. Quite so. And sometimes it might be safer and a lot more comfortable for us to keep our mouths shut, and carefully conceal our light under a bushel (basket). But some poor soul stumbling along in the resultant darkness might fall headlong into the bottomless pit.

Then there arose certain of the synagogue, which is called the synagogue of the Libertines, and Cyrenians, and Alexandrians, and of them of Cilicia and Asia, disputing with Stephen.

These synagogues were established by foreign Jews for their own use when they were in Jerusalem, and for the use of their sons who were sent there to complete their education at the schools and colleges which were usually attached to the synagogues. The "certain" mentioned could easily have been these bright young foreign students who were not about to let this fanatical upstart wreck the sacred traditions of their fathers. **And they were not able to resist the wisdom and the spirit by which he spake.** Which must have been very frustrating to the bright young students; and since they couldn't win the debate by fair means, they resorted to foul—charming people. We are not told anything about Stephen's formal schooling, but we are told that the men chosen to be deacons had to be "full of the Holy Ghost and wisdom," attributes which will enable a man to win very nearly any debate.

Then they suborned men, which said, "We have heard

him speak blasphemous words against Moses, and against God."

"Suborn." Ever stumble over a word for twenty-five years, and then get unbearably curious about it? I'd never seen the term except in the King James Version of the Bible, and had somehow acquired the notion that it was one of those archaic leftovers from the Elizabethan era, and probably couldn't even be found in a modern dictionary. But it's there: "Suborn. (Verb, transitive) To induce to commit perjury; to hire or persuade to swear falsely." The gentlemen of the foreign synagogues were really out to get Stephen. And they got him!

And they stirred up the people, and the elders, and the scribes, and came upon him, and caught him, and brought him to the council. And set up false witnesses, which said, "This man ceaseth not to speak blasphemous words against this holy place, and the law: for we heard him say, that this Jesus of Nazareth shall destroy this place, and shall change the customs which Moses delivered to us."

Sound familiar? It should. Perhaps two of these false witnesses were the same two whom the "chief priests, and elders, and all the council" finally found to testify against Jesus when He was before Caiaphas (Matthew's Gospel). You remember those two worthies testified, "This fellow said, 'I am able to destroy the temple of God, and to build it in three days.'" Apparently, determination and money could always find at least two cooperative witnesses in those days. Also, the idea comes through that the Jews were much more concerned about their magnificent temple than they were about God to whose worship it was allegedly devoted.

And all that sat in the council, looking stedfastly on him, saw his face as if it had been the face of an angel. The face of an angel. Shining, holy, beautiful, pure. Do you suppose that some of the council may have had a couple of qualms about the veracity of the accusing witnesses at that point?

Then said the high priest, "Are these things so?"

Stephen is being allowed an opportunity to answer his accusers. Instead of promptly and emphatically denying the charges, he begins tracing the history of the Jews. We wonder if the people in his audience were surprised. We suspect that the reaction of a modern audience to a recital of history would be absolute boredom enlivened by the nodding of a few heads of listeners who had dropped off to sleep. Stephen's hearers were probably mystified, and also lulled and soothed: it is pleasing to hear of the glory and greatness of one's forebears.

This young man with a face like an angel, recounting national history, rendering due honor to Abraham, Isaac, and Jacob—the Patriarchs—and Moses and David and Solomon, has not even mentioned the name of Jesus, and certainly has not made any threats against the temple. So why, some of his hearers might have wondered, why has he been arrested and brought to trial? Has somebody made a mistake?

And then they had their answer, and if any had been soothed to sleep they must have been jarred into a rude awakening by the shower of accusations flung at them like stones from David's slingshot.

"**Ye stiffnecked and uncircumcised in heart and ears, ye do always resist the Holy Ghost: as your fathers did, so do ye. Which of the prophets have not your fathers persecuted? and they have slain them which shewed before the coming of the Just One; of whom ye have been now the betrayers and murderers: who have received the law by the disposition of angels, and have not kept it.**"

Stubborn. Jews by physical ritual only. Resisting the Holy Ghost. Persecutors. Betrayers and murderers of the "Just One"—Israel's Messiah.

Stunned silence perhaps for the fraction of an instant, and then, **They gnashed on him with their teeth.** Teeth-grinding rage—they were about to explode.

What was Stephen's reaction to the gnashing of the teeth? In all probability, he didn't even notice it; he was occupied with much more important things. But he, being full of the Holy Ghost, looked up stedfastly into heaven, and saw the glory of God, and Jesus standing on the right hand of God. . . . Then, against an accompaniment of muffled sounds of fury, these words, "**Behold, I see the heavens opened, and the Son of man standing on the right hand of God.**"

The teeth gnashing opened into a concerted shout which swallowed up the prisoner's words as council, witnesses, and

spectators ceased to be a court and became a mob. **They** . . .
ran upon him with one accord.

Hands shot out to seize the young man with the glory of
God in his face. Pale, aristocratic hands that never touched
anything harsher than a sheet of papyrus, pudgy hands that
lovingly fondled coins, calloused hands that shed honest dirt
with the ceremonial washings, all yearned now for the feel of
huge rough stones in their grasp. They pushed and pulled and
buffeted Stephen out of the building. Did they stop in the
street outside and look about for missles? Not at all! Even
their consuming rage did not make them forget the legal
nicety which forbade stoning inside the city's walls; they
were a law-abiding mob: they **cast him out of the city.**

Stephen, being hurried along to the place of the stoning,
knew that death was reaching out to bury him under a heap
of bloody stones. But he was still looking at his risen and
ascended Lord, that One who had reassumed the majesty laid
aside for a veil of flesh and a death of disgrace to redeem the
world. Jesus, the Christ, still wearing that veil of flesh which
will forever identify Him with man, was *standing up,* waiting
for Stephen to join Him. This mob with its flying stones was
God's chosen way for lifting Stephen across the intervening
space to that place where the Son of man stood waiting.
Therefore with joy Stephen moved toward his appointment
with death.

**And cast him out of the city, and stoned him: and the
witnesses laid down their clothes at a young man's feet,
whose name was Saul.**

The witnesses, according to Jewish law, were required to
hurl the first stones, and then to lead the others of the assemblage in the execution of sentence. These men removed their
outer garments for greater muscular freedom, and they
placed the clothes on the ground at Saul's feet. Saul didn't
hurl any stones, he merely guarded the coats of those who
did. To me, it is a fascinating commentary on the honesty of
these terribly law-abiding people that the clothes of the witnesses had to be watched!

The scholarly young Saul watched the clothes. He also
watched Stephen. Stephen was naked. Stephen was bruised.
Stephen began to bleed horribly; he began to sag and sway

under the stoning, but his face was still lifted toward heaven, and his voice rang clearly: **"Lord Jesus, receive my spirit."**

The sound of the hated name renewed the mob's frenzy; the stones came faster, and with even more telling accuracy. But the doomed man knelt among them and raised his disfigured hands in a gesture of supplication to God, and again his voice rose above the sounds of hatred: **"Lord, lay not this sin to their charge."** His head dropped upon his breast; his eyes closed.

The stones kept coming down. Stone against flesh . . . stone against stone . . . stone upon stone. The heap grew higher. The top stones were not stained with blood.

The panting witnesses returned to the place where Saul was standing. They retrieved their mantles, and began adjusting them carefully, exchanging small talk about their disheveled appearance. Saul of Tarsus had a sudden feeling that his soul had touched defilement. He turned blindly away, and ran.

Great Christian thinkers have told us that Stephen traded his life for the soul of Saul. Saul who became Paul. Let us trace the precious line: Stephen to Paul . . . to Lydia . . . to Luther . . . to you and me—that thin, scarlet stream of martyr's blood cutting across the sands of time to bring salvation to me!

Chapter Six

And Saul was consenting unto his death. Saul helped Stephen's executioners; Saul watched him die. And for more than thirty-five years, until that day when his own neck was bared to the axe of the madman Nero, Saul of Tarsus never forgot the dying face and the dying words of Christ's first martyr.

And devout men carried Stephen to his burial, and made great lamentation over him. Devout men, strong men with tears running down their sweat-stained faces as they took away the spattered stones and lifted out the body of the beloved Stephen. Were these friends singled out for special fury in the storm that broke loose as if on signal with Stephen's death? Did skulking watchers carry word to Saul?

And at that time there was a great persecution against the church which was at Jerusalem; and they were all scattered abroad throughout the regions of Judaea and Samaria, except the apostles.

As for Saul, he made havoc of the church, entering into every house, and haling men and women committed them to prison.

Saul's conscience was in the saddle, digging with ever-reddening spurs into the soul that reared and plunged in an excess of fury as it sought to destroy the thing which tormented it.

Terrified saints, fleeing before the wrath of Saul, did not realize they were carrying out the second phase of the Lord's great commission, **"Ye shall be witnesses unto me both in Jerusalem, and in all Judaea, and in Samaria. . . ."** Saul, ferreting out the hapless saints and forcing others into flight, was even then serving the purpose of Him whose name he sought to purge from the minds of men.

If we had to leave our homes and our cherished possessions and flee for our lives from persecution, what would we think about? What would we talk about?

Therefore they that were scattered abroad went every where preaching the word. Luke seems to take for granted that wherever they paused, they would preach the Word. Would we? We might, after we got over being outraged at the injustice of it all. Then again, we might hide in some convenient village and brood in permanent silence.

Then Philip went down to the city of Samaria, and preached Christ unto them. One commentator (Butler) says, "We do not know what city, but we may well infer that it was Sychar where Christ had privately taught for two days with wonderful results."

It was the city of Sychar where our Lord matter-of-factly shattered the taboo of the Jews "having no dealings with the Samaritans" by engaging a Samaritan woman in conversation at Jacob's well. So, if Sychar was the city, we can easily understand Philip's warm welcome. Four or five years had passed since the day when Jesus told the woman plainly that He was the Messiah, and she had left her water pot at the well and rushed back to the city to tell the good news to the men. (The women probably had nothing to do with her because of her reputation.) Two years, possibly, had elapsed since the Jews had delivered the Messiah up to be crucified. Did the Samaritan people know of that? Quite probably. Had they heard the wonderful news of His resurrection? Probably not; not directly, anyway, and certainly not from somebody who had *seen* Him, who knew that it was true. They must have been hungry to hear more.

And the people with one accord gave heed unto those things which Philip spake, hearing and seeing the miracles he did. For unclean spirits, crying with loud voice, came out of many that were possessed with them: and many taken with

palsies, and that were lame, were healed. And there was great joy in that city.

Indeed there was joy. Joy of demented people made sane again, joy of people whose useless limbs had been made steady and strong, joy of the families of those who were healed; indeed there was joy. And beneath this ecstasy, the deep, abiding joy of all who realized that Jesus was truly the Messiah because even though He was not present, the servant whom He had baptized with the Holy Spirit could perform miracles by calling on His mighty name.

But there was a certain man called Simon. . . . Now, if Simon lived today, he would have top billing as "Simon the Superb, Simon the Supreme, Simon the World's Master Magician." And people would pay perfectly good money to go inside and see him do his tricks, to be intrigued and amazed at the seeming miracles he did. And they would get their money's worth of good, clean fun, because people simply dote on being fooled in that fashion. But Simon doesn't live now, he lived then; and incredibly enough, people seem to have been even more gullible in those days, so they believed him when he said that his "great gift" was of God!

Simon was a canny soul, a very shrewd businessman. He watched Philip perform miracles in the name of Jesus Christ. He probably looked very closely, studying to discover Philip's gimmicks. There were no gimmicks—this was for real. H-m-m, this magic was more powerful than his; he'd better get in on it!

Contemptible? Certainly. Without modern parallel? Well, I *have* heard of people joining the church because of the marvelous potential. Wonderful place to find new customers, you know, and most of them are likely to be completely honest, even!

Then Simon himself believed, also: and when he was baptized, he continued with Philip, and wondered, beholding the miracles and signs which were done. Of course Simon believed; he couldn't very well help himself. To get completely in on this new thing, you had to go through the ritual of baptism: Simon was baptized. He continued to study Philip; if he applied himself assiduously, in a few months he might be able to do these same miracles and have them quite authentic. Still, there seemed to be something that he lacked, and which Philip had in abundance: an elusive, almost terrifying power. Now, how did he go about getting that?

Quite without intending to, Peter and John supplied Simon's answer. Upon receipt of the joyous news that Samaria had received the word of God, the other apostles sent those two to Samaria that they might bring to perfection the marvelous work which Philip had begun. We read, **Who, when they were come down, prayed for them that they might receive the Holy Ghost: (For as yet he was fallen upon none of them: only they were baptized in the name of the Lord Jesus.)**

John, by the way, is the same John who with his brother James was in a mood to bring down fire from heaven to consume Samaritans of a village that was inhospitable to the Lord Jesus, refusing Him lodging while He was on His way to Jerusalem. Now he is praying for divine fire to be sent to bless, not to destroy, the Samaritans.

Then they laid their hands on them, and they received the Holy Ghost. And when Simon saw that through the laying on of the apostles' hands the Holy Ghost was given, he offered them money, saying, "Give me also this power, that on whomsoever I lay hands, he may receive the Holy Ghost."

It is abundantly evident that Simon himself had not received the Holy Spirit. He believed in Jesus Christ. That was strictly an intellectual assent; he *had* to believe (being an intelligent man) the incontrovertible evidence of miracles performed before his eyes. Simon believed with his mind, but his heart was quite uninvolved; he certainly had not been "born of the Spirit," or he would not have voiced that blasphemous request. In his soul there was no holy awe; he was not even trying to buy his way into heaven, as many pitiable creatures have done down through the ages. He was merely trying to "buy in" on a good thing. In short, Simon was trying to buy his way into the fold of the apostles! Very good business, indeed, if he could guarantee a customer that the mere touch of his hands could impart that incredible, that terrifying power.

Peter, as usual, was the apostolic spokesman. His eyes must have flamed with the very wrath of God as his voice crackled like a whiplash that curled the edges of Simon's soul with terror. **"Thy money perish with thee, because thou hast thought that the gift of God may be purchased with money. Thou hast neither part nor lot in this matter: for thy heart is not right in the sight of God. Repent therefore of this thy wickedness, and pray God if perhaps the thought of thine heart may be forgiven thee. For I perceive that thou art in the gall of bitterness, and in the bond of iniquity."**

Simon's dream of the ultimate in magic shattered into sharp fragments that threatened to cut his soul to pieces. He may or may not have been repentant, but he certainly was scared, too scared even to do his own praying, for we hear his terrified bleat, **"Pray ye to the Lord for me, that none of these things which ye have spoken come upon me."** Gone is the dream of power. Simon is perfectly willing now to settle for simple salvation! Whether or not Peter and John were touched with pity and prayed for the frightened magician, we are not even told. At that point, he is quietly dropped from the narrative. So also we drop him without speculation upon the various legends that surround his later life.

Peter and John preached in many villages of the Samaritans, and made their way back to Jerusalem. But what about Philip? Philip's work in Samaria was done, and he was about to have a new assignment. **And the angel of the Lord spake unto Philip, saying, "Arise, and go toward the south unto the way that goeth down from Jerusalem unto Gaza which is desert."**

What would you do if an angel told you to do something? Ask him to show his credentials? Listen carefully to make sure you could follow instructions? (I'd probably have to make notes!) Or, which is most likely, run screaming to a psychiatrist? We ought to find out more about angels; we'd be less likely to go into shock when we wake up some glad morning to find them all around us.

Philip might have wondered dimly why he was being removed from the scene of a very successful evangelistic undertaking, but there is no record of his having even discussed the matter with the angel. Merely the simple statement, **And he arose and went.**

The place to which Philip was directed was a long way

from the place where he was. How long did it take him to get there? We don't know. How did he get there? He walked. (How long is it since you muttered to yourself because somebody else in the family was using your car, and you had to walk a block for a loaf of bread?) Walking along a desert road would not be the most pleasant way of spending any of the days of one's life.

Now, a modern writer—I mean the kind who devotes four pages to getting a heroine out of bed, bathed, and dressed!— would have told what Philip ate and when, whether or not he used a sleeping bag, how much water he took for the journey, if his feet got terribly blistered, how often he shaved and what he used to keep the hot winds from wrecking his freshly shaved skin, and, of course, a minute-by-minute record of what he thought along the journey. Luke spares us all this. He says, **And he arose and went, and behold, a man of Ethiopia, an eunuch of great authority under Candace queen of the Ethiopians, who had the charge of all her treasure, and had come to Jerusalem for to worship, was returning, and sitting in his chariot, read Esaias the prophet. . . .**

I have no idea why, but that name, Candace, has always held an odd sort of fascination for me. Reading something recently about the mighty doings of Augustus Caesar, I came across a casual reference to a military campaign against Candace, the one-eyed but warlike queen of the Ethiopians, and made a note on the back of an envelope: "Candace, Queen of the Ethiopians—fascinating lady with one eye and a proclivity for making war. Slightly sinister character, and much more interesting than Cleopatra who was merely glamorous, and collected Romans for a hobby!"

This campaign, which Augustus won, I believe, took place a few years after 25 B.C. and Philip encountered Queen Candace's secretary of the treasury in A.D. 34, an elapsed time of approximately fifty-four years which would have made the queen an elderly lady. By that time she probably would have been so absent-minded that she couldn't remember whether her trusted officer was a Jewish proselyte or a mere run-of-the-mill heathen. But then a quick check of a Bible encyclopedia revealed that Candace was quite probably a title (or name of a dynasty) like Pharaoh or Ptolemy, and therefore the eunuch's royal employer was probably not the same queen who engaged in warfare with Augustus. She must have been reasonably tolerant of other people's religious beliefs, else she would not have filled such an important position with a man who worshiped the God of the Jews. It seems unlikely that she herself was of that persuasion, or Luke would have mentioned the fact.

This officer had been to Jerusalem to worship in the temple, a religious pilgrimage which devout Jews and proselytes the world over made whenever possible. That was why there were so many "foreigners" present on the Day of Pentecost. The mood of worship was still upon the man as he made his tedious journey home. He was reading from the Prophecy of Isaiah instead of knitting his official brow over latest tax figures as *our* Secretary of the Treasury would have been doing while his jet screamed homeward across the sky. But then, it is faintly doubtful that our Secretary of the Treasury would have been indulging in a religious pilgrimage in the first place.

Then the Spirit said unto Philip, "Go near, and join thyself to this chariot." And Philip ran thither to him.

The man was reading aloud from the fifty-third chapter of Isaiah, and Philip, probably a little out of breath, asked, **"Understandest thou what thou readest?"**

The man's reply sounds almost petulant, **"How can I, except some man should guide me?"** Then comes the evidence that the Spirit who sent Philip along a desert road for an unrevealed appointment was also preparing the mind of the man He had chosen for His messenger's hearer: **And he desired Philip that he would come up and sit with him.**

Of whom were the tragic words spoken, the prophet himself, or some other man? Again, the Spirit at work, framing the perfect question that cued Philip's sermon, for he **began at the same scripture, and preached unto him Jesus.**

Jesus Christ was Philip's theme, whether preaching to multitudes in Samaria or to a solitary hearer on a desert road, and then as now, that kind of preaching resulted in conversion. When they came to a "certain water"—probably an oasis, since one doesn't find little creeks babbling along in a desert—the eunuch asked to be baptized.

Was Philip remembering Simon who believed only with his intellect when he answered, "**If thou believest with all thine heart thou mayest** [be baptized] "?

And he answered and said, "I believe that Jesus Christ is the Son of God."

Simon had seen miracles performed in the name of Jesus Christ, and this awesome display of power had forced him to believe; the eunuch had witnessed no miracle, only the sudden appearence of this messenger of Jesus Christ to minister to his specific need. And the Spirit who had sent the messenger prompted the answer to the message: "**I believe that Jesus Christ is the Son of God.**"

That was enough. **And he commanded the chariot to stand still.** Command to horses, or to a driver? He isn't mentioned, but most likely there was a charioteer. So important a personage would hardly travel alone on such a long journey, and, too, it is hardly likely that a man could handle a team of horses and read from a scroll at the same time.

Philip and the eunuch went down into the water, and Philip baptized him, but when they came up out of the water, **the Spirit of the Lord caught away Philip, that the eunuch saw him no more: and he went on his way rejoicing.** "Caught away Philip." How? We are not told. The mental image is almost as strong as that of Elijah disappearing from sight as Elisha watched. We see Philip with his garments still wet from the baptismal stream, his face still alight from the solemn beauty of the words he has just pronounced, enveloped as in a whirlwind and being carried away.

The effect of this disappearence upon the newly baptized convert must have been startling indeed. Surely he must have realized that he was a man singled out by God Himself in a very special way, for the divine messenger had materialized as it were from the midst of the barren desert to minister to his need. And when his profession of faith had been sealed by baptism, the messenger had vanished just as mysteriously as he had come. Wherever the eunuch went from that moment on, he would have shining on his pathway the "true Light which lighteth every man that cometh into the world," and in that knowledge, he went on his way rejoicing.

But Philip was found at Azotus. Which furthers the idea

of being propelled along by a whirlwind. **And passing through, he preached in all the cities till he came to Caesarea.** Philip's home was in Caesarea, so he preached all the way home. And in Caesarea we shall find him again twenty years later entertaining Paul and his companions in his hospitable home.

Chapter Seven

And Saul, yet breathing out threatenings and slaughter against the disciples of the Lord, went unto the high priest, and desired of him letters to Damascus to the synagogues, that if he found any of this way, whether they were men or women, he might bring them bound unto Jerusalem.

"Breathing out threatenings and slaughter"—what handling of words! And what a picture of Saul!

Saul was not a placid young man; he seems to have been in a constant state of seething. Here was a young man devoured by the zeal of his convictions, wildly devoted to the religion of his fathers, determined to preserve his faith in its purity no matter what the cost, mounted on a tough-mouthed horse named Tradition, and galloping furiously in the wrong direction. How many times have you heard somebody say it doesn't make any difference what a man believes so long as he is sincere? Saul couldn't have been more sincere!

Saul of Tarsus who became Paul the Apostle is one of the most fascinating characters in Christian history, and one of the rare ones with almost universal appeal. His hairbreadth escapes from death have gripped generations of squirming Juniors and glued them to the edges of their chairs; his brilliant mind has awed scholars of nineteen-odd centuries, and his sublime adoration of the One he encountered on the Damascus road has inspired the souls of millions of just plain people.

Paul is the subject of innumerable books that range from magnificent to mildly absurd, and his enigmatic reference to a thorn in his flesh has provided every Pauline authority—real and imaginary—with a wonderful range for speculation. The guessing runs from near-blindness through epilepsy, and even includes a man who, so the author asserts, was one of the numerous individuals who hindered Paul in his work. Take your pick. It is just possible that the apostle would have been more definite had his divine collaborator, the Holy Spirit, deemed the information necessary for us. At any rate, if Paul had a sense of humor and has taken any notice of the theories about his thorn in the flesh, he must have been mildly amused for lo, these many centuries.

After the death of Stephen, to which he was "consenting," Saul had attacked the new heresy with a ferocious zeal which sent him on a house-to-house search that lodged the hapless disciples in prison. He did not even spare the women.

When things seemed to be coming under control in Jerusalem, word came that the hated cult was spreading like embers from a windblown fire, and had reached even to Damascus and was turning from the true faith the members of the Jewish colony there. This thing must be stopped before it became a holocaust. If defecting members of the Damascus synagogues could be brought to Jerusalem in chains, and a few of them executed for their stubborn heresy, that might be the deluge to drown the embers. Unless, of course, there were many more like Stephen. *Stephen . . . his face when he was dying . . . his prayer for forgiveness for the men who were killing him . . . that prayer included Saul!* His restlessness grew wilder. He went to the office of the high priest for the necessary legal authority for the arrest and extradition of certain Jewish residents of the Roman province of Syria.

The high priest, who had no doubt been breathing a little easier since Saul started on his murderous rampage, gladly gave his consent to the venture. Naturally, if he could have known what was going to happen to his emissary on the outskirts of Damascus, he would have imprisoned *Saul* right then. That was to be the last chance his office would have for some years to lay hands on Saul of Tarsus.

Living casually in the ecclesiastical freedom which is our

heritage from our Lord Jesus Christ, it is next to impossible for us to imagine a situation that would be the equivalent of the moderator of the General Assembly (Presbyterian) issuing warrants for the arrest and extradition of American Presbyterians residing in Canada because they had suddenly decided to become Mormons or Episcopalians or Jehovah's Witnesses. The honorable moderator would be escorted to the nearest psychopathic ward, and the Canadian Presbyterians would laugh and laugh. But in the year A.D. 32 the Jewish "church" and the Jewish state were one and the same thing, and the matter-of-fact Roman mind acknowledged that, and acted accordingly.

We are not told how much time elapsed between Saul's obtaining the "letters" from the high priest, and his departure for Damascus. Considering his temperament, we would be justified in thinking it to be a matter of hours. The distance was 140 miles, and the required traveling time five or six days. Yet somehow the news of Saul's quest got to Damascus before he did, for we shall find Ananias making mention of that fact when he was arguing with the Lord about an assignment.

Once again Luke, the master reporter, takes up an epoch, and with strong fingers around his pen compresses it into a handful of words that are inked with everlasting clarity upon the pages of time.

And as he journeyed, he came near Damascus: and suddenly there shined round about him a light from heaven: and he fell to the earth, and heard a voice saying unto him, "Saul, Saul, why persecutest thou me?" And he said "Who art thou, Lord?" And the Lord said, "I am Jesus whom thou persecutest: it is hard for thee to kick against the pricks."

And he trembling and astonished said, "Lord, what wilt thou have me to do?" And the Lord said unto him, "Arise, and go into the city, and it shall be told thee what thou must do."

And the men which journeyed with him stood speechless, hearing a voice, but seeing no man. And Saul arose from the earth; and when his eyes were opened, he saw no man: but they led him by the hand, and brought him into Damascus.

And he was three days without sight, and neither did eat nor drink.

"Near Damascus." Almost to the end of the long, tiresome journey, which to that point had likely been routine heat and sand and glare, made more acute by Saul's driving urge to get there. "Near Damascus." Probably within sight of the city which was his goal, and then: **And suddenly there shined round about him a light from heaven: and he fell to the earth. . . .**

"A light from heaven." Light whose intensity made the glare of the desert sun at midday seem dim, light whose furious brightness made the men fall on their faces in the hot desert sand; light more powerful than the flash from an atomic blast whose anticipation would send men deep into caves to protect themselves if they had warning. But falling to the earth did not protect Saul from the light, and closing his eyes did not shut out the vision of Him who was in the midst of it. **And he fell to the earth, and heard a voice saying unto him, "Saul, Saul, why persecutest thou me?"**

This One in the center of the unbearable brightness knew Saul by name (He also knows *your* name!), but Saul did not know Him. But he did know that the One who spoke to him was divine, for he asked, **"Who art thou, Lord?"**

How did Saul know this Being was divine? Because his mind was saturated with the history of his people, and he knew that that Light in its terrible majesty bespoke the very presence of God. That Light had attracted the musing curiosity of Moses when a desert shrub flamed furiously but was not consumed. That was the Light from whence had issued the divine commission which ultimately delivered the children of Israel from their slavery in Egypt. That Light, the very Shechinah Glory, was in the pillar of fire, and the tabernacle in the wilderness; that was the Light which prostrated Saul and his companions, and he recognized it. Hence, "Who art thou, *Lord?*"

And the Lord said, "I am Jesus whom thou persecutest: it is hard for thee to kick against the pricks."

In the midst of the Light that meant God's presence, *Jesus!* Saul knew now: *Jesus was God,* and he, Saul of Tarsus in the fury of his zeal had been trying to *destroy God!* He who had worshiped God from his youth with that perfectness which marked a Pharisee, he upon whose soul the Commandments were etched as with a sharpened stone, he had been trying to destroy the One who had given those Commandments to Moses.

Again came the shattering memory of Stephen's dying face, the haunting vision of men and women he had snatched from the sanctuary of their homes and doomed to prison or death. "It is hard for thee to kick against the pricks."

Conscience: a goad in the hands of God, pricking at relentless intervals at the soul of Saul of Tarsus, even as a goad in the hands of a husbandman pricks the hide of a reluctant ox. Jesus: God omniscient who knew what was in the mind of this tormented man.

Saul of Tarsus, who but minutes ago had been bent upon expunging the name of Jesus Christ from the minds of men, in the midst of this awful flash of revelation, capitulated utterly. Henceforth and forevermore he was to be the eager servant of Him who is Lord of creation, only begotten Son of God the Father, shaping with infinite patience the souls of those whom He will call to serve Him.

And he, trembling and astonished, said, "Lord, what wilt thou have me to do?"

And the Lord said unto him, "Arise, and go into the city, and it shall be told thee what thou must do." One step at a time God would lead him; one page at a time the book of his instructions was to be opened. God could have revealed to Saul at that moment the whole pattern and picture of his apostleship, but He does not so work. We in whom patience is not a noticeable virtue would do well to ponder that fact when our efforts at serving God do not remake the earth over one weekend!

When Saul got to his feet and opened his eyes, he discovered that he was totally blind. What a way to start a career of serving God! The men with him who had shared his awesome experience, but did not comprehend it, took him compassionately by the hand and led him into Damascus. Altogether a remarkable contrast to the entrance which Saul had planned, for, whereas he had intended riding in, mounted upon the majesty of Law to devastate, he actually was led in blind and helpless, utterly at the mercy of others.

And he was three days without sight, and neither did eat nor drink—Total fasting in total darkness; complete communion with God unhampered by the distractions of sight and appetite. Saul was alone with the One whom he had just met.

The next bit of narrative should be very comforting to those of us who are obscure, unimportant saints, and will remain so all of our lives. We may be obscure, but to God Almighty we are *not* unimportant! You or I may very well be that tiny fragment which fits between two big pieces of a puzzle to bring the whole thing to completion and make it make sense. That **certain disciple at Damascus, named Ananias** was surely such a fragment, for the man who was to be the mighty Apostle to the Gentiles sat humbly in darkness waiting for him, and praying. Had Ananias stayed at home with his fear instead of going to the street and the house where God directed him, Saul might have begun to have doubts. He had **seen in a vision a man named Ananias coming in and putting his hand on him that he might receive his sight.**

But Ananias did not go until he had fully discussed the matter with the Lord! Ananias reminded the Lord that this Saul of Tarsus was the one who had wrought evil among the saints at Jerusalem, and that moreover his very presence in Damascus was for the purpose of doing the same thing there. God's patience with His fearful and reluctant saint should also be a source of comfort to us who are not always teetering on our toes to be on our way for Him. God did not say to Ananias, as many parents did to their children in my childhood, "You do this because I said so." God, who alone has the right to require instant and unquestioning obedience, deigned to explain things fully to His terrified child.

But the Lord said unto him, "Go thy way: for he is a chosen vessel unto me, to bear my name before the Gentiles, and kings, and the children of Israel: For I will shew him how great things he must suffer for my name's sake."

The Lord not only explained the matter to Ananias but— it would seem from pondering the above words—Ananias knew what Saul's work was to be before Saul himself knew it.

Ananias went.

Saul was expecting this God-directed caller who was to come and lay hands on him to restore sight, he even knew his name, but we wonder if he was prepared for his caller's very first word: "**Brother Saul. . . .**" That might have been the first time that the phrase, "The grace of our Lord and Saviour, Jesus Christ" came to Saul's mind. Certainly, that grace was the only thing which could have made a man marked for possible death address his persecutor as "brother."

"**Brother Saul, the Lord, even Jesus, that appeared to thee in the way as thou camest, hath sent me, that thou mightest receive thy sight, and be filled with the Holy Ghost.**"

Confirmation! The encounter had been quite real, and not a figment of his overwrought imagination, nor the result of a sunstroke. Nor had the vision been compounded of shock and terror and darkness. *Here was the man!* Here was the man laying hands on him; strong hands, gentle hands, hands of compassion. An obscure layman put his hands on a blinded giant, and with that touch the mighty power of the Holy Spirit surged through the prostrate Saul and pushed off the scales that had sealed his eyes, and lifted him to his feet.

And he received sight forthwith, and arose, and was baptized. The face of Ananias must have been a beloved image in the mind of Saul for the rest of his life. This was the gentle brother God had sent to corroborate his vision and restore his sight. This was the man who baptized him, the man whose testimony was to convince the other disciples in Damascus that Saul of Tarsus was in truth one of their very own now, and not a contemptible spy using this means to worm his way into their confidence that he might the more fully betray them.

Saul did not waste any time. **And straightway he preached Christ in the synagogues, that he is the Son of God. But all that heard him were amazed. . . .**

Small wonder they were amazed. This was the man who hobnobbed with the high priest and the chief priests in Jerusalem; this was Saul of Tarsus whose fury had laid waste the church in the holy city, and whose very presence here presaged the same fate for them. How was it, then, that he was forcefully declaiming that this Jesus of Nazareth was the Son of God?

The rulers of the synagogues probably smiled quietly into their beards: Saul had resorted to trickery to bring the heretics out of hiding and declare themselves, so that they might be the more easily scooped up when the time came. A most resourceful young man, this Saul. Then they began to wonder as Saul's preaching became more powerful, more convincing. Really now, couldn't he achieve his goal without adding more converts to the hated cult before he closed in on its adherents?

The rulers waited, their patience beginning to wear thin, their apprehension growing. At last the awful truth dawned upon them: Saul was *not* playing a part, *he believed what he was preaching!* They had been duped, they had wasted precious time, and now they had better act, and fast. They **took counsel to kill him.** Apparently, these people never acted on the impulse of hot outrage, they talked things over to figure out a saner approach. But apparently, also, there was a traitor in their midst, or an apprehensive ear glued to the door of their chambers, for, **but their laying await was known of Saul.**

Here now begins the deadly game of trying to destroy Saul of Tarsus. When the news got back to Jerusalem, the high priest probably cursed the day when he had signed the letters that had taken Saul out of his grasp. Oh well, patience; they'd catch him sooner or later. Nonetheless, the loss of a man of Saul's intellect and ability was a thing that would hurt, for his talents would be turned to hammer blows smashing against the traditions of Moses to destroy them. The sooner he was silenced by death, the better.

And they watched the gates day and night to kill him. They would hunt him down if he stayed in Damascus (even as he had hunted down disciples in Jerusalem!) and they would grab him if he tried to leave. Saul might as well give up and admit he was a dead man. But they failed to reckon with two things: the power of God Almighty, and the resourcefulness of their fellow Jews.

Those who were watching for Saul were not private citizens only, there were also soldiers of "the governor under Aretas the king [who] kept the city of the Damascenes with a *garrison,* desirous to apprehend me. . . ." as Paul was to write many years later to the Corinthian Christians. Then, as now, when church and state join hands to persecute, the Christian has good reason to quake in his sandals, and to look for a basket and a "window on the wall."

God's chosen apostle settled himself in a large basket, was lowered by strong hands from the **window on the wall,** and disappeared in the desert's night shadows while authorities of church and state watched vigilantly at every gate in the city's wall. Even as the mighty forerunner, John the Baptist, was "in the deserts till the day of his shewing unto Israel," so Saul hid himself in the lonely wastes to wait, to pray, and to prepare.

We know that at least three years elapse between verses 25 and 26 of the ninth chapter of The Acts, for we read in Paul's letter to the Galatians: "Neither went I up to Jerusalem to them which were apostles before me; but I went into Arabia, and returned again to Damascus. Then, after three years I went up to Jerusalem to see Peter, and abode with him fifteen days. . . ."

Saul had been away for three years, but memories of the horrors he had wrought among them were still fresh in the minds of the disciples. They knew nothing of the blinding light and the revelation, or the changing of roles from persecutor to persecuted; they knew only that here was the man who had killed their people, and they were afraid of him. They, too, thought that the haughty minion of the high priest had stooped to the role of spy that he might discover beyond doubt the ones he would destroy. They **believed not that he was a disciple.**

Remember Barnabas **(which is, being interpreted, the son of consolation)** who sold his land and turned the money over to the apostles for the care of destitute saints? At this point he comes back into the picture. Why he believed in Saul's sincerity, we do not know; whether he had known Saul personally before, we are not told. Some suggest that the two of them were quite likely members of the same synagogue with the martyred Stephen. But we can pick up enough authentic information (from the Scriptures) to know that later when Saul needed a sponsor, a defender, or a friend, Barnabas was right there.

Barnabas took him to the apostles (apparently only Peter and James, for Paul's account of the incident says he saw only those two) and told the story. They trusted Barnabas, therefore they accepted Saul and he immediately began to **speak boldly in the name of the Lord Jesus, and dispute against the Grecians,** which suggests strongly that he preached and debated in the same synagogue where Stephen had preached. Whether or not it was the same audience, their reaction was the same: they couldn't silence the opposition by force of argument, therefore, they'd kill the man. Devastatingly simple—one-track minds, these people apparently had.

Here we have escape number two. Saul's work for God had hardly begun, and he would not know martyrdom till it was finished. The plan to kill him was discovered by his newly found "brethren," and they took him down to Caesarea and put him on a boat headed for Tarsus. Saul was going "back home," apparently having failed. And when we meet him again, it will be in company with Barnabas who went to Tarsus to look for him, because he had discovered the place where Saul belonged.

Chapter Eight

Then had the churches rest throughout all Judaea and Galilee and Samaria, and were edified; and walking in the fear of the Lord, and in the comfort of the Holy Ghost, were multiplied.

This "rest" did not result from a sudden switching from persecution to sweetness and light on the part of the priestly hierarchy: it was pretty much the same thing that would happen if a man plagued for a year by minor headaches should suddenly discover he had a cancer. He would, quite naturally, forget all about the headaches.

The menace of the moment was not Christianity, but Caligula. That enterprising young man had succeeded the aged and unpopular Tiberius as emperor of Rome. Some historians assert that Caligula hastened the succession somewhat by smothering Tiberius with a convenient pillow case (or some such thing) when the old gentleman rallied from what had appeared to be the long-awaited death. It is hardly likely that the Jerusalem people were unduly concerned about the new emperor's penchant for murder; what disturbed them was that he took much too seriously the business of being one of the gods.

It seems that this young man, who was somewhat more insane than some of the other emperors—and that's a large statement!—was actually convinced that he was a god. And since any god worthy of being invited to tea on Olympus must needs have statues here and there, the new god had statues of himself placed here and there for the convenience of his worshipers.

Now, the temple of the Jews in Jerusalem, Caligula reasoned, would be an absolutely ideal place for one of his more imposing statues. The Jews would have hysterics, naturally, since their peculiar monotheistic nonsense forbade the use of statues, but that really was ridiculous. He would have one of his statues placed in the temple, and their priests could offer daily sacrifice. Augustus and Tiberius had humored their stubborn whims by accepting daily prayers *for* the emperor; but he, Caligula, would end that absurdity once and for all time. They'd pray *to* the emperor who was the God Gaius, or else!

So, while the officials at Jerusalem were busy trying to keep their heads, their high office, and the purity of their religion intact, the new church had "rest."

Simon Peter now returns to the narrative. When we last saw him, he and John were on their way back to Jerusalem from that city in Samaria where Philip had preached, and they were preaching in Samaritan villages as they went back. Now, he is on another journey, a rather extensive one for somebody traveling on foot, as Peter quite likely did.

We read, **As Peter passed throughout all quarters, he came down also to the saints which dwelt at Lydda.** Lydda was a village six miles inland from Joppa, that ancient city on the Mediterranean about forty miles from Jerusalem whose port city it had been since Solomon's time. Both Lydda and Joppa were some thirty miles from Caesarea, which was to be the next "point of interest" to Peter. Lydda to Joppa to Caesarea—Simon Peter was being drawn into position for his date with destiny, but he, leaving destiny in the hands of God, was concerned with what immediately confronted him: **A certain man named Aeneas, which had kept his bed eight years, and was sick of the palsy.**

The man named Aeneas was quite likely a Christian believer, because Peter **found** him when he **came down to the saints which dwelt at Lydda.** Now why hadn't God healed Aeneas earlier? Well, for one thing, nobody had pointed out to him that he had access to healing in Jesus Christ. Peter did that. He looked down at the helpless man who was doomed to lie there till he died—probably of old age—and made what sounds like an almost matter-of-fact statement: **"Aeneas, Jesus Christ maketh thee whole. . . ."**

Did Aeneas wail petulantly, "Well, why on earth didn't *somebody tell me sooner?*" No. He was far too busy acting on Peter's next words: **"Arise, and make thy bed."** Luke says simply, **And he arose immediately.** And adds, **And all that dwelt at Lydda and Saron saw him, and turned to the Lord,** leaving us to imagine the details. A vivid picture of that comes easily: A man paralyzed for eight long years, lying flat and helpless, living, perhaps, by virtue of the fact that somebody literally put food in his mouth. That man gets up from his pallet on the floor. His now-supple body moves easily as he bends to roll up his bed, his fingers move with complete facility as he smooths the roll. Then he seizes the arm of the man who pronounced his deliverance, and moves silently through the door.

Once outside, he begins shouting praises to God, and calling his neighbors. Within minutes a cluster of excited villagers rushes along with Peter and Aeneas; before nightfall, all the village of Lydda knows about it.

And all that dwelt at Lydda and Saron saw him, and turned to the Lord. Not only in his village did he testify of the miracle, but in the whole region of the plain of Sharon he went, and people, seeing and hearing, turned to the Lord.

And then there came two men to see Peter. Two men from the nearby city of Joppa, half numb with grief, had come to implore Peter to come quickly to Joppa where death had taken a beloved woman: **A certain disciple named Tabitha, which by interpretation is called Dorcas.**

Luke does not say here, but other sources tell us that Dorcas was a widow. The name means "gazelle," which immediately conjures up a picture of a small, deer-like creature with luminous eyes. *Dorcas* was a term of endearment which Greek men used for their women, but because of this woman the name, to us, means selfless generosity and endless work for other people—usually poor people.

Dorcas was dead. Did the disciples think that Peter could restore her to life, or did they hope only for the comfort of his presence? We do not know. We only know that **Peter**

arose and went with them. Somehow, we can see his gnarled, sandaled feet striding toward Joppa, moving so fast that the messengers almost had to run to keep up with him.

Weeping friends met them at the portals, and escorted Peter, hot and breathless, to the upper chamber where the body lay in state. **And all the widows stood by him weeping, and shewing the coats and garments which Dorcas made, while she was with them.** There were old widows whose withered hands shook against the coats Dorcas had made to keep the chill from their blood; there were young widows clutching the garments made for their children by her benevolent hands. What would they do now? Dorcas was dead.

Peter wept with them. And then he motioned them gently from the room. For the work before him, he needed to be alone with the One who had said, "Simon, son of Jonas, lovest thou me? . . . Feed my sheep."

"Yea, Lord," Simon might have answered now, "I would feed Thy sheep with the bread of Thy pity, I would feed these grieving ones with the bread of Thy consolation; I would feed them with physical bread, and clothe them again with the warmth of wool fashioned by the hands of this Thy daughter whose life has gone back to Thee. Lord of pity, Lord of love, Lord of all-conquering life, restore, I beseech Thee, this one. . . ."

Peter kneeled down, and prayed. Sweat, weariness, agony, the great burden of compassion pressing down upon a soul lodged against the indisputable fact of death. "Lord of life, Source of life, Maker of heaven and earth, *God!* Let Thy Holy Spirit whom Thou hast put in me go forth from me and touch and permeate this rigid clay that it may pulse and throb again with life. . . . O God! O God! *O God!* . . ." **And turning him to the body said, "Tabitha, arise. . . ."**

"Glory and praise and majesty to Thy conquering name, O Lord of heaven and earth! Color of blood moving through idle veins to touch this pallid face . . . movement of pulse beating gently in the throat . . . motion of eyelids lifting . . . *O God . . . victory!*"

And she opened her eyes: and when she saw Peter, she sat up. "Who are you?" she must have asked, "and where are those who stood by me weeping when I fell asleep?"

Peter extended his hand, and Dorcas grasped it eagerly as he answered, "I am Simon Peter, an apostle of our Lord Jesus who in tender mercy and mighty power has awakened you from the sleep of death. Those who were with you are in the outer room, weeping and praying." Peter's strong hands lifted her up and his voice boomed against the closed door. "Come! Come and see this thing which our God has done!"

The door opened and the **saints and widows** filed in. They saw Dorcas standing with Peter, Dorcas alive and strong standing by her own bier, holding out her hands, smiling at them. They fell on their knees and with one voice raised a mighty shout of thanksgiving and exultation.

And when the wild fervor had calmed somewhat, Dorcas probably reached quietly again for her needle and thread.

"Peter, our Lord's apostle, through His holy Name, has brought back to life Tabitha who was dead!" The joyful word flashed from one household to another among the believers, and, passing to nonbelievers, became, "A man named Peter has called upon the name of one, Jesus of Nazareth, a prophet and teacher whom Pilate crucified at the high priest's wish, and through the power of that name has brought back to life a woman who was dead. We went to see the woman. We saw her sewing for the poor. A hundred witnesses testify that she was truly dead, and now she is truly alive. Is not this Jesus in truth our Messiah?"

And it was known throughout all Joppa; and many believed in the Lord.

Chapter Nine

Things don't just happen; God arranges them. Peter remained in Joppa for a considerable time, and he was the house guest of **one, Simon, a tanner.** A tanner's trade entailed the unclean business of skinning animals so that their hides could be worked and cured and softened into leather, and this, quite naturally, required contact with dead animals. Consequently, this work was dishonorable in the estimation of a careful Jew. Nonetheless, Peter was the houseguest of Simon who was a tanner.

God was about to switch Peter from dead animals to live Gentiles, and the one idea was, to a Jewish mind, about as repugnant as the other. God belonged to the Jews, and the Gentiles strictly didn't count, except the few who became Jewish in soul by the physical ritual of circumcision. Peter, without Christ, would hardly have remained in association with a man whose trade was unclean; but to send Peter to a Gentile required a shocking vision and a very sharp and definite command. **"Ye shall be witnesses unto me both in Jerusalem, and in all Judaea, and in Samaria, and unto the uttermost part of the earth,"** the Lord had told them before He was taken up into heaven. Of course they'd be witnesses—to the Jews, but naturally. Certainly there were Jews in the **uttermost part of the earth,** and of course that must have been what the Lord meant.

Thirty miles north of Joppa on the Mediterranean coast there was a city called Caesarea. The very name must have been hateful to the patriotic Jew because it called to mind Caesar, the all-powerful head of the all-powerful state, Rome, the mistress of the world. To Rome, the area of Palestine was merely a fertile, if frequently irritating, speck of empire. Caesarea was the Roman capital of the province of Palestine, and the official residence of the Roman governor. Naturally it was also military headquarters of the occupying power. It had been built by Herod the Great, that canny monarch who retained his political head by an uncanny instinct for licking the right Roman boot at the right moment, and by pouring into the always-outstretched Roman hand wealth wrung from an oppressed people.

In this very Roman place there lived a man named Cornelius who was a centurion of the Roman army, the head of a group called the "Italian Band," which is thought by some to have been the governor's bodyguard. If this supposition is correct, the Roman governor must have been an indulgent soul, or else have figured that the God of the Jews lacked sufficient power to do any appreciable damage to a Roman, because the commander of his bodyguard had definitely come under the influence of this Jewish Deity. On the other hand, the governor might have reasoned that this was a pretty good thing good-will wise, for Cornelius was forever making donations with a lavish hand to needy Jews in the area. Since Cornelius represented Rome, this might even help to prevent rebellion. Certainly, a good governor had to figure all the angles.

Cornelius was **a devout man, and one that feared God with all his house, which gave much alms to the people, and prayed to God alway.** He was not a Jew nor even a Jewish proselyte, but he prayed to God, and God heard him. He was a good man, a devout man, a generous man, but he was still a Gentile and no Jew would have eaten at table with him any more than you would get down on the floor and drink milk from the dish with your cat.

Cornelius saw a vision and was instantly obedient to its message; Peter saw a vision, and gave the Lord a good brisk argument before he was ready to obey orders. Both men were at prayer when the visions came, Cornelius at three o'clock in the afternoon, and Peter about noon the next day.

Cornelius prayed, and an angel came and called him by name, "Cornelius!"

The man was frightened, and blurted out, "What is it, Lord?"

The angel's answer was reassuring: "Thy prayers and thine alms are come up for a memorial before God."

God had heard his prayers; God was pleased with his compassionate generosity. Was that not enough? Apparently that was but a prelude to greater blessing. The worship of God and the good works that resulted were about to bring to Cornelius a more complete revelation of God. But there was something that he must do to bring this about. He was to send messengers to Joppa for a man named Simon Peter who was staying in the home of another man named Simon who was a tanner by trade, and lived on the waterfront. This same Simon Peter would tell Cornelius what he should do.

We who are bored and weary of "church work," if we were completely honest with ourselves, would probably wonder why Cornelius was so eager to send for a man who was going to tell him something else to *do*. The answer is quite simple: God was of supreme importance in the life of this Roman soldier. Our attitude is that if we attend church once each Sunday we're doing pretty well, if we go to prayer meeting we're extraordinary, and if we spend fifteen minutes a day reading the Bible we're doing God Almighty a downright favor. The pitiable truth about our "church work," however, is that far too much of it is at the behest of our busy-minded brethren who must bat our brains out along with their own in doing things that have no connection with God. There is a possibility that if Cornelius had been as soul-weary of committee meetings as is the active Christian of today that the edge of his eagerness would also have been somewhat blunted. As it was, we somehow get the impression that he could hardly wait for the divine messenger to leave before going into action!

He called three people—two household servants and a personal aide from among his soldiers—and told them in detail of the divine visitation, and sent them to Joppa to look for Simon Peter.

The next day about noon as the men were nearing Joppa, Peter went up on the housetop to pray.

In case you might be thinking that a housetop would be a strange place to pray, the houses of that area had completely flat roofs which were as much a part of the family living area as any other room in the house. In many places in Palestine a roof would have been an unmercifully hot place in the middle of the day, but Simon's house was **by the sea side** and probably quite comfortable. However, it is not too likely that Peter was concerned about physical comfort in the place where he prayed. The last time we saw him praying, he was on his knees beside the body of Dorcas. This time, we are not told anything about the burden of his prayer, but we may be quite sure that it did not require a crisis to send the apostle to his knees. This spot on the roof could very well have been his private prayer chamber while he was a guest in Simon's house, and if it was he had been there many, many times during the **many days** of his visit.

While Peter was still on the roof, he became very hungry. Now, since it was about noon and therefore time for the midday meal, this should not have been surprising. But Luke says, **And he became very hungry and would have eaten,** which suggests unusual, almost unnatural, hunger. He "would have eaten," but the food wasn't ready.

Parenthetically, as a hostess whose meals are seldom exactly on time, my sympathy flits back over the centuries to Mrs. Simon who must have been in something of a flurry when she discovered her distinguished guest was terribly hungry before lunch was quite ready. I wonder if she also put the flat silver in the wrong place by the plates, and quite forgot to add dressing to the salad!

Mrs. Simon could have relaxed: her guest had forgotten all about lunch. He had fallen into a trance, and was seeing a vision. The hunger had nothing to do with the trance, but it was shockingly tied to the vision.

Peter was in a trance. People, circumstances, events, and surroundings were temporarily blocked off from his mind and senses in order that he might see and hear and feel and understand the staggering thing God was about to reveal.

Quite suddenly the sky was cleft and an enormous square

of fabric began coming down. Peter gasped. Was this object, whatever it was, about to fall on him? Instinctively he tried to squirm out of the way, but a relentless force held his feet to the spot like a mighty magnet gripping steel. Swiftly the object descended, but its pace did not accelerate as it came closer. Why, Peter wondered numbly, didn't it fall faster as it came closer to him? And then he saw: The square of fabric was fastened together at its corners as though it had been fashioned on gigantic knitting needles, and it was being suspended by these corners as if mighty hands were letting it descend at a precise and predetermined rate of speed.

Like a great tent turned upside down, the object came closer until Peter could see what was inside it: Animals! All sorts of animals—cattle, asses, bears, jackals, conies, snakes, swine, eagles, vultures, partridges, doves—all sorts of animals, clean and unclean.

A vision. A vision of animals. Why? Before he had time to ponder overmuch on that, a voice cut through his consciousness with a brisk, incisive order: **"Rise, Peter; kill and eat."** He, Simon Peter, was being told to eat something that was filthy! From the depths of shock, his answer was automatic: **"Not so, Lord; for I have never eaten anything that is common or unclean."**

The Voice came a second time, and its words struck the dazed Peter like a slap in the face: **"What God hath cleansed, that call not thou common."**

And again, the order came: **"Rise, Peter; kill and eat."** And the still-dazed Peter, perhaps wondering if God had rescinded His instructions to Moses, nonetheless responded with the same answer.

Again, the third time, the Voice spoke the same words, and Peter, perhaps a little uncertain by then, gave the same answer **(This was done thrice,** Luke says.) and then the great sheet with its burden of animals was lifted up and up and out of sight.

Wondering, worried, apprehensive, Peter watched the sheet disappear. What did it mean? Was the command literal? Was the Lord instructing His disciples to discard the dietary habits of centuries, and if He was, why? Were the animals symbolic? What did they represent? **"What God hath cleansed, that call not thou common."** What did it mean?

While Peter was still on the housetop pondering, the messengers from Cornelius had located Simon's house and stood at the gate, calling in to ask whether Simon Peter was staying there.

God works out every detail, He does not leave loose ends dangling. While the messengers of Cornelius were talking through the gate with Simon's servants, the Spirit spoke to Peter who was still thinking about the vision: "Three men are looking for you, so get up and go downstairs and go with them in complete confidence, for I have sent them."

From force of long habit, Peter was by now almost mechanically obedient to the Holy Spirit. He got up from his knees and started down stairs, wondering how the men looking for him would fit into the vision he had just seen. Or were they completely apart from the vision? This only he knew: *God had sent them to him!* That was enough. If they fitted into the unbelievable thing he had just seen and heard, well and good; if they had nothing to do with it, God would make the matter clear in His own good time.

With steady and certain steps, Peter descended the stairs and moved toward the gate where the three men were waiting. He opened the gate and saw the Roman soldier with the two household slaves who had accompanied him. Gentiles! Unclean people! The voice of the Spirit saying, **"Go with them, doubting nothing: For I have sent them."** Unclean animals in the vision, and the voice of command, **"Rise, Peter, kill and eat. What God hath cleansed, that call not thou common."**

In Peter's mind, the voices merged: "What God hath cleansed, that call not thou common; go with them, doubting nothing: for I have sent them."

Simon Peter stepped through the gate and held out his hands and smiled. "I am he whom you seek; why have you come?"

God had sent an angel to Cornelius, their master and commander, with instructions to send for Simon Peter to come into his house and speak.

Peter held the gate open and beckoned. "We will leave

tomorrow morning to go to your master. But you must be hungry and tired from your journey; come in, and eat and rest."

I cannot help wondering what Mrs. Simon's reaction to that was. The three extra luncheon guests she probably could have taken calmly in stride; but two of them were slaves, and all three were *Gentiles!* You didn't eat at table with Gentiles, you didn't have them in your home, yet here was the great leader and apostle who had honored her home as its guest, bringing the three inside. Mrs. Simon was at that moment quite probably one of history's most distraught hostesses.

The next day they left for the return trip to Caesarea, accompanied also by other Christians from Joppa. (God was providing Peter with extra witnesses for what was to come.)

Seven Jews and three Gentiles setting out upon a journey, walking together from Joppa to Caesarea, journeying with eager but wondering steps into the brotherhood of all men who believe in Jesus Christ. "How beautiful upon the mountains are the feet of him that bringeth good tidings, that publisheth peace." Buoyant feet of young discipleship following the Master along the seashore and the hard-packed paths across the fields of Galilee; resolute feet of maturity tramping across the desert's scorching sand with the good tidings of the resurrection; weary feet of age treading Rome's hard paving stones, moving to a martyr's cross that even in the dying he might follow his Lord: The calloused, gnarled, and utterly beautiful feet of Simon Peter!

Cornelius was waiting for the man whom God had promised to send him, and with him waited all his near relatives and his intimate friends. He either waited at the gate himself or instructed his porter slave to call him the instant his divinely sent guest came in sight, for we read, **And as Peter was coming in, Cornelius met him, and fell down at his feet, and worshipped him.** Cornelius thought Peter was divine because he was the promised messenger of God, but Peter reached down instantly and lifted him up, assuring him that he also was merely a man and by no means to be rendered any such homage.

Thus Peter found himself in the court of the house of a

Gentile, and was not in the least ill at ease because it was God who had sent him there.

Inside, he found the "many people" whom Cornelius had called together to share this thrilling experience with him. Sensing that they were wondering why he, a Jew, was there with them, he explained that God had broken the fetters of legal custom by showing him that men of "other nations" were not to be regarded as common or unclean. And this revelation was the reason for his being there. All of this time, Peter had not known definitely why God had sent him to Cornelius, and having concluded his explanation, he asked, "Why have you sent for me?"

Cornelius eagerly recounted his vision in minute detail. Why had he sent for Peter? Because God ordered it. Why had God ordered it? Peter was to talk; Cornelius was to listen. **"Now therefore we are all here present before God, to hear all things that are commanded thee of God."**

Then Peter opened his mouth, and said, "Of a truth I perceive that God is no respecter of persons, but in every nation he that feareth him and worketh righteousness, is accepted with him." And thus began the first sermon to the Gentiles.

The people before him were not pagan in their souls: they worshiped the true and only God. We are not definitely so told, but it is quite possible that they, like their noble host, **gave much alms to the people** [i.e., needy Jews] **and prayed to God alway**. A great many people in our day would consider that attitude and those actions utterly sufficient for their souls' salvation, but the people of Peter's audience knew better. They lacked something essential; their religion was a beautiful building without a foundation, shaky, unsafe, and tragically impermanent.

These Gentiles knew *about* God; they knew something about Jesus Christ. They had heard that God, in some mysterious way, through Jesus Christ established peace in the human soul. They had heard of the work of Jesus of Nazareth, how He went from place to place healing and helping because of His mighty compassion for people, and they had heard that His life ended on a cross.

Peter says to his Gentile audience, "You know (dimly)

about these things, for you have heard of them. I was there. *I*
was with Him. I saw Him healing lepers; I saw Him feed five
thousand men from five loaves and two small fishes; I saw
Him call forth from the tomb a man dead four days; I saw
the soldiers of the high priest seize Him after one of His own
disciples betrayed Him; I know that He was crucified and
dead and buried. But I also know that God raised Him up the
third day. *He is alive!* I saw Him. I touched Him. I ate with
Him. After His resurrection, He was not seen by unbelievers,
but only by certain witnesses chosen beforehand by God, and
I was one of the chosen. After His resurrection, He commanded us to preach to the people, and to testify that He is
the One ordained of God to be the Judge of both living and
dead.

"Moreover, I know that this is He of whom all the prophets speak, saying that through His Name, whosoever believeth
in Him shall receive remission of sins."

With one mind the people before him believed the words
of Peter, and at that instant (while he was still speaking) the
Holy Spirit fell upon them and they began to glorify God,
speaking in **other tongues** even as the disciples themselves had
done on the Day of Pentecost. This, then, was the Day of
Pentecost for the Gentiles.

The six Jewish disciples who had come with Peter looked
on with amazement and awe. They would not have believed
it if they had not seen it with their own eyes: The matchless
gift of the Holy Spirit was being poured out on *Gentiles!*
Through the numbness of shock, their minds groped back to
the words of the prophet Joel: "And it shall come to pass in
the last days, saith God, I will pour out of my Spirit upon *all
flesh. . . .*" Was it possible, then, that God regarded Gentiles
with as much favor as He did His own of the chosen seed of
Abraham?

Peter answered their thoughts with a challenging question: Could any mere man dare to forbid water for baptizing
these people whom God Himself had so obviously baptized
with the Holy Spirit? Would any of them presume to question the workings of God? The six men shook their heads in
dazed silence, and then for the first time in history the sacred
ritual of baptism in the name of Christ was performed for

men not circumcised. The hand of God, using Peter the Rock, had battered down the middle wall of partition.

Peter was shortly to have need of his six witnesses, for when he went **up to Jerusalem,** he was called to account for his actions in going into the house of a Gentile, and eating with him.

Peter recounted his experience in minute detail, emphasizing over and over again the fact that God had poured out upon Gentile believers the Holy Spirit, and ended with the simple question: **"What was I that I could withstand God?"** If they were going to call somebody to account for this thing, it would have to be God Himself—answering to mere man for His acts!—and not Simon Peter.

When they heard these things, they held their peace, and glorified God, saying, "Then hath God also to the Gentiles granted repentance unto life."

Chapter Ten

"And ye shall be witnesses unto me both in Jerusalem, and in all Judaea, and in Samaria, and unto the uttermost part of the earth." Thus the Lord had spoken to His dimly comprehending disciples immediately before He was taken up.

The Word was preached in Jerusalem, and thousands believed there before the first great persecution came with the death of Stephen. The storm of that persecution blew believers wildly in all directions, and wherever they came to rest, they preached Christ. Thus we find "all Judaea and Samaria" evangelized, and now we are turning toward the "uttermost part of the earth."

Some of the Jerusalem disciples really scattered! As far as Phenice, and Cyprus, and Antioch. Why those particular places? Perhaps some of them had relatives there who could shelter them until they could become reestablished; perhaps some of the places held hope of employment for their particular skills; or maybe some of them were part of the pilgrims who had witnessed the birth of the new church on the Day of Pentecost and who then had remained at Jerusalem as believers. If there were any of these latter, they were simply going back home. Phenice was a province of Syria on the Syro-Palestinian coast of the Mediterranean; Cyprus was (and still is, naturally!) an island in the Mediterranean sixty miles from the coast of Phenice; Antioch was a city in northwest Syria, and at that time was among the three or four greatest cities of the world.

A province, an island, and a city, and they had one thing in common: a segment of the population was Jewish. It was to these people and to them only that the Jerusalem refugees preached, at first. But now, **And some of them were men of Cyprus and Cyrene, which, when they were come to Antioch, spake unto the Grecians, preaching the Lord Jesus.**

Men of Cyprus and Cyrene. Cyprus is the island mentioned above; Cyrene was on the north coast of Libya in Africa, across the Mediterranean Sea from and due south of Greece. Cyrene was a Greek city, Greek in population and culture, that is, but it belonged to the Roman Empire. Why didn't the men of "Cyprus and Cyrene" go back home when they had to leave Jerusalem in a hurry? We are not told. They went instead to Antioch, that beautiful and cultured Greek city in Syria (which also belonged to Rome, but naturally!) that rivaled the city of Rome in everything, including its filthy wickedness.

These Jerusalem refugees preached Christ to the Greeks. Having in all likelihood heard of the conversion of Cornelius and the gift of the Holy Spirit to the Gentiles, they brought to Greeks the wonderful news of salvation, and the startling news that men did not have to become Jewish proselytes to have access to that salvation. Wonderful tidings, indeed! **And the hand of the Lord was with them: and a great number believed, and turned unto the Lord.**

These men who brought Christ's message to the Greeks in Antioch were not apostles, they were not even preachers—they were laymen. Ordinary laymen, filled with wisdom and power by the Holy Spirit, began bombarding the ramparts of Satan with the showered stones of Truth. And eventually, they forced the worship of Ashtaroth with its immoral filth into the dark corner of obscurity to be forgotten by everybody except historians and others of an inquisitive nature.

What would happen if we similarly tackled Satan in one of his glittering strongholds? We'd probably fall flat on our well-kept faces. Why? Terrifyingly simple: Those laymen were filled with the Holy Spirit. We are not.

The church in Jerusalem heard the glad tidings of the Word planted in Antioch by ordinary saints, of the good seed sprouting and thrusting tender green tips through pagan soil, and they hastened to send a man to help tend its growth. Again, the man they sent was not an apostle: they chose Barnabas. How they must have loved and trusted that man who gave recklessly of his great wealth to nurture the infant church; who vouched for Saul when the church feared him; who was full of gentleness and strength and wisdom.

Barnabas saw the tender new growth reaching up eagerly toward the Light, and with great gladness of heart helped beam that Light upon it. With strong hands of exhortation he steadied the new growth against the blasts of doubt and indecision which Satan blew upon God's newborn ones in those days also. Barnabas stayed; he talked; he worked; he loved. People heard him; they watched him; they studied the man. Here was something genuine. Luke puts it, **For he was a good man, and full of the Holy Ghost and of faith.** The result? More tender new sprouts pushed up for Barnabas to tend.

The crop was beginning to be too big for one husbandman to handle—he must have help; where would he seek it? Who can doubt that the Holy Spirit spoke to Barnabas as He had spoken to Ananias? " . . . **Saul of Tarsus, . . . for he is a chosen vessel unto me, to bear my name before the Gentiles and kings, and the children of Israel.**"

God's newborn here were Gentiles. Who, then, but Saul to preach and minister to them? **Then departed Barnabas to Tarsus for to seek Saul.**

Saul was right there. He had been waiting. We have no day-by-day, or even year-by-year account of Saul's life during the stay in Tarsus, but we can take for granted that he was busy while he waited for the "greater call." The more you study the life of that man, the more certain you become that he never wasted ten minutes during his whole lifetime! For one thing, it is reasonably certain that he worked at making tents, since he was not one to sit on a cushion and wax philosophical and expect the Lord (or anybody else) to feed him. Saul took quiet pride in the fact that he worked for a living.

There is no formal record of Saul's activity in connection with his divine calling, but we do have illuminating glimpses here and there. When he writes to the Corinthians (in the second letter) he mentions three shipwrecks, five Jewish scourgings, three Romans scourgings, and one stoning. Of these the stoning (at Lystra) and one scourging (at Philippi) are recorded in the Book of Acts. The other sufferings he experienced during his stay in Tarsus.

In all probability Saul operated in Tarsus as he did in other cities: he went first to the Jews, and then to the Gentiles. In spite of (or perhaps because of) the terrible persecutions he suffered, he gained converts. It was quite likely he who established the churches in **Syria and Cilicia** which he, with Silas, **went through, confirming** as recorded in Acts 15:16.

It is also quite likely that Saul made converts of numbers of people whom he contacted through his tentmaking—which should suggest something to us! If he had made tents and kept his mouth shut, he would have avoided suffering. But he had not been called to make tents, but to preach Christ.

Then departed Barnabas to Tarsus, for to seek Saul: And when he had found him, he brought him unto Antioch. How very simple is the narrative which tells us of it; how very simply began the larger work of the most influential Christian the world has ever known! Saul was waiting; Barnabas found him; Barnabas took him back to Antioch.

For an entire year Barnabas and Saul worked in Antioch, teaching people who were added to the growing church. The body of Greek disciples must have been large enough to make a distinct impression upon the pagan population of the city, for it was the pagans who gave the adherents of the new religion the title which set them apart from Jews. **And the disciples were called Christians first in Antioch.** A title of pious respect and regard? Hardly! An epithet hurled at a group of wild-eyed fanatics? Possibly. A distinct term, matter-of-factly distinguishing this strange new sect from proselytes of the Jewish religion? Quite likely. In any event, it is the name which Christ's followers have worn from that day onward, sometimes to His glory and sometimes, alas, to His embarrassment.

The Gentile Christians in Antioch were shortly to have an opportunity to demonstrate the love of Christ which dwelt in them. Prophets came from Jerusalem to Antioch, and one of them named Agabus foretold—through the Spirit—of a coming famine which was to be worldwide. The famine came during the reign of Claudius Caesar, and the disciples of Antioch decided to send help to the disciples in Judea. The Gentiles gave **every man according to his ability** to help their famine-stricken brothers who were Jews, a magnificent example of that love of Christ in whom there is "neither Jew nor Greek." They took up their collection, and sent it to the elders in Jerusalem by Barnabas and Saul.

Chapter Eleven

Here we encounter another king named Herod, of the third generation in that charming line of cutthroat politicians. He was a grandson of the Herod who killed all the boy babies in Bethlehem in an effort to destroy the infant Jesus. This same "Grandfather Herod," by the way, destroyed some of his own sons when he thought they threatened his kingdom. The particular Herod with whom we are concerned at the moment was Herod Agrippa I, and his father, Aristobulus, was one of the princes so destroyed.

Herod Agrippa I enjoyed great popularity among his Jewish subjects whom he tried valiantly to please. He discovered that one sure way to favor was to eliminate Christians, so . . . **about that time Herod the king stretched forth his hands to vex certain of the church. And he killed James the brother of John with the sword.** Just like that!

James the brother of John—how very little we are actually told about this man. He was a son of Zebedee and Salome; he and his brother John were partners in the fishing business with Simon Peter; with Peter and John he made up the "inner circle" of disciples always closest to the Master. These were the only three to witness His transfigured glory on the mountain and His supreme agony in Gethsemane. Before His death and resurrection, these three sparred every now and again for favored positions in His government, believing that Rome's doom was imminent and Israel's prophesied glory at hand.

Our Lord called James and John "Sons of Thunder." Solemn commentators solemnly comment that this was probably because of their temperament and their zeal in preaching. Now, the solemn commentators are far wiser than I, yet when I read that title, I always think of Jesus as chuckling when He said it, even as you and I chuckle when we refer to cherished young ones as the "thundering herd." We tend to forget that the Savior was completely human.

So James, one of the three closest to the Lord, was the first apostle to suffer martyrdom. John, his younger brother, was the only apostle who was not martyred, and in between we will find Peter dying on a Roman cross.

Another Herod's hands were stained with blood, and it was the blood of one of God's very special people. The work that God Almighty had assigned to James the apostle was done, else a petty little king would not have been allowed to take his life. But that same petty little king, puffed up beyond measure, was riding the crest of a wave which was sweeping him toward a painful and remarkably humiliating death.

Herod, seeing that his butchering of an apostle pleased the Jews enormously, decided to do a repeat performance. But this time, he'd grab a more prominent one, the one who was said to have done many miracles including the restoring of life to a woman over in Joppa. This one was named Simon Peter. Accordingly, he seized Peter early in the week of the Passover season, and had him put in jail.

Peter's death was to be what Hollywood would call a spectacular, a treat for all Jerusalem to witness. But Jewish custom forbade the execution of criminals on festive days, so Herod put Peter in jail for safekeeping till the **days of unleavened bread** were over. But he was taking no chances on an escape! He **delivered him to four quaternions of soldiers to keep him.** A quaternion was a group of four soldiers constituting a watch, and each group was on guard duty for three of the twelve night hours. Two of these stood sentry duty by the door of Peter's cell, while the other two were inside with the prisoner, one on either side of him, and fastened to him with chains linking his arms to their arms in what Herod fondly believed to be the bonds of absolute doom.

But there were two things Herod could not hear: the prayer of the church, and the laughter of God! Peter was watched constantly, but the church prayed constantly: "Lord, we beseech Thee, keep Thy servant Simon Peter in safety, and deliver him from the hand of Herod the king."

And from the throne of God, quiet laughter. God was watching a puny little king's efforts to destroy His servant before the appointed time.

Peter, soundly asleep between his sleeping guards, was awakened by a gentle but insistent slapping against his side. Through the fog of somnolence, he was reminded of the way his mother used to awaken him before dawn on a day when he was supposed to get up early. Then he felt himself being lifted to a sitting position. That was odd, his mother never did it that way, she always just kept slapping gently till he yawned and sat up. He opened his eyes and saw that the one who had lifted him was not his mother, but an angel.

"This isn't real, of course," Peter said to himself, "I'm seeing another vision; but this time, I'll do what I'm told to do, and I won't argue about it."

"Simon, get up; hurry!" The angel directed briskly, and Peter obeyed; and since he was acting out his part in the vision, he was not in the least surprised to see both chains fall off his hands, but stay firmly fixed to the guards' hands.

"Get into your clothes, and put your sandals on. See to it that you fasten the thongs, for you don't want to have to stop for a dangling shoe latchet."

Peter put his clothes on without answering, and was careful to secure his sandal thongs.

"Splendid," said the angel, "Now throw your garment around your shoulders, and follow me. Watch your step, the guard is nearly under your feet!"

Again, Peter obeyed silently, thinking how wonderful it would be if this vision were real. He was careful not to stub his toe against the sleeping guard as he followed the angel from the cell. The cell door was open and the sentries stood at attention, their eyes glazed and unseeing, their sinews rigid in the fixed immobility of catalepsy. The angel nodded his head toward them and said sympathetically, "This will be hard for them, I fear, but that's not my department. Come, Simon, follow me. Make haste!"

Peter still followed in numb silence, still convinced that he was acting his part in the vision, but illogically thankful somehow that he hadn't kicked the guard, even in a vision.

They progressed from the inner, or maximum-security, section of the prison toward the outer gate, and guards were either asleep or elsewhere for the moment. Then they reached the sturdy iron gate which was the last barrier to freedom, and it opened for them as automatically as the Out Only door of a supermarket swings wide for you on your way out with a cart of groceries.

The angel started down the street with long, swift strides, and Peter was suddenly aware that his legs felt as if they were being overused after a period of cramped inactivity. This was odd: in a vision, one was not aware of anything *that* acutely physical. At the end of the block, the angel turned around and stopped, and patted Peter's shoulder. His face began to be an indefinite blurr, but his kindly, matter-of-fact voice was still incisive.

"Very well, Simon; I've rescued you—you're safely out of Herod's prison and Herod's hand—and now my work is done." The voice also began to blur, "The Lord be with thee now and always; farewell, Simon Peter." The angel took a few steps beyond Peter, and then simply vanished.

Simon Peter shook his head sharply, and then reached down to rub his aching legs. A predawn breeze blew against his face bringing gentle coolness and familiar odors of the outside world. Those were not prison smells, and moreover, the ache in his leg muscles was beginning to disappear with the rubbing.

This was not a vision, the whole thing was blessedly real!

Peter lifted his face to the sky, and the stars were blurred by his tears. "O Lord, my God, of a truth Thou hast rescued me, for Thou didst send Thine angel to deliver me out of the hand of Herod, and from all the expectation of the people of the Jews." Almost automatically his feet turned toward the house of John Mark's mother. He lifted his tear-filled eyes once more toward the stars, and words were torn from the breath of a muffled sob: "James! James! Oh, James, our beloved brother!"

Mary, the mother of John Mark, had nearly a houseful of company and they were staying very, very late. They were not eating, they were not drinking, they were not playing games; they were not even amusing—or boring!—each other with tall tales. They were praying. They were all praying for the same thing, and had been for some time: the safety and the release of Simon Peter.

Some of these same people had been in Mary's house for nearly a week, hardly eating, hardly drinking, but praying, praying always. The thin edge of desperation was beginning to show in their voices; not only were Peter's days numbered, his hours were nearly spent. Very soon now he would be dragged from the prison, a toothsome dainty for Herod's howling mob. Tears gushed from under their swollen eyelids and ran down cheeks seemingly eroded by rivulets of former tears. Some prostrated themselves in frantic, fervent silence, their faces almost touching the floor. How many hours till dawn? How long till sunrise? Nobody paused to find out. They kept on praying.

Was the **damsel named Rhoda** one of the group praying in the house? If she had been inside the house, she wouldn't have heard somebody knocking at the small door by the street gate. Perhaps she had been impelled to leave the room to go out into the court and gaze fearfully toward the east to see where dawn was. Then again, perhaps she had been left there by the street gate to watch for danger. The authorities must have known of some of the places where the disciples met, and they would have known where to swoop down, just in case King Herod should decide to have another victim after he had finished with Simon Peter. In any case, Rhoda was in the court and near enough to the door to hear knocking.

The knocking came, and somehow I can hear the slight quaver in the girl's voice as she called, "Who's there?"

"It is I, Simon Peter," a voice answered urgently, "Open quickly, and let me in!"

"God has heard us, God has heard us, the Lord has heard our prayer!" Rhoda wheeled around and ran full speed across the courtyard, having quite neglected to either unlock or open the door where Peter still stood knocking. She dashed pell-mell into the room where the disciples were still praying, and cried out, "God has heard us! Peter is at the gate!"

Their answer to tidings of answered prayer was one of church history's most extraordinary statements. They said flatly, "You're crazy!"

"But I tell you, Peter *is* at the gate! I heard him, I know his voice; and anyway, he told me who he was."

"You poor child! This has been too much for you. You're hearing things that are not there because you can't bear the awful truth."

"The knocking was not in my mind, and the voice was not in my imagination, I tell you, both were real. And I was so excited, I forgot to open the door. Peter is still standing there knocking, and Herod's soldiers may be after him—please, come on!"

"It is the voice of Peter's angel that you heard, for he himself is either with the Lord, or still in Herod's prison."

"Well, come with me and let the angel in, then! But I tell you, *it is Peter himself.*"

Finally persuaded, but almost grudgingly as if to humor the feeble-minded, they followed Rhoda into the courtyard.

Steadily, insistently, Simon Peter had continued to knock. If he kept at it long enough, somebody would come to unlock the door. When the company heard the knocking, they rushed en masse toward the door, and somebody managed to unlock it.

"Thanks be to our God for that which He has wrought, for this is a miracle!" A voice cried out in exultation, and the others echoed, "Thanks be to our God!"

But Peter raised his hand for silence, and beckoned for them to lock the door behind him. Then he told them quietly how the Lord had delivered him from Herod's prison, and since he was not one to tempt God by staying in a place where Herod could grab him a second time, he was leaving. They were to report these things to **James and the brethren.** The James mentioned here is the brother of our Lord. He is the same man whom we shall encounter presiding over the council in Jerusalem at a later date.

Then Luke reports succinctly, **And he departed, and went**

into **another place.** It almost seems that even at the time of his letter to the "most excellent Theophilus," about twenty-three years after the divinely contrived jail break, Luke was reluctant to reveal Peter's hiding place. It was also possible that Peter didn't even tell them where he was going, knowing that the glad tidings were to be spread to all the church, and that some minion of the enraged Herod might be listening at an unguarded keyhole.

We are left to imagine the wild joy and thanksgiving that went with the people from that prayer meeting as they left Mary's house. They must have knocked at many doors on the way home, and spoken in half whispers to the sleepy house-holders who answered: "The Lord has delivered Peter from Herod's prison, and sent him in safety to a secret place." Or perhaps some of them also were still up, praying for Peter. Perhaps dim lights were still burning in the house of James, the brother of our Lord.

The waves of exultant joy ascending from the saints in Jerusalem must have reached to God's own throne to mingle with the joy of Stephen and of James and all the other martyred saints, and of the angels gathered there.

But we are definitely not left to imagine Herod's reaction!

In a masterly bit of understatement, Luke says, **Now as soon as it was day, there was no small stir among the soldiers, what was become of Peter.** It is not difficult to picture the frantic confusion which followed the awakening of the guards. They had been blissfully asleep with an important prisoner chaining them together, but now, the chains were still present, but the prisoner was gone.

The luckless prison officials knew perfectly well what would happen to them if this man destined for a spectacular execution could not be located before the hour the king was ready for him to be brought out. And they were quite right! **And when Herod had sought for him, and found him not, he examined the keepers, and commanded that they should be put to death.** The fact that the prison officials were quite innocent apparently had no influence on his majesty: they not only had allowed an important prisoner to escape, but this had all the earmarks of an inside job.

Then (still speaking of Herod) Luke says, **And he went down from Judaea to Caesarea, and there abode.** Sounds almost as if the king had had it, and in a fit of pique was washing his hands of Jerusalem and all Judea. His popularity with the ruling Jews must have suffered considerably, at that, when he failed to produce Simon Peter for the hungry sword. So he'd go live in Caesarea where Roman military dignity made life a little less hectic for a Jewish monarch.

About two years later, in A.D. 44, we find Herod putting on another spectacle for the people. This time, the show was not the execution of an apostle, but games in honor of the Emperor Claudius when there was "a certain festival celebrated to make vows for his safety," as Josephus puts it. Subsequent events proved that Herod should have been much more concerned for his own safety.

On the second day of this spectacular, the king appeared, garbed in what Luke refers to simply as "royal apparel." Josephus (who probably could not have kept a job as a reporter—too wordy!) is again more specific, saying, "He put on a garment made wholly of silver, and of a contexture truly wonderful, and came into the theatre early in the morning; at which time the silver of his garment being illuminated by the fresh reflection of the sun's rays upon it, shone out after a surprising manner, and was so resplendent as to spread a horror over those that looked intently upon him." The man Josephus had a way with words!

Herod . . . made an oration unto them. And the people gave a shout, saying, "It is the voice of a god, and not of a man!" And immediately the angel of the Lord smote him, because he gave not God the glory. . . . Herod was enough of a Jew to know better than that, in spite of his Roman upbringing! Now, his mad friend, the Emperor Caius Caesar (Caligula), had *really* thought himself to be a god, but Herod had no such delusions of immortal grandeur. But oh, how perfectly lovely just for a moment to be *called* a god! He neither rebuked nor corrected his blaspheming audience—and instantly he was seized with agonizing pains in his belly. His wondrous silver garment was nothing more than extra weight upon his outraged flesh as he was carried back to his palace. There, five days later, he died of the same loathsome disease which had claimed the life of his grandfather, Herod the Great.

And immediately the angel of the Lord smote him, because he gave not God the glory: and he was eaten of worms, and gave up the ghost.

Josephus describes in graphic and revolting detail the illness which killed Herod's grandfather. Oh, yes indeed, there were worms—lots of worms!

Chapter Twelve

But the word of God grew and multipled. Herod was dead. Simon Peter still lived. We wonder with a gentle sort of speculation if the angel who released the one from prison was the same one who struck down the other. (As I have said before, we really ought to become reaccustomed to the idea of angels. We'd be much less embarrassed when we open our eyes some perfect morning to find them all around us if we didn't have to blurt apologetically, "Oh, dear! You really *are* after all, aren't you?")

God through His Holy Spirit wrought mightily in the lives of His children, and His Word grew and multiplied in the hearts and minds of new believers.

Now we get back to Barnabas and Saul.

You remember that when the Gentile Christians in Antioch knew of impending famine they sent "relief" to their Jewish Christian brethren in Jerusalem. Barnabas and Saul were the ones chosen to deliver the money for distribution among the needy. Now their work was done and they were going back to their posts in Antioch. They took with them John Mark who was the nephew of Barnabas and the son of that Mary whose home was a sort of unofficial headquarters for the disciples.

We are now about to witness the official beginning of the missionary work of Saul of Tarsus and of Barnabas. The Holy Spirit did not send these forth from the Jewish Christian church in Jerusalem; He sent them from the Gentile Christian church in Antioch.

Three men are mentioned in connection with the prelude to the Spirit's call: **Simeon that was called Niger, and Lucius of Cyrene, and Manaen, which had been brought up with Herod the tetrarch. . . .**

Remember Herod the tetrarch? He was that weak-willed monarch who allowed his wife to maneuver him into murdering John the Baptist. Manaen was his foster brother. He had been **brought up with Herod**; therefore he must have grown up in that atmosphere of political chicanery and intrigue which were the breath of life to brother Herod. But Manaen had chosen God, and was helping in God's great adventure of saving the world. Herod had chosen the world, the flesh, and the devil; he had lost his kingdom and his power, and was living out his days in exile and disgrace.

Simeon and Lucius and Manaen and Saul and Barnabas fasted. We don't fast. We're much too concerned with eating. How many people do you know who use the backyard barbecue a lot more than they use the Bible? Don't bother to count them, you'd probably need an adding machine. We think that fasting is a strange, archaic fragment from an era in church history in which Christians were said also to have been filled with the Holy Spirit. The fasting and the filling were not necessarily unrelated. When people fasted, they also usually prayed. Let me tell you a secret: If we ever get so busy praying that we forget to eat, this nation will become a *Christian* nation in fact as well as in name!

As they ministered to the Lord, and fasted, the Holy Ghost said, "Separate me Barnabas and Saul for the work whereunto I have called them."

How did the Holy Spirit speak to them? Does that matter? The important thing is that they *recognized the voice of God.* And so can you. How do you accomplish that? You keep God always in the undercurrent of your thought (and if you do that, my friend, you're not going to get into too much trouble!). You read the Bible thoughtfully enough so that precious fragments of it will be stored in your subconscious mind. And you pray. There is always a completely clear channel between you and God. You pray with your mind and your soul; you cannot always pray aloud. Then you empty your mind and your soul of every vestige of thought.

You are completely still. And the words which flash across your mind are the words of God speaking to you. Usually, it will be words from the Scripture. How do I know this is not the voice of my own yearning? Because sometimes the words will be totally unrelated to anything that's been in my mind! For example: One night when I couldn't sleep, I was praying for two friends, an old couple who were sick, nearly forsaken, and worse than childless. (Praying, by the way, is an excellent way to make use of insomnia.) I kept praying for God to do something for this tragic pair and finally, like a frustrated child, cried out (in my mind, I mean), *"Lord, answer me!"*

Instantly there flashed through my mind these words: "I will open the windows of heaven and pour out upon you such a blessing that you will not be able to receive it." Answering me with what my mind retained of a phrase from the third chapter of Malachi. Answering my frantic plea for help for my friends with a promise of blessing for me. My startled reaction to that was, "But, Lord, I'm asking something for *them,* not me!"

No, you don't always know the meaning of the answer; the disciples closest to our Lord didn't always know what some of His more cryptic answers meant, either. But you certainly do know that the answer didn't come from the voice of your own yearning. Usually you will find, however, that the words which come to you are a very recognizable answer.

The church at Antioch recognized the voice of God, and obeyed its directive. **And when they had fasted and prayed, and laid their hands on them, they sent them away.**

So they, being sent forth by the Holy Ghost, departed unto Selucia; and from thence they sailed to Cyprus.

And now begins an epoch of adventure with God.

Selucia was the port city for Antioch. It was near the mouth of the Orontes River and on the Mediterranean Sea. Antioch was about as far inland as Los Angeles is from San Pedro, its port city. But seafaring travelers from Antioch did not have to cope with freeway traffic to get to the port city: it was much simpler to catch a connecting boat down the Orontes.

At Selucia, they boarded a ship for Cyprus. Did they go through the first-century equivalent of typhoid shots, birth certificates, and passports complete with odd photographs? Could be. The Caesars also dealt generously in red tape.

The journey from Selucia to Cyprus was not a long one, and was apparently uneventful. Barnabas and Saul and John Mark entered the island at the city of Salamis. Preachers going into Cyprus today would have to convince the Greeks that they were not too friendly to the Turks, and the Turks that they were not too friendly to the Greeks, as a Very Important Person from our government found to his chagrin—though this gentleman could hardly be called a preacher! But in those good old days the Romans had everything well in hand.

The Romans were, in fact, very handy to have around to keep peace in the world so that the gospel of Jesus Christ could be spread. Naturally, if anybody had hinted of such an idea to the reigning Caesar, that person would have been banished, or ordered to commit suicide. The very idea of Caesar doing anything to further the interests of the God of the Jews—unless, of course, it might be politically expedient for the moment! Those royal gentlemen had no way of knowing that God Almighty uses all sorts of quaint heathen to further His inexorable purposes.

In Salamis, Barnabas and Saul went into the synagogues and preached to the Jews. This seems to have been the custom they always followed, and may, at first glance seem strange for those who were sent to the Gentiles. But the glad tidings of the Messiah always went *first* to the Jews: "**Jerusalem, Judaea, and Samaria**" were before the "**uttermost part of the earth**" in the Lord's command. (No, the Samaritans were not Jews, though part of their remote ancestry was Jewish.) And there were in the synagogues Gentile proselytes to be reached with the gospel, and through them other Gentiles might be reached. The three passed on through the length of the island till they came to Paphos. Here they encountered opposition—and opportunity.

The Roman proconsul, Sergius Paulus, was in Paphos. A great many intelligent Romans, and especially of the higher classes, had ceased altogether to believe in the multiplicity of gods who were the official deities of the Roman state. They rendered outward homage whenever homage was required, and that was that. It must have been a little difficult, at that, to render worship to a living emperor whose hands were stained with the blood of his rivals, and whose soul oozed the nauseous filth of immorality.

Intelligent men were groping for, hoping for, seeking, immortal Truth, and sometimes they grasped eagerly at a rotten straw. Such a man was Sergius Paulus, and the rotten straw to which he was clinging for salvation was **a certain sorcerer, a false prophet, a Jew, whose name was Bar-jesus.** Bar-jesus— *Son of the Savior!* Blasphemy? Certainly. Saul soon labels him properly: *son of Satan.*

News traveled ahead of Barnabas and Saul and their young assistant, John Mark. Word reached the proconsul that two Jews, teachers with an extraordinary message, were in his island. These men were preaching about a Savior for all mankind, One who was none other than the Son of God. With eager anticipation, Sergius Paulus sent for the two men, and asked to hear the word of God. He listened intently, his mind open for Truth.

Another man listened also, listened carefully, listened apprehensively. The sorcerer, Elymas (for he was also called by that name), was intelligent enough to recognize Truth when he heard it. He knew that unless he could prevent the proconsul's believing the message of God, he, Elymas, would lose a rich and influential patron and a very comfortable berth. In short, he'd have to move on and look for other suckers.

So Elymas began heckling Barnabas and Saul in an effort to convince Sergius Paulus that these two were blasphemous charlatans trying to discredit the very Son of the Savior! Satan was daring to challenge God Almighty in open conflict for the soul of a man. Satan appears to have been remarkably stupid; or perhaps it was a final thrust of fury from one who knew he had lost a battle.

Abruptly, Saul stopped talking. In the quivering silence, the sense of power which flooded his whole being made him to understand quite clearly that he had ceased to be himself, Saul of Tarsus, and had become a voice, even the Voice of God.

109

Saul's hypnotic eyes sought and chained the gaze of the startled sorcerer whose babbling ceased on a half-finished word. Almost childishly he tried to lift his hands to shield his face from the penetrating fury of Saul's eyes, but his hands seemed too heavy to lift. There was nothing left in the world but those penetrating eyes, and slowly, ever so slowly they grew larger; slowly, ever so slowly, they came closer. Elymas could not see the stern mouth forming words, but he could hear them crackling like a whiplash in the silence:

"O full of all subtility and all mischief, son of Satan, thou enemy of all righteousness, wilt thou not cease to pervert the right ways of the Lord? And now, behold, the hand of the Lord is upon thee, and thou shalt be blind, not seeing the sun for a season."

Elymas finally found that he could move his hands. He lifted them to claw at the white mist that had suddenly settled like a heavy curtain over his eyes. The mist did not part, but grew thicker and thicker, and then began turning black.

With a scream of rage and terror, Elymas turned to run from the room; he crashed into a marble column and fell sprawling on the floor. Whimpering, cursing under his breath, he got to his feet, and with the groping awkwardness of the newly blind sought with his hands for familiar objects to guide him toward the door. He finally made his way outside, and they heard him crying out, "Help! Have pity! Take my hand and lead me, for I am blind."

Saul turned toward the proconsul. "And now, most noble Sergius Paulus, if we may continue to speak. . . ."

The Roman smiled. "In my language, your name is the same as mine. I will hear you gladly, *Paul.*"

Luke finishes the narrative with **Then the deputy, when he saw what was done, believed, being astonished at the doctrine of the Lord.**

From here on in, we find **Paul and his company** instead of "Barnabas and Saul."

This switch in leadership appears not to have ruffled Barnabas in the least, but something was definitely gnawing at the mind of his nephew, the young John Mark; and that something could have been resentment at the change. Some guess that he was merely homesick. However, some writers suggest that Mark's dissatisfaction stemmed from the fact that ministry to the Gentiles was being over-emphasized. But since he must have known all the while that Saul's call was peculiarly to the Gentiles, that Barnabas had been working with Gentiles since being sent to Antioch, and that the church of Antioch which was sponsoring this mission was a Gentile church, that attitude would seem completely illogical in even a very young man.

Luke leaves us guessing.

Paul and his company, taking ship again, **loosed from Paphos**, and having sailed north across nearly two hundred miles of Mediterranean water, they sighted the mainland of Asia Minor. They were nearing the shores of the province of Pamphylia and, turning in at the mouth of the river Cestrus, they sailed the seven miles upstream to the city of Perga. There isn't a word or even a hint of any preaching or teaching in Perga, but it was there that John Mark left them and went back to Jerusalem.

From Perga, Paul and Barnabas went to Antioch in Pisidia.

By the way, there were sixteen cities named Antioch. The only two with which we are concerned are Antioch in Syria, from whence Paul and Barnabas set out on their journey, and Antioch of Pisidia, where we find them now.

... **They came to Antioch in Pisidia, and went into the synagogue on the sabbath day, and sat down.** They sat down quietly, and waited to be asked to speak.

When they were invited to speak, it was Paul who responded: "**Men of Israel, and ye that fear God, give audience.**"

(I can't help wondering what would happen if a visiting minister in our church were to get to his feet abruptly, make one single gesture, and say—without preamble—"You Presbyterians, and everyone else who holds God in awe, listen to me"!)

Paul, a son of Israel, speaking to his brothers, the sons of Israel, was picking up beloved fragments of history of the house of Israel. He was dropping the fragments into the ever-receptive pool of Jewish minds and fitting them there into the tear-stained mosaic of Jewish history.

"God chose our fathers. . . . God brought them out of Egypt. . . . God suffered their manners in the wilderness. . . . God destroyed seven nations in the land of Canaan and divided the land among His people. . . . God gave them judges until Samuel the prophet. . . . God gave them Saul as king. . . . God removed Saul as king and raised up David instead." Ah, David! David the magnificent, the man after God's own heart, David whose dynasty would be established forever, for from his seed would spring Israel's Messiah.

And "of this man's seed hath God according to his promise raised unto Israel a Saviour, Jesus."

"Of [David's] seed, a Saviour"—*He has come!* The eagerness, the hope, the wild yearning that must have been stamped on the faces of Paul's audience. Jesus, the Savior has come! Where is He? When will we be able to see Him? And on the wistful faces of the Gentile proselytes is written the question, "Will we, not actually being the children of Abraham, be allowed to see Him also? Will He accept us?"

What is the messenger saying now? "Children of the stock of Abraham, and whoever among you feareth God, to you is the word of this salvation sent." The Gentiles exhale a concerted sigh of gratitude—yes, the message is for them also; they will not be excluded from the presence of the Savior. Is He in Jerusalem? They will go to Jerusalem. No matter how grave the hardship, no matter how great the cost, they will go and find Jesus the Savior.

But something is going wrong with this narrative! The rulers at Jerusalem failed to recognize Him in spite of the prophets whose words they heard read every sabbath; they, in fact, turned Him over to Pilate for the Romans to execute as a common criminal. "It is written, 'Cursed is every one that hangeth on a tree.' " Israel's Messiah, the Son of David, accursed? Somebody has erred wildly.

Down from the tree and into a tomb. From the women's gallery comes the sound of sobbing. Israel's Messiah dead and buried, the precious fruit of Rachel's womb putrefying in the fetid earth; has God become a cruel Father who mocks His children?

The speaker's next words dry their tears with sheer astonishment: **"But God raised him from the dead."** Can the man be certain of that? How does he know? **"And he was seen many days of them which came up with him from Galilee to Jerusalem, who are His witnesses unto the people."** Witnesses. More than one witness. "At the mouth of two witnesses, or at the mouth of three witnesses, shall the matter be established."

Jesus the Savior has come into the world. The rulers in Jerusalem murdered the Messiah. God raised Him from the dead. " 'Thou art my Son, this day have I begotten thee.' " And again, " 'Thou shalt not suffer thine Holy One to see corruption.' " *With David the king let us render praise unto our God, for this longed-for Fruit from Rachel's fecund womb did not decay in earth's relentless bosom. He lives!*

And now the messenger is saying, **"Through this man comes the forgiveness of sins: and by him all that believe are justified from all things, from which ye could not be justified by the law of Moses."** Through a man, forgiveness of sins? But sins were forgiven by the offering of sacrifice. How could these things be?

After the services were over, many members of the congregation, proselytes as well as Jews, followed Paul and Barnabas, eagerly asking questions, eagerly listening to the answers. And they pressed about the messengers begging them to repeat the same message the following sabbath.

Luke tells us, **And the next sabbath day came almost the whole city together to hear the word of God.**

Multitudes thrilled at the prospect of hearing this new message from God; multitudes were intrigued by what they had heard of this strange new doctrine which would transplant Gentiles into the garden of God merely by their believing on the Messiah. Antioch of Pisidia was a good-sized city, the crowd must have been enormous.

But evidently a lot of the Jews and proselytes had been doing some serious reconsidering during the week. This could not be right: The Messiah was not to be for mobs. He belonged to the faithful children of Abraham and the patient proselytes whose observing of the Law of Moses made them adopted children of the covenant. Why should these heathen be granted the privilege of salvation merely by believing? Why should they not also be required to come to God by way of circumcision and observing the whole Law? Why should salvation be made cheap and easy for anybody, and most especially for a Gentile?

Paul did not get to preach his sermon that sabbath. The envy and bitterness in his hearers boiled over into noisy heckling, contradicting, denying, even blaspheming. He stopped preaching, and looked slowly around his audience with penetrating fire in his eyes. In the sudden and breathless silence that ensued, he beckoned to Barnabas, and the two spoke to the silent people.

"God sent us to you first with this glad news," said Barnabas, "and so to you we came. But you seek to hide the Light of God within the circle of yourselves; that Light cannot be so contained—it will break forth."

"Yea," Paul added tersely, "with your blasphemy you have pronounced judgment upon yourselves: You have made yourselves unworthy of everlasting life. Lo, we turn now to the Gentiles."

"For so hath the Lord Himself commanded us, saying, 'I have set thee to be a light of the Gentiles that thou shouldest be for salvation unto the ends of the earth.' " Barnabas concluded.

Gladness in the hearts of the Gentiles broke out in a great shout.

In Antioch of Pisidia as in Antioch of Syria, the majority of the new disciples were Gentile. Many believed, and throughout the whole area the Word was preached.

But here we have the beginning of a very familiar pattern of persecution.

Bitterness and envy in the heart of the synagogue increased proportionately with the success of Paul and Barnabas among the Gentiles. Having determined to rid the region of the two messengers of the new faith, the Jewish leaders knew how to accomplish that feat without undue difficulty: They simply worked on the emotions of the women proselytes, some of whom were wives of heathen husbands. Some of these husbands could very well have been the **chief men of the city**, as Luke puts it.

Then as now, regardless of what history says about her legal or technical status, a woman had ways of influencing the decisions and conduct of her husband. Whether she merely nagged him over the morning mush or took a subtler tack and appealed to his broad mind and his compassionate soul (either of which could have been purely imaginary!) the results were the same: The lady usually got what she wanted. And so, the "chief men of the city" began the persecution of Paul and Barnabas which forced them to leave the area. So they **shook off the dust of their feet against them, and came unto Iconium.**

Paul and Barnabas were forced to leave, but the precious Word they had sown among the Gentiles grew and flourished, for we read, **And the disciples were filled with joy, and with the Holy Ghost.**

Chapter Thirteen

Iconium, Lystra, and Derbe were all cities of Lycaonia, a section of what is now Turkey. Iconium was the most important of the three and was nearest to Antioch of Pisidia, being about a hundred miles east and a little south. To Iconium Paul and Barnabas went next and, quite undeterred by their recent experience in the synagogue, they went again and preached. Their efforts were rewarded with what Luke calls a great multitude of both Jews and Greeks who believed.

But the familiar pattern was being laid out again: The unbelieving Jews began stirring up trouble for the messengers. This time, however, Paul and Barnabas stayed right where they were and kept on preaching. They remained in Iconium for a considerable period of time, and the Lord set His special seal of approval on their work here, authenticating it by allowing His servants to perform many miracles.

These signs and wonders helped strengthen the faith of the new believers, and helped to turn still others to the Truth which was being proclaimed. But the miracles further embittered the unbelieving Jews whose hatred finally reached the point of plotting to kill Paul and Barnabas by stoning. Some of the new converts heard of the plot and warned the missionaries, and so they moved on again, this time to Lystra which was only about twenty miles away.

There were not enough Jews in Lystra and Derbe to have synagogues, so Paul and Barnabas preached wherever they could find people to listen. Among their listeners was a young man whose name was Timothy. There was another prominent listener whose name we are not even told. Luke, with his matchless gift for brevity, tells the man's life story in twenty-three words:

And there sat a certain man at Lystra, impotent in his feet, being a cripple from his mother's womb, who never had walked.

"Who never had walked": A little boy who sat under a tree and watched wistfully as other little boys played base-ball—or its Lystran equivalent. A teen-ager who sat and watched gangling boys amble by with giggling girls, if that was the way of adolescence in Lystra. A man who sat and watched life pass by unheeding.

Had he heard of the two Jewish teachers who were in town with a strange story of a Son of God who had assumed human form? Had he heard that the followers of this God had power to heal cripples?

If the cripple of Lystra had heard of these strange things, he wanted more than anything else to see and hear the Jewish teachers for himself: If they healed others, could they not also heal him? It is even possible that the person who carried him when he had to be moved would also be eager for a meeting with the teachers; after all, if this man could be cured, it would save a lot of trouble!

At any rate, the crippled man was taken to a place where Paul and Barnabas were to preach. While Paul was speaking, he saw the man. His pitying glance took in the useless legs stretched straight out on the ground, the wistful yearning, the hope stamped on the eager face. His magnetic eyes caught and held the eyes of the cripple while God's imperishable gift of faith was being planted in the soul behind them.

"He believes! He believes even unto healing!" Paul's heart exulted, even as his voice boomed out, **"Stand upright on thy feet!"**

Like electric current released by an unseen hand upon an unseen switch, life flowed through the man's believing mind and energized his flaccid members. He leaped up (the utter, dizzying glory of being able to *stand!*) and walked (the utter, unbelievable joy of placing one foot firmly in front of the other, and *moving!*). "Look!" he shouted, "Look at me. Hear what this man says, and believe him, *for he has made me walk!*"

Joyful bedlam broke out in the crowd. Somebody said, "The strange men's God did it; let us hear more about their God!" That word traveled through four or five other people and became, "The strange men are not men, but gods who took on human form to visit us. The tall, glorious one must be our Father Jupiter. The one whose speech would move a stone? He is none other than Mercurius!"

The crowd began shouting, "Happy are we, how happy are we of Lystra, for this day have the gods come down to us in the form of men!"

What were Paul and Barnabas doing during all this? Quite probably waiting for the crowd to settle down so they could finish their discourse. All this excited babble was in the **speech of Lycaonia**, which was a colloquial mixture of Greek and Assyrian. Under the strain of strong emotion, the people reverted to their dialect, and Paul and Barnabas, who spoke pure Greek, did not know what was being said.

Jupiter was the special protector and patron of the city of Lystra, and a temple to him had been erected just outside the city gates. Mercury, according to the information which had been given the Lystrans, was the frequent traveling companion of Jupiter, so there was nothing strange about his appearing with the great chief of all the gods.

A messenger, panting with exertion and bursting with importance, halted at the temple and told Jupiter's priest what had happened. If that worthy gentleman wondered petulantly why the gods had chosen to materialize in the middle of town a mile or so away instead of appearing in the place appointed for their worship, he didn't have time to brood.

This probably would never happen again in his lifetime, and he'd best snatch the finest sacrificial materials he could lay hands on and get downtown in a hurry, lest the gods should vanish before he could make it. White oxen with gilded horns? That he could manage. Tender grapevines with bunches of grapes?—(Jupiter was the "giver of wine"). There were none; he'd have to substitute a libation of rare wine. Heads of wheat or barley with their stalks to be woven into the garland for the neck of Mercury's ox?—(Mercury was, among other things, "protector of the grain trade"). There were none. After all, this was a temple of Jupiter. Perhaps Mercury would accept a wreath of flowers and greenery instead. The priest was grateful for a staff of votaries and slaves sufficient to handle an emergency in a hurry.

In a remarkably short time glistening white oxen, their gilded horns glittering in the bright sunlight, their unsuspecting necks laden with wreaths of sweet-smelling flowers, lumbered through the city gates goaded and guided by excited temple slaves toward the spot where the "gods" had materialized and performed a miracle.

Wondering, Paul and Barnabas watched the procession draw near. Men, women, and children, in an apparent frenzy of joy, flowed along behind the priest and the oxen, chanting, "Happy are we, oh, how happy are we! This day the gods are come down to us in the form of men!"

Answering them, the priest intoned, "O Jupiter, O Mercurius! Accept we pray, the sacrifice we are about to offer!"

Paul's strong hands tore at his mantle, and he dashed into the midst of the crowd, crying out, "Hear me, sirs, hear me! What is this that you are about to do? Stay your hand; do not slay your beasts. You must not, you *must not* do sacrifice to us, for we are men like you. We feel, we eat, we sleep, even as you do. We know joy and we know fear; we are not gods, for we also worship. But He whom we worship is the only God, the living God. It is He who has created all things, heaven and earth and sea, and everything in them. He also created us, and we are His children. Hear me, men of Lystra. . . ."

Barnabas ran into the crowd from the other side, tearing at his garments, crying the same frantic message at the top of his voice: "Men of Lystra, we are *not* gods! There is one God, and we are His messengers. He it is who shows Himself to you by giving rain from heaven to touch the fruitful earth and make it yield glad harvest that man may have food and beauty. Hear me, men of Lystra: there is but one God!"

If you are one of those people who become faintly distressed when your preacher raises hands or voice, or moves more than five inches from his microphone, think what it

120

would do to you to be in an open-air service where *two* preachers preach at the same time, running wildly around among the people of the audience, and conveying their message in a not-too-well modulated shout! And there wouldn't even be any choral "amen" at the end of the service.

An unholy substitute for the choral "amen" was the rumbling of curses straight from the soul of Jupiter's priest. He had been tricked. These cursed Jews had made a fool of him in front of the whole town. What had promised to be the most important performance of his whole life had turned into an absolute flop. He tested the edge of the sacrificial knife against his pudgy thumb, and yearned to plunge it into the throat of the wiry little Jew who refused to play god. Apoplectic with frustration, he waved the glittering knife with one hand and the bottle of rare wine with the other in a vague gesture toward the rear. "Back!" he bellowed, "Back to the temple!"

The still unsuspecting white oxen, their necks still laden with fragrant garlands, lumbered back toward their temple pastures and life. Part of the crowd followed along, almost silent except for the gentle slapping of their sandals against the paving stones.

As they approached the gate of the city, the priest saw something that raised his blood pressure even higher: more Jews coming through the gate. He handed the bottle of wine to a slave. "Hold here," he commanded the crowd, "Mayhap our father Jupiter would as soon have a Jew as an ox with a wreath around his neck!" He tested the knife point again, and walked to meet the strangers.

Five minutes later he returned, accompanied by a handful of Jews. The Jews looked quite happy, and the priest's face wore an expression of absolute bliss. The people, who had logically expected a sacrifice of *some* sort to come from all this, waited in bewildered but respectful silence. The priest explained: These honored gentlemen were an official deputation from the cities of Antioch and Iconium, and they had come to Lystra for the express purpose of capturing and punishing two renegade Jews who were trying to overturn the government and upset the world with their false teaching.

Would they, the patriotic citizens of Lystra, be willing to help?

The patriotic citizens of Lystra were very willing!

The white oxen were left to browse, or trample happily upon whatever shrub or flower they could find, while the crowd once more reversed its direction and headed back toward town. As they moved along, the official deputation explained smoothly that it was the custom of the Jews to execute criminals by stoning. Would the people, perhaps, be willing to assist?

Again, the people were willing. They paused, or turned aside to look for suitable missles; they would yet see sacrificial blood this day!

Paul and Barnabas were speaking earnestly, quietly, to the few people who had remained with them when they looked up and saw the mob approaching. There was no doubt as to its mood or intent—the stones were poised for hurling.

"Get the little one first!" the priest yelled, "He makes the most trouble."

"Flee!" Paul said tersely, "Every man of you get to the safety of his own house!"

"I will not leave you." Barnabas sought to shield Paul with his own body.

"Go, beloved friend, O Son of Consolation. Shall we waste two servants of our Lord when one will suffice? Go with these. If God so wills . . . " Paul did not finish the sentence. The last thing he remembered was the image of love and terrified concern stamped on the face of Barnabas. The first hurled stone had struck him on the head.

More stones rained down on the apparently lifeless body crumpled on the blood-smeared paving stones, while the handful of faithful disciples fled as Paul had directed.

"Dead!" Jupiter's priest said contemptuously, kicking the inert heap on the ground, "We might as well drag him beyond the gates for the dogs and the vultures to finish off!"

Was Paul dead?

Lazarus was dead.

Jairus's daughter was dead.

The son of the "widow of Nain" was dead.

Dorcas (Tabitha) was dead.

Christ's chosen Apostle to the Gentiles had not yet finished his work.

About fifteen years later, we find him writing from Philippi in his second letter to the church at Corinth: "I knew a man in Christ above fourteen years ago, (whether in the body, I cannot tell; or whether out of the body, I cannot tell: God knoweth) such an one was caught up to the third heaven. And I knew such a man (whether in the body, or out of the body, I cannot tell: God knoweth;) how that he was caught up into paradise, and heard unspeakable words, which it is not lawful for a man to utter."

Was Paul "absent from the body, and . . . present with the Lord" when he heard "unspeakable words, which it is not lawful for a man to utter"? He probably was dead, but even if he was not, surely miraculous healing etches these words in fire: **Howbeit, as the disciples stood round about him, he rose up, and came into the city: and the next day he departed with Barnabas to Derbe.** A man who had been pelted with stones till the mob had satisfied itself that he was dead, and had then been dragged for perhaps the distance of a mile with his unprotected head banging against paving stones—would that man have been able to **rise up and come into the city?** Hardly!

Paul with Barnabas and the disciples moved in quiet triumph back past the temple of Jupiter, through the gate and into the city of Lystra.

The priest of Jupiter, recognizing the man he had helped toss dead on a rubbish heap a few hours earlier, felt his stomach harden to ice. He collapsed on a small couch because his rubbery legs refused to support his bulk, and reaching for Jupiter's bottle of rare wine opened it recklessly. "I saw him dead!" he muttered, "I tell you I saw him dead on a rubbish heap, and there he goes *walking* back without even so much as a limp, and there isn't a bruise nor a cut on his face! I don't care what he says, *that man's no man, but a god—Oh, Jupiter, I'm scared!*" He emptied the sacred wine into a huge goblet and downed it in unappreciative gulps, and in due time the ice in his stomach melted and warmed, and a measure of strength returned to his limbs. "I still say the bouncy little

one's Mercurius," he murmured drowsily, "Oh well, I . . .
tried. . . ."

How the news of Paul's miraculous recovery must have
electrified the Lystran disciples with joy, and what an everlasting mark it must have made on the soul of the young
Timothy! Were Paul and Barnabas guests that night in Timothy's home? Was that when the apostle met the mother,
Eunice, and the grandmother, Lois? The only thing we hear
about Timothy's father is that he was a Greek. Evidently he
did not accept the Christian faith, for we think that Luke
would have said so. But he must have been very kindly dis-
posed toward the faith of his wife and her mother, else he
would not have allowed his son to go forth with Paul when
the apostle visited Lystra on his second missionary journey.

The next day, Paul and Barnabas moved on to Derbe, and
in this city they were allowed to teach and preach in peace.
The Jewish "deputation" from Antioch and Iconium probably figured that Paul was dead and Barnabas silenced, so
there were no riots, no stonings, no persecution of any sort.
This must have seemed blissfully strange to them. In this
place, which was the last stop on their first missionary journey, they **preached the gospel, and taught many.**

From Derbe, they could have gone down into Tarsus and
sailed directly "home" to Syrian Antioch; but they went
back through the cities where they had preached, Lystra,
Iconium, and Antioch. In all those places, they sought out
the disciples to strengthen their faith, to encourage them to
grow and continue in the faith, to remind them that the road
into the kingdom of God is fraught with peril and tribulation.
And they ordained elders in every church that had been born
of their ministry. From now on in, these new disciples might
be on their own, and the strongest and wisest men among
them must be sought out and ordained to watch over the
churches.

Luke says, . . . **They came to Pamphylia, and when they
had preached the word in Perga. . .** , which reminds us that
Perga was the point where John Mark left them so many
months before to return to Jerusalem, and that no word was
said about preaching or teaching there.

From Perga, they turned their faces toward home. Back

124

down the river Cestrus to the port of Attalia they went, and there they took ship for Antioch from whence they had been sent out such a long time before—somewhere between two and three years.

Thus does the writer Luke condense into two chapters the account of that magnificent journey which began to evangelize the Gentiles in Asia Minor. And the home church in Antioch heard with great joy of the work its missionaries had wrought.

Chapter Fourteen

And certain men which came down from Judaea taught the brethren and said, "Except ye be circumcised after the manner of Moses, ye cannot be saved."

Have you ever encountered self-righteous people who were grimly intent upon making the lesser saints over into their own remarkable image? If you haven't, you're fortunate; if you have, you've prayed for more of the graciousness of God to rub off on you to keep you from exploding. To me, these people are much more trying than the "carnal Christians" they're seeking to reform. Don't misunderstand, please. Carnal Christians need to change and they need to grow, but one does not ordinarily encourage an infant to grow by batting it over the head!

These "certain men" had quite probably heard—or heard of—Peter's report of his God-commanded visit to the home of the Gentile Cornelius, and how the Holy Spirit had fallen upon all the Gentiles there who heard the Word and believed. *God* accepted the uncircumcised Gentiles, but they were not up to the standards of the "certain men" who went down from Judea to set the heathen straight in Antioch. We wonder if any of these messengers were a part of the Jerusalem saints who had been succored in famine by help previously sent by these same Gentile Christians in Antioch! Anyway, they went down to Antioch to browbeat and befuddle the Gentile Christians there.

Their timing was wrong: Paul and Barnabas were back!

They should have known better than to tangle with Paul; people who got into arguments with him were usually left trying to pick up the pieces of their shattered logic. They argued. They disputed. Words flew thick and fast. Eyes flashed. Flowing sleeves fluttered with the quick motions of gesturing hands. And the people were bewildered.

There must have been great relief when it was decided that the apostles and the elders of the mother church in Jerusalem should decide this question, and that the views of the Antioch Christians would be presented by Paul and Barnabas. Who could be more able than these two who had nurtured them in the faith, and had in turn been sent by them—under the direction of the Holy Spirit—to bear the joyful news of salvation to men in far-off places?

And being brought on their way by the church, they passed through Phenice and Samaria, declaring the conversion of the Gentiles: and they caused great joy unto all the brethren.

With what prayerful care the Antioch church must have prepared its delegates to that fateful first council of the church! With what joy tinged with anxiety they must have brought their offerings that the needs of Paul and Barnabas and Titus might be met along their journey! (Titus is not mentioned in Luke's account, but Paul speaks of him in Galatians 2:1.)

The delegates stopped in many places in Phenice (Phoenicia), and recounted to eager disciples the thrilling news of the conversion of the Gentiles. The Lord Jesus, the Messiah of Israel, accepted them as they were when they turned from their sins and believed on Him. The Gentiles rejoiced, and on this tide of joy, the messengers were swept along through Phenice and through Samaria, until they finally arrived in Jerusalem.

They were received of the church, and of the apostles and elders.

First, perhaps at a public gathering of the church, Paul and Barnabas were "received" and given audience. Again, they told the story of their work.

It is hardly likely that the people in the Jerusalem church had heard any except the vaguest account of the journey of

Paul and Barnabas. Perhaps the homesick youth, John Mark, had given a report of the journey as far as Perga in Pamphylia; on the other hand, the young man may not have been too anxious to talk of the matter. Reading Luke's terse, vivid account of the travels and the work of Paul and his companions, we tend to forget that their contemporaries in Jerusalem had no such record, and had to depend upon word-of-mouth reports. They probably did not know too much about the work and the progress of the church in Syrian Antioch, for that matter; so they listened eagerly to all that the missionaries had to say.

After the "reception" by the church, Paul and Barnabas and Titus had opportunity to speak individually to the apostles and the elders. Titus, an uncircumcised Greek, probably did little talking except to answer questions about conduct and doctrine. This was the first time Paul had met any of the apostles except Peter and James the brother of our Lord whom he met during his first visit to Jerusalem after his conversion. His second trip to the holy city when he and Barnabas took the famine relief offerings from Antioch, was so near to that terrible time when James the brother of John was murdered by Herod that we may assume that there was little opportunity for fellowship. Peter was either in prison or in hiding, and the other apostles had probably gone "underground" for the time being.

The apostles and the elders were in hearty accord with Paul and Barnabas, for in the letter to the Galatians we find a record of "James, Cephas [Peter], and John, who seemed to be pillars" having given their blessing through the "right hands of fellowship" for Paul and Barnabas to "go unto the heathen," and they (the three apostles) "unto the circumcision."

But the matter was not settled. It had to be debated in public and settled in public, and we of the church today should be most grateful for that.

There were Pharisees among the believers, and they could not be reconciled to the idea that Gentiles could be saved without keeping the Law of Moses, including the ritual of circumcision.

More than a decade had passed since Peter had stood

before the church in Jerusalem to defend himself against the charge of mingling with Gentiles and heard his brethren glorify God because the Gentiles also had been granted **repentance unto life**. Had they forgotten Peter's testimony that uncircumcised men were accepted of God by the simple act of *believing?* Or were they so zealous for the traditions of their fathers that their Messiah had to be a continuation of, instead of a culmination of, those traditions? And naturally, if that was the way in which salvation came to them, that would also be the way in which salvation came to all men.

And the apostles and elders came together for to consider of this matter—the first council of the church, and it was called to decide a matter of vital doctrine. Is a man saved by *believing* something, or by *doing* something? And in spite of the clear-cut decision reached a little more than nineteen hundred years ago, people still argue heatedly about the same question! Man is an odd little creature.

And when there had been much disputing, Peter rose up. . . .

Who spoke for the Pharisaical believers? The record doesn't say. Evidently, they had their say first. Then Peter stood before the council. To render a verdict? No. To pronounce sentence? No. *To give testimony, like any other witness!* If Peter had supreme authority in the church, he evidently didn't know a thing about it. And neither had he known anything about it eleven years before, when he took Jewish witnesses with him to answer the divine summons to the Gentile, Cornelius.

In simple words, Peter reminded the council again of his experience in the home of the Gentile, Cornelius. He reminded them that God who sent him to the Gentiles knew their hearts, and set the seal of His acceptance on them by giving them also the Holy Spirit. God had not required circumcision of the Gentiles. God purified their hearts by faith. No outward sign of inward purification was needed, for God knew their hearts. They were saved because they had believed on Jesus Christ for remission of their sins.

Was it logical for the church to put upon the necks of the Gentile disciples the yoke by which they themselves had been trying unsuccessfully for generations to pull the burden of the Law? It couldn't be done; no man could observe the whole Law as laid down by "the scribes and the Pharisees, sitting in Moses' seat," as Jesus Himself had pithily expressed it.

"**But we believe that through the grace of the Lord Jesus Christ we shall be saved, even as they.**" Christ kept the Law; He observed the whole Law in its essential purity and perfection, the Law as it had been delivered to Moses. His grace made those who believed in Him also partakers with Him in that perfect keeping of the Law—they were henceforth and forevermore identified with Him in His perfection, because they were a part of Him. The grace of perfect holiness draping the garment of salvation over the nakedness of any sinner who came to Him across that sturdy but very plain footbridge of faith—"We shall be saved, even as they." Jew or Gentile, black, white, brown, or yellow, educated or ignorant, cultured or crude—by that same grace of the Lord Jesus Christ, shall be saved.

Peter sat down, and a great silence filled the place.

Then all the multitude kept silence, and gave audience to Barnabas and Paul, declaring what miracles and wonders God had wrought among the Gentiles by them. Many danger-laden months, hundreds of danger-packed miles, precious new fruit for the kingdom of God pressed by the hand of the master-reporter Luke into one small paragraph!

An interesting sidelight on this chapter is that while they were in Jerusalem, Barnabas is again mentioned before Paul is. This probably has no particular significance, and might simply have been because Barnabas was well known and much beloved in Jerusalem, while Paul was a stranger to most of the disciples there.

Paul and Barnabas were the final witnesses. After their testimony was finished, the matter was summed up and a verdict rendered. Who made the summation? Who pronounced the verdict? James! James, the brother of our Lord, also called James the Just. He was loved and respected by the Pharisee Christians, as well as all the others, because he was careful to observe all the Law and traditions of the Jewish heritage. Here was a Jew's Jew, a Pharisee's Jew, whose opinions and judgment would be respected by the traditionalists.

Here was a pious and just and holy man whose opinions and judgment would also be accepted by those of the opposing school of thought. James appears to have been the undisputed head of the Christian church in Jerusalem.

"Simeon hath declared . . . " James called Peter by his Hebrew name, "Simeon." **"Simeon hath declared how God at the first did visit the Gentiles to take out of them a people for his name."**

It was *God* who "visited the Gentiles" through the ministry of Simon Peter. It wasn't Peter's idea; in fact, God had had to condition Peter drastically for the journey to Caesarea. And the beginning of this "people taken out for his name" was accepted by Him, through the pouring out of the Holy Spirit, without any hint of circumcision, by simple *belief* in Christ.

Why did God "visit the Gentiles to take out of them a people for his name"? Because that was a part of His "master plan" for humanity from the very beginning: **"Known unto God are all his works from the beginning of the world."**

James quotes from the prophet Amos: " **'And I will return, and will build again the tabernacle of David, which is fallen down; and I will build again the ruins thereof, and I will set it up: That the residue of men might seek after the Lord, and all the Gentiles, upon whom my name is called, saith the Lord, who doeth all these things.' "**

How pathetic the ruins of the "tabernacle of David"! How many weary generations since a man from David's loins had reigned upon a throne! But that King, unknown to all save an insignificant handful, has come, and the rebuilding of the ruins has begun. And that magnificent structure which God is building has ample room for all the "called out" ones of the world, even for Gentiles.

"Wherefore my sentence is . . . " In exquisite simplicity; without a trace of the bombast or pomposity which would accompany such a verdict in our day—in fact, with what seems to us an almost matter-of-fact humility—James settles the matter.

"My sentence is, that we trouble not them, which from among the Gentiles are turned to God: But that we write unto them, that they abstain from the pollution of idols, and

from fornication, and from things strangled, and from blood."

The Gentile Christians in Antioch and Syria and Silicia were to be counseled by letter to abstain from those practices which identified them with paganism: The eating of meat that had been offered as sacrifice to heathen gods; the consumption of blood, which was a feature of heathen feasts; the eating of animals which had been strangled to death instead of slaughtered; and the almost casual practice of personal impurity. All of these things which they were counseled (but not commanded!) to avoid were an outrage to the sensibility of the Jewish Christians with whom they would freely mingle now in all things. And as a gesture of love and gentleness— even simple courtesy—they were to avoid those things which offended their brothers in Christ.

It comes as a shock to most of us that the sin of gross immorality was mentioned in the same breath with dietary customs. Among the Gentiles, chastity was not something to be cherished, nor impurity a sin to be avoided. They simply did not know any better. How could they have known? Their very religions were filthily immoral.

We know better. Nonetheless, we are moving swiftly toward that abyss of immorality from which those Gentiles were rescued by the grace of our Lord and Savior, Jesus Christ.

The letter which was written by the Jewish church in Jerusalem to the Gentile churches in Antioch and (the rest of) Syria and Cilicia was the first written document of the New Testament, and it was for the purpose of telling Christians that they did not have to observe the Jewish ritual nor keep the Law of Moses to obtain salvation.

Further, the letter repudiated the "certain" (ones) who had gone out from Jerusalem. It commended Barnabas and Paul as **"beloved men who have hazarded their lives for the name of our Lord Jesus Christ"**—implying quietly that the troublemakers had not risked anything—and it named the two official delegates who were to take the letter to the churches: Judas and Silas.

"It seemed good to the Holy Ghost, and to us." The Holy Spirit was with them in their deliberations and in their decision. Then followed the list of recommended prohibitions. The Gentile brethren were not commanded, they were counseled: Advice dictated by the Holy Spirit, sent in the spirit of meekness and gentleness, and received with gratitude and joy by the people to whom it was written. If we pondered that message long enough, we might find something which could be used for a church which is following the secular trend to be governed from the top down instead of from the bottom up. Ecclesiastical freedom can be lost by yawning indifference just as definitely as political freedom can be. And terrifyingly *is!*

When that letter was read in Antioch, joy broke out, joy born of comfort and reassurance. Their salvation was real, their salvation was perfect, their salvation was Jesus Christ. Salvation had indeed come to the Gentiles.

Paul and Barnabas were back in Antioch again, free to teach and preach in peace.

At length, Judas and Silas were reluctantly allowed to go by the church in Antioch, so that they could return to Jerusalem, but Silas decided to stay awhile longer. It is not likely that Silas knew at the time how momentous that decision was for him: It meant that he was to be the companion of Paul in his next missionary journey.

Chapter Fifteen

Paul wanted to revisit the cities where he and Barnabas had preached. His love for his converts and his anxiety for their spiritual growth are evident in all his letters to them. He knew that those who are young in the faith need a strong hand to steady them, a tender hand to feed them. Believers in the churches he established—or helped to establish—were not an indefinite blur of faces to the apostle Paul. They were individual human beings, they were *people* whose images were etched with love on the pages of the diary he kept in his heart.

Paul said unto Barnabas, "Let us go again . . . "

Barnabas was willing, but he wanted to take John Mark with them again. Paul objected to that: Mark had failed them miserably before, why try him again? Neither would yield, and we read with amazement and sorrow of the quarrel between these spiritual giants whose work together had accomplished marvelous things for God.

Even so, there is comfort for ordinary saints in the matter-of-fact record of the failings of great men of God. In the first place, it should help to understand that this account which Luke was penning was dictated by the Holy Spirit, since books by human authors tend to minimize or ignore the failings of their heroes. Then, too, it should give us a nice glow of being identified with these whom we hold in awe when we reflect that they, too, had glaring faults.

But this must have been bewildering to the Antioch

Christians; bewildering and saddening, for they loved both men deeply. But God used even this unhappy occurrence, for instead of two people going forth on one journey, four set forth on two journeys.

Barnabas took young John Mark and set sail for Cyprus. Paul chose Silas for his companion and fellow worker and left, **being recommended by the brethren unto the grace of God.** Since Luke said nothing of Barnabas and Mark being so recommended, we may believe that the church of Antioch "took sides" to a degree in the quarrel, and that their sympathies were with Paul.

And he went through Syria and Cilicia, confirming the churches. What churches? No definite account is given of the establishing of any churches in those places prior to this time, except the one in Antioch. It seems to be universally taken for granted that the others referred to are those which resulted from Paul's ministry while he waited in Tarsus for his summons to a fuller ministry to the Gentiles. These churches would be preponderantly Gentile, and the letter from the Jerusalem church, read to them by Paul and confirmed verbally by Silas, must have evoked the same joy and relief it had brought to the disciples in Antioch.

Then came he to Derbe and Lystra. Five or six years had passed since the day Paul was stoned in Lystra and dragged outside the city and left for dead. During those years the young Timothy—who undoubtedly had been converted by Paul's preaching—had matured physically and spiritually. He had been brought up with pious zeal for the God of Israel under the tutelage of his grandmother, Lois, and his mother, Eunice. He had been brought to the knowledge of Israel's Messiah by Paul and Barnabas, but he was not considered a true son of Israel because he had never been circumcised.

Aside from his purely spiritual qualities, there must have been in Timothy a winsomeness whose tendrils instantly encircled the heart of the lonely, childless Paul. A child of his spiritual begetting, a "son in the faith" Paul found in Timothy. **Him would Paul have to go forth with him.** Timothy was willing and eager to go with Paul, but under the circumstances he could do nothing of the kind! Why? Because in every city where he took the gospel, Paul went first to "the lost sheep of the house of Israel"—to the synagogue—and his chosen helper would not even be admitted into the synagogue: Timothy was an uncircumcised Jew. Therefore, Paul **took and circumcised him.**

Was this completely inconsistent with the message Paul and Silas were taking to the churches from the apostles and the elders in Jerusalem? Not at all. The "decrees for to keep" set forth the truth that *Gentiles* did not have to be circumcised to be saved. Timothy did not have to be circumcised to be saved, nor to preach to Gentiles, but he did have to be to preach to Jews. A Gentile did not have to become a Jew to become a Christian, but neither did a Jew have to stop being a Jew to become a Christian.

So Paul and Silas went out from **Lystra and Iconium,** and with them went the young Timothy.

And as they went through the cities, they delivered them the decrees for to keep, that were ordained of the apostles and elders which were at Jerusalem. And so were the churches established in the faith, and increased in number daily.

The churches in "Syria and Cilicia," and all the churches that Paul and Barnabas had established on their journey together, heard the blessed letter from Jerusalem, and listened to verbal corroboration by Silas. Their salvation was assured, the counsel sent to them was wholesome advice; they were "established in the faith," and their souls had rest from doubt and uneasiness and bickering. And so they grew.

Up to this point, Paul seems to have had no intention of doing anything more than revisiting the churches to strengthen and confirm them. Now, he seems ready to plunge into untouched territory.

North from Iconium and farther into Galatia they went. Luke gives no great detail here, but in Paul's letter to the Galatians, he speaks of having preached to them "through infirmity of the flesh," and "I bear you record, that, if it had been possible, ye would have plucked out your own eyes, and have given them to me." So it would seem that physical illness forced him to pause in Galatia, and that the warmhearted, impulsive (and, alas, fickle!) Galatians received his message and received him with real affection. In fact, their love for him was so fervent that they would have given their healthy eyes to replace his ailing ones if they could have done so.

This strongly implies that the disease from which Paul suffered had the effect of impairing his eyesight; otherwise, why would his converts have been willing to give their *eyes?* Near-blindness was probably the reason for Paul's dictating his letters. There is something poignantly touching in his personal note near the end of the letter to the Galatians: "See how large a letter [or with what large letters] I have written unto you with my own hand." A person almost blind would write laboriously, and the letters would be large.

Success in Phrygia and Galatia, but forbidden by the Holy Spirit to preach in Asia, or even to go into Bithynia. How? We don't know. Why? We don't know that either, not definitely. But if *we* had been stopped in our tracks while on an errand for the Almighty, we'd have headed for the nearest wailing wall to remind the Lord that, everything considered, He wasn't treating us right. And we would never have made it to Troas!

And they passing by Mysia came down to Troas— Alexandria Troas, a port city on the Aegean Sea approximately in the northwest corner of Asia Minor. Paul and Silas and the young Timotheus were facing toward the sea. Which way would they be sent? And what effect would that direction have upon *us?* If that brilliant, half-blind little Jew had *not* proceeded northwest, I might not be writing, and you might not be reading; and if our children were stricken suddenly ill, we'd send across the forest for the nearest witch doctor. The apostle Paul was about to enter Europe, and most of us are of European ancestry. The beginning of our Christian civilization stems from that particular sea voyage.

Paul must have been waiting for definite instructions: he had been told where not to go and where not to preach. Now, he was waiting for something positive. It came: **And a vision appeared unto Paul in the night; there stood a man of Macedonia, and prayed him, saying, "Come over into Macedonia, and help us."** The suppliant hands were shackled with chains of pagan superstition, and the yearning eyes were the eyes of one who looks through prison bars at a strong man with a key.

And after he had seen the vision, immediately we endeavoured to go into Macedonia, assuredly gathering that the Lord had called us for to preach the gospel unto them.

Note the "we."

Unobtrusively, as becomes a good reporter, Luke has joined the party of missionaries—Luke the writer, Luke the physician, Luke the faithful and beloved friend. What was he doing at Troas? He doesn't say, probably figuring it didn't matter in the least. Was this his first meeting with the great apostle? Quite likely not. Some writers say positively that Luke met and worked with Paul in Antioch (of Syria); others say the two had probably met in Antioch. At any rate, they are going together on the first missionary venture into Europe.

We do not know how long Paul had to wait in Troas before the vision came, but we can almost feel the surge of relief and eagerness in the words, "immediately we endeavoured to go into Macedonia." Down to the waterfront they went, Paul and Silas and Timotheus and Luke, looking for a ship that might be sailing right away. They found one without difficulty, and even the winds were favorable, for Luke says, **We came with a straight course to Samothracia, and the next day to Neapolis.** Thus, they made the journey in two days, whereas later on we shall find them making the same trip in reverse and using five days from Neapolis (seaport of Philippi) to Troas.

From Neapolis they traveled inland some ten miles and came to the city of Philippi, **the chief city of that part of Macedonia, and a colony.** Roman colony, that is, established by Augustus Caesar to honor his victory—with Antony—over Brutus and Cassius after those two had killed Julius Caesar.

There were few Jews in Philippi, so few that there was no synagogue, and so Paul and his companions went to a spot on a river outside the city where godly people were accustomed to gather for prayer. On that particular sabbath, apparently the only people there were women, and so the missionaries sat down and talked to them.

Paul had entertained a most compelling vision of a *man*

from Macedonia appealing for help, but when he hastened to answer the appeal, he found a handful of apparently insignificant women congregated by the riverside to pray. Paul, the mighty preacher, sat down and talked to the women. Luke says, **we sat down and spake unto the women. . . .** Paul, Silas, Timothy, and Luke, all talked to them.

When they went to that place of prayer, the women had expected nothing more than the usual blessing from prayer and whatever bits of Scripture they could recite (they had no books). What must have been their excitement when they saw the four strangers and learned where they came from. What must have been their joy when they discovered the reason for that visit: To proclaim that Israel's Messiah had come, and that the blessings of His kingdom were also for the despised Gentiles. Not only to those Gentiles who had come to God through Israel and her law and ritual, but even to Gentiles who came with their unwashed filthiness to be cleansed by the sacrifice of His blood.

A handful of women, some Jewish by birth and some by "adoption," and among the latter was Lydia, **a seller of purple, of the city of Thyatira.** Lydia was a wealthy business woman who worshiped God. Wealth did not satisfy the cravings of her soul—she looked for something better. Her "household" is mentioned, but nothing is said of her husband, so she was in all probability a widow. God unlocked her heart to receive the treasure of Paul's words, and thus she became the first Christian convert upon the European continent.

This, the firstfruits of a mighty race of Gentile Christian women, brought her "household" with her into the faith. Her household probably consisted of her children, other relatives who lived in her home, household servants, and quite possibly some or all of her employees.

The river outside of the city must have been the scene of a mighty baptizing when Lydia and her household were baptized. Elderly people, little children, even slaves, sealed in one faith to one Lord by that sacred rite. What a marvelous thing for human beings who were *property* to learn that they were accepted by God through Jesus Christ on the same footing with their masters—and princes and kings. Centuries before

man, by virtue of Christian civilization, got around to pro-
hibiting slavery by law, a man was free in his spirit because
Jesus Christ made him free.

Lydia began immediately to demonstrate her faith by her
works. She saw that the missionaries had no place to stay,
and she not only invited them to her home, but insisted that
they should make it their headquarters. How willing, how
eager must have been the hands in Lydia's home that tended
the needs of these men of God. These were the messengers
who brought hope and salvation to slaves. How gracious, how
companionable must have been the conversation of God's
ministers with the slaves of Lydia's household. I think there
was not a trace of condescension there.

Chapter Sixteen

As the work progressed and grew, the missionaries began to have publicity of a sort that was not only embarrassing to them, but an insult to the God whom they served. Satan appeared to be trying to get into the act, trying to identify himself with the Most High God by means of the twisted mind and the shrill voice of a slave girl who was a fortune-teller. Fortunetellers have nothing to do with God, and God has nothing to do with fortunetellers. It was true then, and it is true now. The ones who are fake deceive their silly customers with clever tricks of psychology; the ones who are genuine belong to the devil, and God's people will do well to avoid both. Twice, and twice only in my life, do I remember encountering the spirit of evil so absolute that it was almost as tangible as the hissing of a snake. On both occasions I was spoken to by women who probably called themselves "ministers," and they were mouthing "messages" which were supposed to add to the store of my general happiness. If you have nothing in your hand with which to destroy it, you move out of a rattlesnake's range: I did not linger for chit-chat with the ladies!

On their way to the place of prayer, Paul and his company encountered a fortunetelling slave girl. Gullible people paid good money then just as they do now to have their fortunes told, and the girl's owners had a good financial thing going.

The girl turned around and trailed along after the mis-

sionaries, crying her shrill singsong, **"These men are the servants of the most high God, which shew unto us the way of
salvation!"** Her masters were quite naturally present to collect fees, and to prevent their valuable slave's escaping, so
why they allowed her to do this is something of a mystery.
The first time, they might have been stupid enough to think
the missionaries would pay them for the "favorable publicity" which was advertising their work (as it no doubt did,
for that sort of thing gets around). But after no fee was
forthcoming, it is strange that they allowed this oracular message to continue day after day. It could have been, of course,
that the owners were as superstitious as the gullible dupes
whose money they were pocketing, and didn't dare stop the
message.

How did the unfortunate girl know that "these men were
the servants of the most high God"? Evil spirits always recognized Christ, and proclaimed that recognition through the
voices of their tortured victims. They seemed to be under a
terrible compulsion to proclaim the deity of Christ. James in
his epistle remarks pithily, "Thou believest that there is one
God; thou doest well: *the devils also believe, and tremble.*"

These Spirit-filled servants of God were so completely
identifiable with their Master, that the devils had no difficulty recognizing Him in them.

The "message" was true, all right. But Paul wasn't any
happier than your pastor would be if some "medium" should
receive a message from the spirit world exhorting those assembled in seance to begin attending services at the First
Baptist Church! Your pastor would figure that the cause of
Christ set forth in His church was being profaned, and he
would be right. Paul felt the same way.

And this she did many days. But Paul, being grieved . . .
Paul was filled with indignation and pity. Indignation, because the name of the Most High God was being linked in the
minds of the Philippians with "Python," which was the name
of the heathen god, Apollo, in his oracular character. The
pity was for the poor, demon-possessed girl because her mind
and soul were imprisoned, shut up securely in a locked cell
while the devil used her to parade his own personality. This,
too, was a part of the appeal of the "man from Macedonia."

Paul turned around and looked at the girl. Sullen apprehension and resentment stared back at him through her eyes. In the suddenly electric silence, Paul looked steadfastly at the demented girl, and somewhere in a dark and slimy corner, her imprisoned mind began stirring feebly. "His eyes . . . his eyes," she thought, "sore eyes . . . sore eyes . . . make me sick . . . I will not look at his eyes . . . I can't stop looking . . . sore eyes . . . sore eyes . . . I feel sick!"

Articulate thunder exploded from the mouth of the man with the ailing eyes: **"I command thee in the name of Jesus Christ to come out of her."**

Steel bands seemed to tighten around the girl's head. Pain pierced the nape of her neck and widened into a swirl of screaming agony in the crown of her head. With long-nailed, dirty fingers she tore at her disheveled hair, as though trying to make room for the pain to escape. And then she collapsed on the ground, writhed in convulsion, and lay as one dead. The slave girl opened her eyes and saw two strange, hard-faced men bending over her. "Who are you?" she asked her masters, "Where am I? Where is my mother?"

"We are your kind masters; you are in Philippi, and through your lips the great god Apollo foretells the future for favored ones. Come, young man," they wheedled a passing youth, "for a fee—for such a small fee—the Pythoness will read your future."

She stared at them blankly. "Your words mean nothing to me, and I know nothing of the great god, Apollo."

Her masters looked at each other over her head. "That Jew!" they raged, "That cursed little Jew with his mouthings . . . he has robbed her of her great gift! She is empty; she is useless; and she will bring no more in the market than an ordinary kitchen slave. The Jews have robbed us; after them!"

They caught Paul and Silas, and drew them into the marketplace unto the rulers, and brought them to the magistrate, saying, "These men, <u>being Jews,</u> do exceedingly trouble our city, and teach customs, which are not lawful for us to receive, neither to observe, being Romans."

Why didn't the infuriated owners also catch Timothy and Luke? Why did they take Silas, when Paul was obviously the one who had rendered their property worthless? Because he, also, was a Jew! Timothy was half Greek, and it is quite possible that he did not look Jewish; Luke also was probably a Gentile. (There is no completely definite information in Scripture concerning that, but Paul does not list him among those "of the circumcision" who are with him in Rome when the letter to the Colossians is written. "Luke, the beloved physician, and Demas" are listed separately, as also sending greetings to the Colossians.)

Paul and Silas were obviously Jews, therefore it would be easy to stir up public resentment against them.

Aside from the fact that they were quite likely liars by nature, why did the owners lie in the charge they brought against Paul and Silas? Because they knew they hadn't a legal leg to stand on. True, their property had lost its value by virtue of Paul's action, but the law had no remedy for property rendered worthless by exorcism. If they had stated their true case they would have been thrown out of court, so they resorted to the time-tested trick of screaming "Jews!" in accents that made it a dirty word.

The old trick still worked like a charm. **And the multitude rose up together against them; and the magistrates rent off their clothes, and commanded to beat them.**

One little phrase from Paul and Silas would have stopped the magistrates in their tracks and sent them scurrying for report blanks to fill in and send to their superiors. That little phrase? "We are *Romans.*"

The gospel of Jesus Christ was not being proclaimed under the protecting shadow of Rome. (And a few centuries later when Rome officially espoused her, the church lost her purity and her power.) So Paul and Silas were stripped and beaten.

Being beaten was not a casual thing. The lictors went about their business with a savage efficiency, and they used rods. Since they belonged to a civilization which entertained itself by watching human beings kill each other in the arena, it is even possible that they derived a sadistic joy from striking naked human flesh with a rod, and watching the welts raise and redden, the outraged skin tear and bleed.

I don't know whether or not Luke witnessed this horror;

I find myself hoping that he did not. The mental anguish from standing by in helplessness while his friends were being barbarously used would have been almost unbearable. Add to that the outrage of a physician watching human bodies reduced to a mass of bleeding flesh, and you can imagine that his suffering would have been almost as acute as that of the victims.

Paul and Silas were allowed neither balm nor bandage. Straight from under the lictor's rod they were taken to prison, and the jailor was evidently given to understand that they were dangerous prisoners, violent men who were about to have the whole city in an uproar. He **thrust them into the inner prison, and made their feet fast in the stocks.** Desperadoes, malefactors, rioters—men who would overthrow the government of Caesar by force and violence; well, he could handle them. He rather thought that in his maximum security ward they'd stay put! The jailor went about his business, and in due time, went to bed.

It doesn't take a very vivid imagination to make us realize the intense pain which Paul and Silas endured as the day dragged on. If the "stocks" used in the prison were the same sort we see in pictures of primitive things, the men were either sitting or lying on the floor with their legs stretched out stiffly and their feet locked in the wooden device. And there is no reason to believe that the floor was not crawling with rats and vermin, since authorities in ancient governments were not overly concerned about sanitation in their prisons. Tormented flesh and lacerated skin were at the mercy of prison fleas and rats and lice.

What would you or I have done under such circumstances? We would, quite probably, have gone into shock and died, or into hysteria and teetered on the brink of complete insanity.

What did Paul and Silas do?

The answer to that is one of the most extraordinary statements ever written: **And at midnight Paul and Silas prayed, and sang praises unto God: and the prisoners heard them.**

God's lonely servants, sitting in utter darkness, singing and praying above their suffering and pain. Remembering the suffering and the loneliness and the humiliation of their Lord, they rejoiced that they could share that suffering.

When God's people hit bottom, and look up and pray, things happen. Elijah, that solitary old man on Mount Carmel, mocked the filthy hordes of Baal arrayed against him, and prayed God to send down fire. And the fire came down. The disciples in the home of John Mark's mother prayed for Peter's release when he was hours away from execution. And a delivering angel came.

In the dark prison in Philippi, the awe-struck inmates listened to men who, if they had been "normal," would have been reviling and cursing their persecutors. Instead, their unfaltering voices rose in prayer and songs of praise, "Hallelujah! Hallelujah! Blessed be the name of the Lord from this time forth and forevermore. Hallelujah! Hallelujah! Holy is His name!"

Angels over Philippi? Who knows? Choirs of angels massed above, listening to the voices from the prison, answering with antiphonal "Hallelujahs" whose majestic cadence shook the very earth beneath them?

And suddenly there was a great earthquake, so that the foundations of the prison were shaken: and immediately all the doors were opened, and every one's bands were loosed.

Did the prisoners scatter madly through the opened doors to freedom? They did not! That was phenomenal. Why didn't they? Because they sensed that the earthquake was in answer to the prayers of the two strange men. If those men had *that* kind of power, the God who sent an earthquake to shake their bonds off was looking after them very carefully. It would be safer to stay close to this God's men than to dash out into the night and perhaps break their necks falling over loosened stones and timbers.

The jolting of the earth, the violent shaking of his bed, the creaking and groaning of timbers, all served to jar the prison keeper into instant wakefulness. Earthquake! Had it been severe enough to loose the doors of the prison? Were his prisoners still there, or had they escaped? He buckled on his sword, seized a lamp, and went to investigate. The doors were open. Roaming the streets of Philippi by now, dodging behind piles of debris, waiting to rob or murder unsuspecting

Roman citizens were the felons who had been delivered into his custody.

With the steely resignation of a Roman who had failed in the performance of public duty, the jailor unsheathed his sword. Self-inflicted death would blur the harsh shadows of disgrace.

But from the depths of the building, there came a strong cry: "**Do thyself no harm: for we are all here!**"

Nobody gone? That couldn't be! Prisoners always escaped when there was opportunity. Moreover, that cry had come from the direction of the men he had confined in stocks, the ones who had been dragged in bleeding from the lictor's rod. *Why should they be distressed because he was about to commit suicide?* He had subjected them to additional pain and misery. By all natural reckoning, they should have been ready to gloat over a sword thrust into his vitals. *What manner of men were these who returned solicitude for cruelty?* Suddenly, he was more terrified than when he had first seen the opened doors.

With a swift flash of insight, he coupled the Jewish prisoners with the earthquake; he recalled the reports of the outcries of the pythoness: "**These men are the servants of the most high God, which shew unto us the way of salvation.**" Most High God. Most High *God! Who was the Most High God?* The One above all other gods, and he, an obscure official of Rome, had dared to add outrage to the servants and messengers of this One.

By then the jailor's personal slaves and deputies were approaching with more lamps, and he motioned them to follow him toward the center of the building. They watched in amazement as their master rushed into the presence of the two strange prisoners and fell on his face before them, reaching out in absolute silence to touch their swollen feet.

Paul laid his hand gently on the man's head. "Nay, my child; do not prostrate yourself before us, for we are also men."

"I hurt you, I hurt you," the jailor muttered, and kept repeating almost childishly, "I hurt you, but you saved my life! Come," he got to his feet and extended his hands to them, "come; let me lead you out of this place." And he added almost matter-of-factly, "Your God has loosed the shackles from your feet."

Crowded around the still-gaping outer door a group of people stood looking fearfully into the brightly lighted interior of the prison. Members of the jailor's household, worried, had come to check on him. The flaring lamps threw grotesque shadows on a motley group of men, unshaven and unwashed. Not a man of them moved. They stood, or sat, or lay on the floor, frozen into position by a mighty hypnosis that kept their eyes fastened on their jailor and the two Jewish prisoners whose hands he touched with the reverence accorded only to royalty. They saw him lift his own hands suddenly in supplication. "Tell me, my lords," he implored Paul and Silas, "tell me, I pray you: What must I do to be saved?"

How utterly strange that question must have sounded to the ones outside the door! It was obvious to them that the master of their household was *already* saved! He was standing there alive; he was not crumpled on the floor with the hilt of his sword protruding from his body. He was safe. His prisoners had not escaped, therefore his position was not in jeopardy. There were enough armed guards on the scene by now to prevent any attempted break, even if the men had been of a mind to escape, which they obviously were not.

The guards were about to close and lock the door again, but the jailor's family surged in. They had to hear the answer to that fantastic question.

And they said, "Believe on the Lord Jesus Christ, and thou shalt be saved, and thy house."

In its magnificent simplicity, that is the mightiest text in history. It is so simple that it is difficult for us to grasp. We are saved because we *believe* on the Lord Jesus Christ.

God's servants ignored the pain of their tortured flesh. Here were souls looking for the Way; here were minds seeking the true Light. They stood and preached.

And they spake unto him the word of the Lord, and to all that were in his house. And he took them the same hour of the night, and washed their stripes; and was baptized, he and all his, straightway.

We do not need to worry too much about faith and

works. Faith, itself newborn, gives instant birth to good works! **And he took them the same hour of the night, and washed their stripes. . . .** At long last, their wounds were treated. Did the jailor perform this service with his own hands? Or did he call his personal slaves whose work was to attend him in the bath, and massage him afterward with their gentle, skillful hands? Did he send for a doctor? Did he, perhaps, send slaves through the night to the house of Lydia to fetch one, Luke, who was the dear friend and personal physician of the man, Paul? Did he find fresh clothing to replace their blood-soaked and vermin-infested garments? I think he did.

I also love to speculate upon the *place* where the jailor and his family and people were baptized. Was there an eerie, torch-lit procession winding through the dark streets of Philippi, out to the **riverside where prayer was wont to be made?** Did the apostles ever make use of the private "baths" of that day, which were somewhat similar to our own swimming pools? Or did they sometimes baptize their converts by means other than immersion? When I was a small child, such questions would have touched off heated arguments about the proper mode of baptism. Now, most sincere Christians feel that it truly does not matter.

After belief, ministry—**and he took them the same hour of the night, and washed their stripes . . .**—then baptism—**and was baptized, he and all his, straightway. . .**—then fellowship and rejoicing—**and when he had brought them into his house, he set meat before them, and rejoiced, believing in God with all his house.**

Food. Good food. Clean food served from a clean table by clean hands. Conversation; questions; wholesome laughter; fellowship; animated joy—this was comparable to a meal in Lydia's beautiful home. The night that had begun in humiliation and pain was ending in healing joy.

The next morning, the magistrates of Philippi apparently decided that the beating of the afternoon before plus a night in jail constituted sufficient punishment for the Jewish malefactors who actually had done nothing more heinous than irritate the mob by simply *being* Jews. So these conscientious gentlemen sent their lictors ("serjeants") to the prison to convey to the jailor a message which, in modern parlance, would have run, "Turn those jerks loose."

In due time, the lictors returned to headquarters, and we may imagine a part of the conversation which ensued. A lictor, standing before his superior who was reading a report, cleared his throat apologetically, and the superior finally looked up in irritation, and asked, "What's the trouble, sergeant?"

"It's those Jews, sir."

"Well, what about them?"

"They refuse to leave the prison, sir, unless the magistrates who had them committed come themselves and free them."

The magistrate's face reddened, and veins knotted dangerously on his forehead. "By Jupiter, I'll have their hides for this! Just who do those Jewish tramps think they are, anyway?"

"That would seem to be the trouble, sir—they're Roman citizens."

The veins on the magistrate's forehead emptied instantly, and pallor crept up from the neck of his tunic and advanced to his receding hairline. This could literally mean death for him! He bellowed feebly, "Well, why in the name of Minerva didn't they *say* so?"

"I don't know, sir. Being Jews, they're stubborn and peculiar; perhaps they wanted to get us into trouble."

The magistrate chuckled wryly. "I can't imagine even a Jew being stubborn enough or peculiar enough to get himself beaten to a pulp to get somebody else in trouble! Go call the others, will you, and then order the litters; we'd better get over there in a hurry. Even if we survive this with our hides intact, we'll be writing out reports for the rest of our natural lives as to why we permitted this outrage upon Roman citizens. Jews! Oh, woe; why was I born?"

With horrified apology the magistrates brought Roman citizens Paul and Silas out of prison, and asked them humbly if they wouldn't please leave the city.

With dignity, Paul and Silas received the apology; with compassion, they assured the frightened officials that no complaint would be made to their superiors; with graciousness, they consented to leave the city after they had visited their friends and companions in the home of Lydia.

Why did Paul and Silas, who had submitted quietly to savage beating and unjust imprisonment, now demand public apology and exoneration? Perhaps it was to vindicate Christianity. They had shown their willingness to suffer; now they wished to make clear that they had been guilty of no crime. They wished to impress the officials and the citizens of Philippi with the fact that Christians were quiet, law-abiding people, not dangerous seditionists. They were seeing to it that the young church they were leaving in Philippi would not be branded with the stigma of criminal association.

Chapter Seventeen

Timothy and Luke did not go with Paul and Silas, but remained in Philippi to give direction and nourishment to the newly founded church. If the young Timothy had expected to be constantly with his spiritual father, this first parting must have been attended by keen disappointment. And yet, what joy must have been his when he was given so soon this place of very real responsibility.

Along the great Roman highway, "Via Egnatia," Paul and Silas set out to bring the gospel to another city.

It is quite likely that they left Philippi either the same day on which they were released from prison, or very shortly thereafter. They would, therefore, have been in very poor physical condition for a long trip on foot, and in all probability transportation was arranged for them by that efficient and gracious Christian business woman, Lydia.

Their destination this time was Thessalonica. About a hundred miles a little south of west from Philippi, it was a large city, beautiful and wealthy, and the capital city of the Roman province of Macedonia. It was named for a woman, Thessalonica, the sister of Alexander the Great. I can't help wondering if they *called* that lady by her whole name!

In those days, people traveling from Philippi to Thessalonica usually divided the journey into three stages. The first day they made Amphipolis, which was thirty-three miles. (Half an hour's driving distance for us, if the traffic lights were right. But I can remember using ten hours to drive forty miles, and so, probably can you—if you also are a hangover from the horse-and-buggy days!) The second day brought them to Apollonia, thirty miles from Amphipolis; and the end of the third day found them in Thessalonica.

So we find in the text, **Now when they had passed through Amphipolis and Apollonia, they came to Thessalonica, where there was a synagogue of the Jews.** The Jewish population of Thessalonica was quite large.

We don't know what day of the week Paul and Silas arrived. But we do know that they went to the synagogue on the first sabbath, and that Paul carried the glad tidings first to the lost sheep of the house of Israel. We know also, from his second letter to the Thessalonians, that he lost no time in finding work when he arrived in their city, so that he and Silas "might not be chargeable" to any of them. Paul frequently worked with his hands to support himself and his fellow workers as they carried Christ's message to the ends of the earth.

By now the pattern of events must have been so familiar to Paul that he knew exactly what would happen when he went into a new synagogue: The rulers of the synagogue would ask him to speak. He would unfold to them the same sublime truth, that the long-awaited Messiah had come, and had been crucified. Skillfully and patiently, he would prove to them from the Scriptures that Christ **must needs have suffered, and risen again from the dead, and that this Jesus, whom I preach unto you is Christ.** Some of the Jews would believe his message, and joyfully cleave to him and Silas. The majority of them would not believe. Great numbers of the proselytes would believe, including a number of influential women. The Jewish majority, resenting his success with the Gentiles who accepted the gospel which they themselves had spurned, would try by any means—no matter how foul—to discredit and injure him.

Paul preached in the Thessalonican synagogue only three sabbaths, but he was in the city about four months. He turned to the Gentiles, and we know from his letters to the Thessalonians that his gospel emphasized the imminent return of the Lord Jesus as King.

The unbelieving Jews, **moved with envy,** used Paul's

words against him, even as the Pharisees had tried to trap our Lord with His own words.

It is remarkable how easily a mob can be assembled when skillful and determined agitators are on hand to manipulate human emotions. (Mobs, you understand, are not mobs in our day—they are "demonstrators.") I like Luke's description of the "demonstrators": **certain lewd fellows of the baser sort.** Riffraff; trash; idlers who hung around in public places and ogled passing women. These, inspired by eloquent and well-chosen words of the agitators, were transformed in the twinkling of an eye into righteous, respectable, and outraged citizens who were "demonstrating" to preserve the foundations of empire and quite likely the sanctity of the home. Which would seem to prove that the human mind changeth not.

Paul and Silas were staying in the home of a man named Jason, who could have been the same Jason Paul calls his "kinsman" in the letter to the Romans. The mob stormed the house of Jason, demanding that Paul and Silas be handed over to them. Whether or not the missionaries had been forewarned and moved to a safer place we do not know; but they were not there.

But the "demonstrators" had to have somebody, so they seized Jason and some of the other believers and dragged them before the city authorities. The charge? Harboring criminals!

These men whom Jason was sheltering were the same ones who were turning the world upside down. Quite without intending to, the agitators were paying tribute to Paul and Silas: They *were* turning the world upside down—and exposing its nauseous iniquity to the probing searchlight of God. These criminals, the mob leaders insisted, were also peddling a new form of treason: Under the guise of religion, they were urging their followers to transfer allegiance from that greatest of all emperors, Claudius Caesar, to one Jesus, a king who was shortly to appear and rule the whole earth. It is truly amazing what can be done with a few grains of truth mixed with the quicksands of an enormous lie.

The city authorities as well as the people of Thessalonica were frankly worried by these reports. Their city was a "free city," that is, self-governing; but the continuing of that status depended on their unquestioned loyalty to Rome. Emperor Claudius had recently banished all Jews from the city of Rome, and he would have regarded with a jaundiced eye a *free* city which showed too much indulgence to Jews accused of treason.

Thessalonica was on the spot. But its officials showed remarkable sense. They evidently listened to Jason's side of the story and decided there was something a bit smelly about the accusations. They allowed Jason and the other accused men to post bond to guarantee good conduct, and turned them loose.

Jason and the other disciples were apprehensive. They knew that the agitators would strike again, and having been thwarted once in their attempt to get Paul and Silas, they would be the more determined and vengeful. The young church was established, and thrusting lively roots into the well-prepared soil; perhaps her founders could return at a later and safer time to water and stake and shape. But now, flight was the prudent thing; and it must be immediate flight. So Paul and Silas left under cover of darkness for the safety of Berea.

At Berea, they found something new and very beautiful—continuing and absolute tranquility *after* Paul's first sermon in the synagogue!

This rabbi (the Bereans said) was saying that the Messiah had already come, and that He had died the death of a criminal, but that God had raised Him from the dead, and he cited Scriptures to prove it. Was the rabbi right? They were eager to know the Truth; their minds were not sealed tight by tradition against a new idea, so they went to the surest place to find Truth: they **searched the Scriptures daily, whether those things were so**. They were completely satisfied with what they found, therefore, **many of them believed**. And as at many other cities, many Gentiles also believed.

These people who "searched the Scriptures daily" evidently were the nucleus of an ideal church, because there is no letter from the mighty apostle to correct, or chide, or instruct. And a church of Bible-searching believers is still the ideal church.

But the familiar pattern began to take shape again; this blessed tranquility was not to last very long. The Jews of Thessalonica heard that Paul was preaching at Berea, and took the usual measures to stop him. Luke says merely, **They came thither also, and stirred up the people.**

It is quite likely that the Berean Christians knew what would come eventually, and were prepared in advance. They escorted Paul **down to the seashore** where they boarded a ship, and some of them went along with their beloved mentor and friend. The ship was about to set sail for Athens, so to Athens they went. Athens was a very long way from Berea, and Paul would be safe there.

Silas remained in Berea. Timothy, whose arrival was not mentioned in the narrative, also stayed behind. Paul was the big prize the Thessalonian Jews were after; evidently they considered Silas and Timothy small fry, and relatively harmless.

The ship arrived at Athens, and when it left for the return voyage, Paul's Berean followers went back home with instructions from him to have Timothy and Silas join him at Athens as soon as they could possibly get there.

Paul looked at Athens.

He saw a place of incredible beauty.

Athens was a city saturated with the quiet insolence which comes with aristocracy of the mind. She was the intellectual center of the world. She was no longer politically free, s-o-o, did she cringe before her conquerors? She did not! The lordly Romans adopted *her* language, sent their sons to *her* schools to be educated, and drooled wistfully over *her* exquisite art. And in all this, they were given quietly to understand that they were uncouth barbarians! The Romans took it. Somewhere, tucked away under their snowy togas, they must have harbored an inferiority complex equal to the weight of their armor.

Paul, a lonely stranger, wandered in a world peopled by sophisticates whose starved souls fed on golden crumbs spilled from the treasury of the mind. And, like starving cattle sated with straw, they did not realize that they were hungry. Paul looked at the magnificent buildings filling the city, and his mind was moved with admiration. He looked at the magnificent statues which filled the buildings, lined the streets, and dotted the market places, and his heart was filled with pity: the statues were the likenesses of the gods of Athens.

The gods of Greece were (like idols of lesser beauty) the creation of the people who worshiped them. They were supermen with supernatural power, but they were also clothed with human attributes of greed, jealousy, love, and hate. The gods were unfaithful to their goddesses, and vice versa. On occasion, it was alleged, both had cavorted with human companions. The Greeks had a deity for everything: gods and goddesses of love and of wisdom, of war and of the hunt, of medicine and of agriculture. And lest they offend some god of whom they had never heard, they had erected an altar to "The Unknown God." We smile at the lovely myths which these deities are to us, and we revel in the literature and art which devotion to them has evoked—but the Greeks brought sacrifices to keep them in good humor!

In Athens, as in all other cities, Paul went first into the synagogue and spoke to the Jews and the proselytes. No hint whatever is given as to their reaction. The apostle also mingled daily with all kinds of people in the agora, or market place, and to anyone who would listen, he talked. His theme here, as everywhere, was Jesus Christ crucified and raised from the dead.

Our civilization, insofar as I know, has nothing which compares with the agora. Certainly, there is nothing of that sort in this country that I have ever heard of. We do not mix business and poetry and art and philosophy and oratory and casual gossip and late news and politics and religious exercises in one big beautiful flat place filled with magnificent statuary, and surrounded by historic hills crowned with buildings which are filled with more statues. In such a setting the average American would, I think, tend to become a little hysterical.

But the Athenians took that way of life calmly in stride. And they must have had more time on their hands than we do even with our forty-hour week, for we get the distinct impression that they had plenty of time to talk, and plenty of time to listen. Luke comes close to humor in his terse parenthetical description of the Athenians: **For all the Athenians and strangers which were there spent their time in nothing else, but either to tell, or to hear some new thing.**

Certain philosophers of the Epicureans and the Stoics heard Paul speak in the agora, and some of them, with priceless arrogance demanded, **"What will this babbler say?"** Babbler? Their lofty term for one whom you would call an educated tramp, a two-bit philosopher who lives by his wits. Others among the philosophers answered that this man seemed to be introducing strange gods. They had heard fragments of his discourse, they had heard reports—possibly exaggerated—from others who had heard more, and they were intrigued.

And so the philosophers conducted Paul up the sixteen steps cut out of solid rock, up to the top of the hill called the Areopagus. In this place was situated the highest court in Athens which sentenced state criminals and—how strange to our ears!—also decided important matters of religion. Here they issued a formal invitation to the apostle to explain the new doctrine.

It is doubtful that the apostle Paul ever faced a more erudite audience. This man who was "all things to all men" was equal to this occasion also. He looked into faces whose expressions ran from supercilious amusement to keenest intellectual curiosity, and began the speech which has fascinated and inspired men through the intervening centuries. The remarkably important philosophers who invited him to speak became mere historical props for this amusing "babbler"!

"Ye men of Athens, all things which I behold bear witness to your carefulness in religion. For as I passed through your city, and beheld the objects of your worship, I found amongst them an altar with this inscription, 'TO THE UNKNOWN GOD.' Whom, therefore, ye worship, though ye know Him not, Him declare I unto you." Using familiar things to draw the mind on to explore the unfamiliar.

That "Unknown God," the stranger told the Greeks, is Creator of the world and all it holds, King of the universe, and certainly does not live in temples erected by the genius of man. Nor does He need any offering from the hand of men. He who is the Source of all things has no need of anything from those to whom He "giveth life, and breath, and all things." God the Creator, the Ruler of all things, the Source of life, made of "one blood all nations of men for to dwell on all the face of the earth." That must have sounded strange to men who considered themselves superior to all other men. As to the Jew there were only Jews and Gentiles, so to the Greek there were only Greeks and "barbarians." "God . . . hath made of one blood all nations of men for to dwell on all the face of the earth, and hath determined the times before appointed, and the bounds of their habitations; that they should seek the Lord, if haply they might feel after him and find him. . . ."

The *Unknown God,* Creator, Ruler of history and of nations, determined and decreed before their creation the time of their existence and the place of their habitation; and to all were given gleams of intimation of His existence and His majesty. "If haply they might feel after him and find him . . . "—gleams of revelation, gropings after the true God who was so close to them actually; so very close "for in him we live, and move, and have our being; as certain also of your own poets have said, 'For we are also his offspring.' "

If men, then, are the offspring of God, God *cannot,* in the very nature of things, be something exquisitely fashioned from stone or precious metal in the hands of His own offspring.

Glimpses of Truth, gleams of intimation of man's sonship to the God of creation: glimpses and gleams, but no revelation to all flesh. Hence, "And the times of this ignorance, God overlooked, but now commandeth all men everywhere to repent . . . " Why *now?* Because God has revealed Himself perfectly in Jesus Christ. " . . . Because he hath appointed a day, in the which he will judge the world in righteousness by that man whom he hath ordained; whereof he hath given assurance unto all men, in that he hath raised him from the dead."

A slight gasp went through the audience. A dead man brought back to life? They were intelligent men, and they knew that dead men do not come back to life. Did this odd little Jew think they were being taken in by his fantastic tale?

Mocking laughter drowned Paul's words, and when it finally subsided, the more courteous among his hearers said that they would hear him again later concerning the matter.

Paul knew that he was being dismissed, and that apparently his sermon had done little good. Yet, there were a few who believed. Two are mentioned by name: Dionysius the Areopagite, and a woman named Damaris. The man's title indicates that he was a member of the highest court in Athens, and therefore a man highly esteemed. Some ancient writers believed that Damaris was the wife of Dionysius, because she is mentioned with him. In the light of the fact that Greek women led very secluded lives, this theory is strengthened, since it is not too likely that women were in Paul's audience.

Paul did not gain many converts among the Greek intellectuals. It is so even today. Men, wise in their own conceits, smug in their self-sufficiency, are not easily persuaded that their souls are wearing filthy rags and feeding on husks. God is only for the weak and the stupid, and they, the intelligensia, have absolutely no need of Him.

Chapter Eighteen

Paul had sent word to Silas and Timothy to come to him as quickly as possible, and his activity in Athens took place while he was waiting for them. We are not told specifically of any further work while he waited, but we may assume that he carefully nurtured and instructed the judge, Dionysius, and the woman, Damaris, and the rest of the little handful who separated themselves from the sophisticates of Athens and **clave unto him.**

Painful and disappointing as it was that his message had been rejected by the Athenians, Paul had at least one crumb of comfort: He did not have to flee the city to escape mob violence. He could remain in Athens as long as he liked. However, when his beloved helpers arrived, he dispatched them to Macedonia to attend to certain matters, and he himself took ship for Corinth. His self-confidence and courage must have been almost washed away by the tide of ridicule in Athens. Battered, scorned, rejected, he was alone again, moving from one great city to another.

Athens fed on the glory of her past. Poor Corinth insulted the wrong Roman at the right time, and got herself buried along with her glorious past. Then, a hundred years later, that remarkable man Julius Caesar began a job of excavation and resuscitation by sending a group of Roman colonists there. In due time, Greek merchants went back. Also in due time, great numbers of Jews were drawn there because business opportunities were practically unbounded, and Corinth was once more a huge and flourishing city. Also, Corinthian immorality was so extraordinary as to be remarkable in a time when immorality was a way of life to most of the world's population.

Into this roistering, earthy city came Paul the Apostle, and even the stench of its immorality was preferable to the odor of decay emanating from dead souls wearing the shroud of philosophy. Men who know they are dirty can be persuaded to wash.

Among the first people Paul met were Aquila and Priscilla, a Jewish couple who had been banished from Rome along with all other Jews there by an edict of Emperor Claudius. For the rest of his life, Paul was blessed with the friendship of these remarkable people. They had much in common, for these two were also tentmakers. They took the missionary into their home, and he worked with them at their trade and was thus able to support himself for the entire eighteen months he was to remain in Corinth. Like many an humble preacher who has followed him down through the centuries, Paul worked with his hands throughout the week to earn the bread that fed his body, and on the sabbath worked with mind and soul and voice to break the Bread of Life to hungry souls. In Corinth, as everywhere else, he went first into the synagogue.

Paul's humiliation in Athens seems to have left deep wounds in his spirit, for we find him later writing to his converts in Corinth, "I was with you in weakness, and in fear, and in much trembling." Nonetheless, he **reasoned in the synagogue every sabbath, and persuaded the Jews and the Greeks.**

Then Timothy and Silas returned from Macedonia with heart-warming news from the churches in Thessalonica and Berea. Anxiety for the welfare of these young churches whom he had been forced to leave suddenly had been another heavy burden upon Paul's heart. When he knew that they were standing fast in the truth and growing sturdily, relief and joy flooded his spirit. The black mood of depression dissolved, and he began to preach again with his wonted fire and vigor, affirming and reaffirming to the Jews that Jesus was indeed the Christ.

The next sentence is tragically familiar: **And when they opposed themselves, and blasphemed** . . . Even as the main body of the Jews rejected Christ, so also did they reject the preaching of His apostle. Paul symbolically shook his garments to show that he was guiltless concerning their impending doom, and turned completely to the Gentiles. After that, he preached in the house of a man named Justus. This house, as Luke puts it, **joined hard to the synagogue.**

And then there began to be significant numbers of converts, the most prominent of whom was Crispus, the chief ruler of the synagogue. It must have been galling to the Jews of the synagogue to see their most influential member turn to belief in the Messiah whom Paul preached. There must have been arguments and hot disputes when the two congregations spilled into the street from adjoining buildings.

Tension was, as usual, building up to the point of physical violence. And then at the point where Paul would have been poised for flight or braced for the attack, reassurance came to him from the only completely trustworthy source: The Lord spoke to him in the night by a vision. **"Be not afraid, but speak, and hold not thy peace: for I am with thee, and no man shall set on thee to hurt thee: for I have much people in this city."**

We can almost feel the tenseness draining from Paul's spirit. The Lord Christ to whom he totally belonged was telling him to stay right where he was, and fight to bring into his Master's fold those foundation sheep of the future flock, the church of Corinth. And he was to fight without fear: the Lord was promising him immunity from physical harm. Paul was not afraid to face danger—it had been his daily bread for years—but a wonderful peace must have filled him when he realized that in this place he was under the special protection of his Lord.

But the Jews of the synagogue went right ahead with their plans for getting rid of Paul. A new proconsul was being sent out from Rome, a man named Gallio. If they could get a hearing before Gallio and convince him that this Paul was breaking their religious law by his teaching, Gallio might get rid of Paul for them. Their right of worship was protected by the Roman state, hence the hope that a man who was undermining that worship might be dealt with severely by the state.

Gallio, by the way, was a brother of Seneca the philosopher, whom most of us probably remember as the tutor of that remarkable young man, Nero. The new proconsul had the reputation of being tolerant, wise, and on the whole a sort of easy-going man. But when a group of Jewish "demonstrators" showed up before his judgment seat, dragging and shoving one of their own number whom they accused of **persuading men to worship God contrary to the law**, his patience snapped. Wasn't it enough that Rome allowed these screwball Jews the privilege of worshiping in their own way? Why were these trying to involve a Roman proconsul in their petty ecclesiastical squabbles? What was it to Rome how they worshiped their strange God who permitted no images?

The little man whom they were accusing was about to open his mouth to tell *his* side of the story, but Gallio lifted an imperious hand: he'd save the small man the trouble. He noted the crowd of Greeks also waiting, to see if the Jews would be put in their place, and told himself wryly that the Greeks hated the Jews and the Jews hated the Greeks, and both of them hated the Romans! But that was neither here nor there. Rome, hated or not, ruled the world, and Rome administered justice under the law. And he, Gallio, at the moment was Rome.

"Hear me, O Jews. Rome is not concerned with your petty religious squabbling. If this man had been charged with a crime against the state or against humanity, I would hear you patiently. But I refuse to be burdened by your long-winded babbling of piling words upon words. Handle these matters for yourselves, for I refuse to judge them. And now, clear out of here!"

Gallio picked up a paper and began reading, and he thought he heard the accused man murmur, "For I am with thee, and no man shall set on thee to hurt thee." Strange people, these Jews. He doubted if anybody really understood them.

The pronconsul heard a small commotion, and looked up from his paper. The delighted Greeks had seized the man who had brought the accusation, and were beating him to celebrate the Jews' discomfiture. H-m-m, what was his name? Oh, yes, Sosthenes, the head of their synagogue. Oh, well, they wouldn't actually do murder, probably not even mayhem. He shrugged his shoulders and resumed his reading.

And in the next verse Luke tells us, **And Paul after this tarried there yet a good while. . . !**

Paul's stay in Corinth was similar to that in Athens in one respect: he did not have to flee suddenly to save his life. That, however, was about the only point of similarity. His labor in Corinth yielded rich fruit in the form of a flourishing church there, and also one in nearby Cenchrea which was one of Corinth's seaports. (Corinth, being on a narrow strip of land between two bodies of water, had a port on each: one on the Gulf of Corinth and the other on the Saronic Gulf.) From allusions in his letters, we learn also of churches in other portions of the Province of Achaia in which both Athens and Corinth were situated.

Also, it was while in Corinth that Paul began that series of epistles to his beloved churches which not only guided them, but have been a priceless source of inspiration and learning to the church in all ages. From Corinth he wrote the two letters to the believers in Thessalonica—First and Second Thessalonians.

"Paul and Silvanus [Silas] and Timotheus to the church of the Thessalonians": An aging man peering near-sightedly at his work, his hands moving swiftly among the threads, but his mind an uncluttered channel into which the Holy Spirit poured words. The words came forth in gentle or flaming sentences to be captured on papyrus by the eager Timothy or the faithful Silas. Paul the Apostle was writing to the churches which the Lord had granted to him to establish.

Eventually, Paul felt that the time had come for him to leave Corinth. Aquila and Priscilla were also leaving to move their business operation to Ephesus, and with them he took ship from the port of Cenchrea to sail to Ephesus en route to Jerusalem.

If Cenchrea sounds familiar to you, it is probably because it was the home of a woman named Phebe, a deaconess in the church there who was entrusted with delivering the letter Paul wrote (at a much later visit in Corinth) to the church in Rome.

Paul was invited to speak in the synagogue at Ephesus, and his hearers, much interested, asked him to remain awhile and explain his message more fully. But undue delay would cause him to be late for the coming feast in Jerusalem, and he was very anxious to be there. There might not be another ship sailing in time, so he reluctantly bade them farewell, promising to return to them if God so willed.

Luke finishes Paul's second missionary journey, and starts him on the third in less than three verses: **And he sailed from Ephesus. And when he had landed at Caesarea, and gone up, and saluted the church, he went down to Antioch. And after he had spent some time there, he departed, and went over all the country of Galatia and Phrygia in order, strengthening all the disciples.**

Ephesus to Caesarea—a very long sea journey, and apparently it was uneventful. Caesarea was the city where Peter preached to Cornelius, and where Paul, later on, would spend weary years in prison. But now he simply passed through on his way to Jerusalem where he "saluted the church." Luke doesn't even tell us if Paul made it to Jerusalem in time for the feast which he had been so anxious to attend. But he probably did. And then, on to Antioch, which was headquarters for Paul because it was the church there which had sent him and Barnabas out in the beginning.

Paul remained in Antioch some little time. We are not told whether he worked at his trade during this period, but it seems reasonable to suppose that the strong church there would have been eager to provide for his needs as he taught and preached among them.

In his history, Luke has kept the spotlight on Paul for so long that it is a bit startling to us to have it turned on someone else. It is at this point that the man Apollos is introduced. Apollos was a Jew born in Alexandria in Egypt, a truly magnificent city named for its founder, Alexander the Great. Alexandria was famous as one of the world's foremost centers of learning, and the man Apollos was brilliant, well-educated, and a gifted orator. Luke tells us also that he was "mighty in the Scriptures."

Some time after Aquila and Priscilla went to Ephesus, Apollos arrived there and began to preach Christ. But his

knowledge was limited, because he preached the same message that John the Baptist had preached: repentance; baptism
with water in preparation for the imminent appearance of
Him who would baptize with the Holy Spirit; anticipation of
the coming of that One. Apparently Apollos had not heard of
John's tragic death *after* he had pointed to the young Rabbi
from Galilee, and cried out, "Behold the Lamb of God,
which taketh away the sin of the world!"

Aquila and Priscilla heard Apollos preaching in the synagogue (and since the Jews had been anxious to hear more of
what Paul had to say, they were undoubtedly giving earnest
attention to Apollos) and instantly sensing his limitations,
they quietly **took him unto them, and expounded unto him
the way of God more perfectly.**

Laymen who knew what they were about, gently and in
private correcting errors in the theology of an eloquent
preacher! That must have taken considerable courage as well
as the highest degree of tact. It speaks well for Apollos that
he received the instruction (and even from a *woman!*) graciously, and profited by it. When he was ready to move on
into Achaia, the believers in Ephesus wrote letters recom-
mending him to the disciples there, and his eloquent preaching convinced many Jews that Jesus truly was the Christ.

Chapter Nineteen

Over a year had passed since the Ephesian Jews had heard Paul preach in their synagogue. The brilliant and eloquent Apollos had come and gone, taking to Corinth with him the knowledge that Aquila and Priscilla had imparted. In all probability, those two were still in Ephesus, quietly plying their trade as they witnessed to the crucified and risen Messiah.

And then Paul arrived. He **found certain disciples.** Did he find them in the synagogue? Did they also know Aquila and Priscilla? Not too likely, else that wise and godly pair would also have "expounded unto them the way of God more perfectly." Paul immediately noticed something lacking in their discipleship and discovered that they, like Apollos, knew only the preaching of John the Baptist concerning Christ.

It is remarkable that nearly thirty years after John was beheaded to sate the vengeance of a royal hussy, his influence still lived in the hearts of men. Apollos of Alexandria was his disciple, and in Ephesus these dozen men had been baptized into his baptism. They had never even heard of the descent of the Holy Spirit at Pentecost, much less of the mighty power He gave to Christ's disciples when His presence filled their lives. They listened eagerly to Paul's explanation that John's baptism was with water, and only pointed to the One who would baptize with the Holy Ghost and with fire. They were baptized in the name of the Lord Jesus. Then **Paul laid his hands upon them, and the Holy Spirit came on them and**

they [like the waiting ones at Pentecost—also] **spoke with other tongues, and prophesied.** These men were the nucleus of the church of Ephesus.

The people of the synagogue listened to Paul again as he preached and taught, persuaded and explained. For three months this continued, but as usual, the seed of opposition sprang up and grew to such ugly proportions that Paul and his teachings were publicly reviled. He withdrew from the synagogue and took the disciples with him to a new place, the school of a man named Tyrannus. This was the official meeting place of the disciples for two whole years. Frequently, I think, we pass over a simple sentence in Luke's account, and so lose sight of the fact that Paul remained in numerous places for considerable periods of time.

How marvelous it would be if our efforts to advance God's kingdom could bear the same fruit in a whole lifetime that Paul's work bore in two years! **So that all they which dwelt in Asia heard the word of the Lord Jesus, both Jews and Greeks.** We keep in mind, of course, that the Asia referred to in The Acts is not Asia as we know it, but a province of the Roman Empire located in a part of what is now Turkey. From the mighty city of Ephesus the Word went forth, carried by Paul's converts, or by his fellow workers, or perhaps in some instances by the apostle himself. In all Asia, then, the name of Christ became known, and with it the name of Paul, His apostle.

Luke continues, **And God wrought special miracles by the hands of Paul: so that from his body were brought unto the sick handkerchiefs or aprons, and the diseases departed from them, and the evil spirits went out of them.**

Why "special miracles"? Was God allowing and encouraging Paul to become a sensation-seeking exhibitionist? Hardly! The special miracles were to combat a specific evil: the magic of Ephesus.

Here again was being fought the age-old war between good and evil, between God and the devil, between Christ and Diana. Here again, as before the cynical Pharaoh, God empowered His servant to work special miracles.

Ephesus was the center of the worship of the heathen goddess Diana, and her temple there was one of the most magnificent structures ever erected. It was over two hundred years a-building, and was one of the seven wonders of the world. Kings and emperors had vied with each other for the honor of contributing some part of the great building—a stately column, or a costly decoration for its interior. The most renowned sculptors of the ancient world had fashioned statues of breath-taking beauty to surround the goddess who, strangely enough, was repulsively, hideously ugly. The Ephesian Diana bore no resemblance to the beautiful Greek goddess of the same name, for the upper part of her body was covered with rows of breasts, picturing her as symbolic of fertility, the great mother of the earth.

Mysterious symbols were engraved on the crown, the girdle, and the feet of the goddess. These signs, called "Ephesian Letters," when formed into words and spoken were believed to be a sort of charm to deliver those who were in the power of evil spirits. In written form, they were used as amulets for protection from bad luck or evil, and to insure success. There was, for instance, the case of an Ephesian wrestler who was always successful against an opponent from Miletus—until he lost his scroll. We would be inclined to ask what *else* he lost, perhaps wind or judgment, but to the superstitious athlete, the loss of his magic amulet was his downfall.

Into this atmosphere where superstition ruled, the mighty name of Christ was brought by Paul the Apostle. Ephesus began to hear strange stories of the sick being healed by the mere touching of a garment from the body of a religious teacher named Paul. So great was the power of this man whose miracles were performed in the name of a God called Jesus, that even those in the grip of evil spirits were set free by touching these same garments.

The city of Ephesus was impressed. So were **certain vagabond Jews, exorcists.** . . . *Jewish* magicians, soothsayers, exorcists? Wasn't that sort of abomination forbidden in their Law? Yes. But before we explode from gaseous self-righteousness, perhaps we'd best look around for a few *Christians* who conveniently ignore Christ's commandments; we might even begin with ourselves.

These Jewish exorcists were canny businessmen who

knew a good thing when they encountered it. Paul, a Jew like themselves, was healing the sick and casting out devils in the name of the Lord Jesus Christ. Very well, if it worked for him it would work for them. So reasoned the seven sons of Sceva, a high priest. This man might have been the actual high priest at Jerusalem at one time, or the chief of one of the twenty-four courses of priests. Whatever his former state, it was evident that he had not done a very good job on his sons.

The seven sons of Sceva decided to do a bit of exorcising on a man who was possessed of an evil spirit, and they used this formula: **"We adjure you by Jesus whom Paul preacheth:** come out of him"—evidently reasoning that it was a good idea to mention Paul, too, so that the demon would not be confused. The demon was not in the least confused—but the formula backfired. The demented man stared ominously at the seven presumptuous strangers before him, and the evil spirit which used his mind and voice stormed at them: "Jesus I recognize, and Paul I know, but *who are you?*"

Too late, the seven realized their error. The man was upon them with the strength of maniacal rage. He seized two and batted their heads together, yanking the girdle from one before dropping both to the floor. Small flecks of foam dropped from his lips to his beard as he opened his mouth to laugh. His long hairy arms reached out with the girdle and made it a noose around the necks of the five who were huddled in a cluster of terror. Tighter and tighter grew the noose made by the hairy arms and the stolen girdle; the man kept on laughing, and the foam from his mouth fell on their faces. They struck wildly, only to discover they were raining blows on each other. They were too close together to fight, and still the noose was drawn tighter. They began gasping for breath; the foam-flecked beard and the open mouth of their tormentor swam hazily from half light to half darkness, and back again. The man loosed his hold abruptly, and all five fell into a panting, writhing mass at his feet; then he began kicking and beating them and tearing their clothes off.

Finally, the first two regained consciousness and began crawling toward the door. They had nearly reached safety before the man saw them, and he left off beating the five and dashed after the two, screaming, "Jesus I recognize, and Paul I know, but *who are you?*" They wriggled through the door and sprinted wildly toward the comparative safety of the street with the man still after them. The other five got dazedly to their feet, grabbed for their torn garments, and fled. The maniac, still holding the girdle and still muttering, "Jesus I recognize, and Paul I know, but *who are you?*" returned to his house, and sat down, and looked at blood and bits of hair and skin. He sat and laughed.

Passersby, some sympathetic, some merely curious, stopped to help or to question the battered exorcists who were so shaken by their ordeal that they didn't have the presence of mind to come up with a quick, plausible lie, but blurted out the simple truth.

The story passed from mouth to mouth, and in a matter of days hundreds of people had heard about a new God so powerful that men who had dared to misuse His name were very nearly killed. The name of the new God was Jesus; it was He whom the strange Jewish teacher named Paul had been telling people about. Men who had misused that name were very nearly killed . . . the name was Jesus . . . fearfully and with awe, superstitious Ephesians whispered the name. They began looking for the man named Paul who could tell them more.

The newly converted Ephesian Christians also heard the story, and Paul may have been a little surprised at the number of them who came and confessed in shame and in fear that they had been clinging to a remnant of their pagan superstitions, their belief in the magical arts.

Fear and awe came upon many of the sorcerers themselves. Their magic was counterfeit, their greatest power was puny weakness before the mighty name of Jesus whom Paul preached. Where could Paul be found? They learned that he preached daily in the school of one, Tyrannus, who had become a disciple.

The group converged on the school of Tyrannus; they asked for the great teacher, Paul. Would the apostle of the mighty God witness what they were about to do? Would he come with them to the courtyard? Would he also bring his disciples for witnesses? Paul beckoned his congregation to follow, and in stunned silence they watched the strangers gather in the center of the courtyard and begin one by one to bring books from the folds of their robes and place them on a neat, pyramiding pile on the stones.

An incredulous whisper came from one of the congregation. "The books! I have seen books like that. They are the costly textbooks of magic—these men are *sorcerers!* Why have they brought their evil here? Why. . . ?" The whisper died as a slender wisp of smoke curled upward from the pyramid.

The sorcerers turned to Paul and bowed somberly. "Witness, O mighty teacher," their spokesman said, "These books which we have deemed treasures have become poisonous trash. They have sustained us; we have lived by their poison; we have infected others with it, but now the earth will be clean of them. We turn to you, O teacher, to learn of your God in whom rests almighty power."

Tears gathered in the apostle's eyes. "Thanks be to God for His wisdom and His power! Forgiveness shall be to you, my children; and grace, mercy, and peace from God our Father and Jesus Christ our Lord."

So mightily grew the word of God and prevailed. Christ, working through the Holy Spirit who flooded the soul, filled the mind, and energized the body of His crusading apostle, had prevailed over the darkness of evil in Ephesus. So Paul began to dream and plan of further journeys into Macedonia and Achaia, and back to Jerusalem, and after that, to Rome. Paul the apostle would lay siege to the mighty city of Rome; the capital of the world he would also bring as the spoil of his warfare to lay at the feet of his Lord.

Meanwhile, he would send two beloved helpers before him into Macedonia and Achaia, so Timothy and Erastus were sent ahead. Paul was ever zealous to collect aid for the impoverished disciples at Jerusalem, and it is quite likely that this was the work Timothy and Erastus were to do. Much later we shall find the apostle confined to prison in Caesarea where Felix held him, hoping for a bribe. The canny governor had heard of the huge sum Paul had collected to take to Jerusalem, and figured he might as well have some of it.

Politicians, it would seem, were no closer to being lily-white in those days than they are now.

Shortly after Timothy and Erastus left Ephesus, visitors came to Paul from Corinth with most distressing news about the condition of the church there.

Some scholars are certain that Paul had already made a hurried visit to Corinth in the earlier part of his stay in Ephesus. They think that this visit was the result of Apollos's returning to Ephesus with a horrifying report of gross immorality among the Corinthian Christians, and that Paul's presence and gentle admonition had not been sufficient to check the filthy tide. Therefore (these scholars say), he had written to them a letter sharply reproving their conduct, and ordering them to purge themselves of "all intercourse with fornicators." This letter has not been preserved.

Now, members of the "household of Chloe" arrived, and upon hearing their report, Paul wrote the letter which has been preserved for us as the First Epistle to the Corinthians. Strangely enough, we can be grateful for the distressing conditions which elicited this epistle, for in correcting them the apostle has left us a sublime set of rules for Christian conduct in every phase of life from Communion observance to lawsuits.

How long it took Paul to write the letter (or dictate it) we do not know, but it was about that time that the devotees of Diana struck back at the gospel which was threatening their religion.

The whole month of May was consecrated to the glory of Diana, and during that time people from the entire province of Asia converged on Ephesus to worship, to celebrate, and to have a gay, good time. The whole occasion was one long festival which combined the characteristics of the Olympics, the World Series, religious antics for which (may God be praised!) there is no modern counterpart, and possibly a dash of the Miss America Contest.

The ancients took their sports events just as seriously as we do, or even more so. The gentlemen who had charge of the games and other events at these festivals were selected by popular vote in formal elections. There were ten of them, and they were not only influential and popular, they were immensely wealthy. Private wealth was a necessary factor since they not only were not paid for their services, but also had to spend great sums of their own money for the amusement and entertainment of the people. These officials were called "Asiarchs," and they were the ones whom Luke referred to as the "chief of Asia."

The hordes of people who attended the festivals bought souvenirs to take home, even as you and I do. But their mementos were not innocuous dolls or ash trays or silver spoons—they were portable images of the goddess and her temple. These small shrines could be displayed in processions, or carried on journeys and military ventures, or set up at home to worship. They were made from wood or precious metals, and their manufacture and sale constituted big business comparable to our Christmas trade.

Paul's impact on Ephesus (and all of Asia) could be measured by the fact that the sale of shrines and images was falling off. There was a man named Demetrius who was not going to take this outrage lying down.

Demetrius had a factory which turned out the shrines to Diana. He and his craftsmen wrought in silver, and their work was much sought after: If *your* souvenir shrine came from *Demetrius,* you were "in." He had watched sales falling off steadily, and had hoped and expected that the great festival would provide customers to take up the slack. It didn't turn out that way; the beautiful silver shrines were still collecting dust on the shelves.

Demetrius called a meeting of his own workmen and others of the trade, and made a little speech. He pointed out to them in a few well-chosen words that "this Paul" was responsible for the decline in their business. Not only in the city of Ephesus, but almost throughout all Asia, this Paul had been persuading people and convincing them that the gods made with hands were not gods at all. Every man within the sound of his voice was feeling the pinch, because people convinced by Paul had stopped buying images. But that wasn't the half of it: If this sort of thing kept up, there wouldn't be any market for their products, and their wives and little ones would be naked and starving. And as if this were not enough evil, their great goddess herself would be outraged by this insult which shamed her in the eyes of her worshipers in all Asia and throughout the whole world.

If there had been a couple of good, old-fashioned Roman cops present, they would have arrested Demetrius for inciting to riot. But Ephesus was also a "free city," and there wasn't a Roman cop on duty. Anyway, they'd have needed a pretty good-sized segment of a legion to stop what was boiling up merrily on the fire Demetrius had set.

The enraged silversmiths started screeching, "Great Diana of the Ephesians!" A mob always gets along better if it has a nice, pithy slogan to screech. Interested spectators joined in the yelling. They didn't know why they were yelling, but it was a heartwarming sentiment. More spectators were attracted. Ephesus was a huge city under normal circumstances, but when it was jammed with festival visitors there was a considerable surplus of people.

When the mob had reached sufficient proportions to handle very nearly anything, Demetrius shouted, "What are we waiting for? Let's go get that Paul right now! *Great Diana of the Ephesians!*"

"Great Diana of the Ephesians!" the mob roared dutifully and started toward the home of the Jews, Aquila and Priscilla.

Aquila and Priscilla stood in the door and quietly insisted that Paul wasn't there. They were pushed aside, and the place ransacked. Paul was not there, but Gaius and Aristarchus, his traveling companions were, and the mob seized them and rushed toward the theatre. This could have been one of the times Paul referred to in his letter to the Romans when he told them that for his life Priscilla and Aquila had laid down their own necks.

Screeching, yelling, sweating, the mob surged toward the theater. Theaters in the ancient world were not buildings, such as we have, but outdoor ampitheaters similar to our huge stadiums. The one in Ephesus is thought to be the largest ever built by the Greeks, and it held fifty thousand people. For this particular spectacle, there is little doubt that every seat was taken and that the STANDING ROOM ONLY sign wasn't put up because there wasn't room to put it.

This definitely came under the heading of an unscheduled

event of the festival, and along about that time all ten of the "Asiarchs" could have used extra aspirin. They were, among other things, supposed to keep order, and it was completely obvious that order was not being kept. They got hold of Demetrius long enough to find out what had happened, and while their opinion of the silversmith is not recorded, it is hardly likely that he was their hero at that moment.

Then, by devious methods, word came that the man whose teaching had caused the riot was determined to come into the theater and talk to the screaming thousands in spite of the pleas of his disciples to dissuade him. Which or how many of the Asiarchs were Paul's friends we are not told; but we do know that all the "chief of Asia" knew that if Paul went into that theater he would not even be spared to be tossed to the wild animals—he'd be torn to bits on the spot.

Hurriedly his friends sent word to Paul imploring him to heed the advice of his disciples and stay out of the theater, *not only because he was their friend, but because they did not want to be responsible for his death.* Only then was Paul dissuaded, and there is little doubt that he and the Ephesian Christians spent the next two hours in frantic prayer for the safety of Gaius and Aristarchus.

Inside the theater, fifty thousand people were still howling, "Great Diana of the Ephesians!"

The Jews of the city, anxious to prove that they were not associated with the group whose deeds had brought on the uproar, **drew Alexander out of the multitude** and brought him forward to plead their cause. Many students think this was "Alexander the coppersmith" mentioned by Paul in his second letter to Timothy; if so, he would have been known to the silversmiths.

Alexander lifted his hand in an appeal for silence, but it was a futile gesture: The crowd recognized him only as a Jew, and they knew that Jews were unfriendly to their gods. Their chant grew even more frenzied, "Great Diana of the Ephesians!" Alexander retired hastily, and the noise continued.

The Asiarchs waited tensely; perhaps the fury would eventually wear itself out. The chances were that not one of these people in a hundred actually knew why they were clamoring, but an hour went by, and there was no sign of any diminishing of the noise. In desperation, the officials finally sent messengers to the office of the town clerk.

The position of town clerk doesn't sound very important to us, possibly because we have no municipal office with which it may be compared. The town clerk was the city's highest official. He represented the city as do modern mayors, but his position was more important than that of mayor. State papers and records were in his keeping, he read important messages to the senate and the assembly, and he had to be present when money was deposited in the temple (of Diana). This official was elected by the voters of the city, and he was known by sight to the Ephesian public.

A full two hours had passed since the crowd screamed Alexander into silence. Some of the people were getting a bit hoarse, but they were still faithfully yelling, "Great Diana of the Ephesians!" when a richly dressed but somewhat paunchy gentleman appeared on the stage. Someone cut a chant in half, and croaked hoarsely, "My, my! And who is *this* large-bellied lad?"

"Quiet, you nitwit!" a hometown Ephesian next to him hissed, "That's the town clerk!"

"Oops, my error; sorry, I didn't recognize him."

The town clerk stood quietly for several seconds, and then as the roar began to ebb, he lifted his hand, and the rest of the noise drifted into silence. "Fellow citizens," he said, "I beg of you, examine and weigh your words. The burden of your speech is a profound truth, certainly. But it is a truth so well known that your screaming repetition insults the intelligence of the civilized world. Where in all the world is there an intelligent man who does not know that the city of Ephesus is the very temple-keeper of the great goddess Diana, and of her sacred image which fell down from Jupiter himself in the dim long ago? Since this truth is self-evident, how is it, then, that you have brought here these insignificant men who not only could do no harm to the powerful goddess Diana, but who have neither profaned her temple nor blasphemed her?

"As for Demetrius and his colleagues: If they have a legitimate complaint against any man, our courts of justice are open and ready to hear their case. But I warn you solemnly that our very status as the free city of Ephesus stands in jeopardy because of this day's uproar, because Rome does not tolerate riots—we may as well call this by its ugly name— and we will have no rational explanation for this one.

"There is one further thing I would call to your attention: For generations, the state of Rome has guaranteed the right of its Jewish subjects to worship after their own fashion.

"Rise to your feet, please. Thank you; you are dismissed."

Like sleepwalkers yanked back from the edge of a precipice, the great crowd filed slowly and quietly out of the theater.

Chapter Twenty

As the noise from the riot finally ceased, the Asiarchs breathed a concerted sigh of relief and set about getting Ephesus and all its visitors back into the normal schedule and spirit of the great festival.

The town clerk's pointed remark about Rome's protecting the right of Jews in their worship had struck Demetrius with the force of wind-driven hail. "This Paul" was a Jew. The fact that he was hardly on theological speaking terms with the Jewish hierarchy did not matter in the least to the logical mind of Rome. This had been demonstrated by the proconsul, Gallio, though it is unlikely that Demetrius knew about that. What is extremely likely is that Demetrius at this point went home and got very drunk, or developed ulcers, or both.

Paul apparently felt that this climax of terror signaled the completion of his work in Ephesus. He had been there three years. The dark religion of Diana, though not completely routed, had nonetheless suffered great loss. The gospel had been preached in all Asia, and many other churches had been established in addition to the one that flourished in Ephesus itself. It was time to go. So, **Paul called unto him the disciples, and embraced them, and departed for to go into Macedonia.**

The apostle did not go directly into Macedonia. He tarried for awhile in Troas, the city from which he had been called (through the compelling vision) to go into Macedonia the first time. There is no record of his having preached in

Troas on the first occasion, but this time (as he writes the Corinthians in the second letter), "A door was opened unto me of the Lord," and he preached with great success. But he also says in the same letter, "I had no rest in my spirit, because I found not Titus, my brother."

Titus was the messenger Paul sent to Corinth, quite probably as bearer of the first letter. He was also to help Timothy and Erastus in the work of collecting the Corinthian offering to be taken to Jerusalem. He was to observe the reaction of the Corinthians to the letter of reproval and correction Paul had written them, and he himself was to do what he could toward restoring tranquility and order in the unhappy church.

Titus was supposed to meet Paul in Troas, but when time dragged on and he did not come, the burden of anxiety and apprehension became too heavy to bear. Paul took his leave of the converts in Troas, and pushed on into Macedonia. Perhaps Titus had gone there instead of to Troas.

As before, he went first to Philippi, entering through the port of Neapolis. He found Timothy, and the beloved Luke (who will shortly begin using the "we" again) but Titus was not in Philippi, either.

Paul was ill from some sort of sickness which had come upon him in Asia. No actual physical harm had come to him from the Ephesian riot, and it is impossible to imagine a man of his temperament giving way to a case of "nerves" after a close brush with death. But whatever its origin or nature, this was a malady so severe that he himself despaired of his life. And while neither of them mentions the matter, it is safe to assume that Luke took over immediately in his professional capacity and ministered to the sick apostle.

Added to the bodily sickness was the gnawing torment of uncertainty. Paul writes to the Corinthians, "When first I came into Macedonia, my flesh had no rest, but I was troubled on every side; without were fightings, within were fears. . . ." He knew that the tender growth which he had planted and Apollos had watered had been set upon by unscrupulous men who were determined to uproot the plants and reset them in the sickly soil of the Judaistic concept of Christianity. These men dogged his footsteps and consistently worked to corrupt his converts. Was the planting of the Lord completely uprooted in Corinth? Where was Titus? Why didn't he come?

At last! "Nevertheless God, that comforteth those that are cast down, comforted us by the coming of Titus." And Titus brought good news from Corinth: The church was not wrecked; the Corinthian Christians, for the most part, had heeded the letter from their founder and had set about correcting the sorry mess they had made.

Paul gathered writing materials and, with Timothy, began joyfully writing a second letter to the Corinthians. This one he also sent by Titus.

Luke says, **And when he had gone over those parts and had given them much exhortation, he came into Greece.** In his letter to the Romans, which was written a few months later, Paul says, "So that from Jerusalem, and round about unto Illyricum, I have fully preached the gospel of Christ." Thus it would seem that he had traveled westward through Macedonia and to the border of Illyricum, preaching as he went. If he did go that far west, he was at the border of what is now Yugoslavia, and he must have looked westward across the Adriatic toward Italy and the mighty city of Rome which he meant to conquer for his Lord.

But Rome was not yet. Paul swung south again and **came into Greece and there abode three months.** These three months were spent in Corinth as the house guest of Gaius, and during this time two more letters were written, Galatians and Romans.

We can very well imagine that Paul and his company of helpers had barely had time to relax in the warm hospitality of the home of Gaius before bad news came in from Galatia. The ecclesiastical busybodies who intended to circumcise all Christian believers had broken into Galatia, and had been very busy indeed. Paul, dismayed and justifiably indignant by the vacillation among the converts who had loved him enough to want to give him their eyes, once again wrote a letter to set a church straight.

After the Galatian letter was finished, he launched into that mighty Epistle to the Romans, a document so full of a theology so profound that we common garden-variety saints candidly admit that we are afraid to tackle it. In fact, I think we are unconsciously relieved when we come to the place near the end of the letter when Paul makes happy plans to visit the Roman Christians, sends special greetings to friends who are particularly dear, and asks all of them to be gracious and helpful to Phebe of the church of Cenchrea.

There seem to be two schools of thought regarding Phebe's financial status, and standing in the church. One says flatly that she was a literal servant of the church, doing such homely chores as cleanup jobs and errands. The other maintains with equal conviction that she was a wealthy widow, a deaconess in the church, and that the reason she delivered the Epistle to the Romans was that she was going to Rome on important business anyway.

Phebe sailed west and north toward Rome. Paul, intending to travel to Jerusalem with the great Gentile offering for the needy saints in Judea, had planned to sail east and south toward Syria. But intelligence came through in time of yet another Jewish plot to kill the apostle, so he changed his route abruptly and headed north into Macedonia.

Luke gives no details of this plot. Some writers speculate that the murder was to have taken place in the Corinthian port city of Cenchrea—where the Jewish population near the waterfront was considerable—either as Paul was boarding the ship, or after it was under way. As long as Paul lived, his enemies among his own countrymen never gave up their hope of killing him.

Back through Berea and Thessalonica Paul went, and finally back again to Philippi.

This time, when Paul left Philippi, Luke went with him. Luke will not leave him again: He will be there in journeyings, in danger, in sickness, in riot, in prison (for though not imprisoned himself, he stood by Paul), in shipwreck, and finally, in Rome.

The other seven men, including Timothy, who were going along on the Jerusalem journey, left Philippi early and waited for Paul and Luke in Troas. Here, again, Luke takes up the "we" in the narrative.

And we sailed away from Philippi after the days of unleavened bread. . . . No hint of the wrench of parting from the church he had nurtured for seven years, no word of the regret at leaving cherished friends who were also his patients. There must have been patients, for it seems illogical to suppose that he would have ceased to minister to men's bodies when he began ministering to their spirits. Apparently, Paul's need of him was greater, and so with Paul he went.

They remained in Philippi until after Easter. It was almost as if Paul already felt the chill of impending disaster in Jerusalem, and wanted to linger in the warmth of love radiated by these, his first European converts. But finally, **And we sailed away from Philippi after the days of unleavened bread, and came unto them in Troas in five days; where we abode seven days.** Five days this time from Philippi to Troas, instead of two days as on another journey. Even the winds seemed to be trying to keep Paul out of Jerusalem.

Paul stayed in Troas seven days this time, almost as though to make up for his hasty departure before when he had left to try to find Titus. This time there would be much precious fellowship with the disciples, much explaining of difficult questions, and probably some warning of the "wolves" who would likely come into the flock to destroy here as they had in Corinth and Galatia.

Then, inevitably, came Paul's last day with them. This was the "first day of the week," and the disciples came together to worship, to hear the apostle's final message to them, and to observe the sacrament of the Lord's Supper. This particular service is interesting for something besides its more spectacular aspect: It tells us that even at that early stage of church history, Sunday, "The Lord's Day," was the accepted day for Christian worship. Also, those of us who are invariably too tired (after an eight-hour day) to attend midweek prayer meeting might give a passing thought to saints who worked a seven-day week and managed to make it to church on Sunday night and spend several *hours* at the service!

The early Christians usually took their food with them to church and had their meal together, and with that meal they took the hallowed bread and wine of the Lord's Supper. This, the disciples of Troas were doing on the last night that Paul was with them.

There is little doubt that Paul was summing up all Christian faith and doctrine in that one discourse, and it took a long time, a very long time. He was preaching to a house so full that at least one person was sitting in a window. The room was a large one on the third floor of the house, but even so, it was not large enough. From being so full of so many people, it was warm and stuffy. It was ablaze with the lights from many lamps, as if to make this solemn occasion a true festival of joy.

The young man sitting in the window was named Eutychus. He listened eagerly, storing the apostle's words in the recesses of his mind. At length, he found to his annoyance that the final words in a phrase were eluding him; he was beginning to get drowsy. He shook his head sharply in an effort to banish the drowsiness, and concentrated once more on the mighty discourse of Paul. There was no use . . . he was so tired . . . the lights were so bright . . . the room was so warm. The fog of somnolence slowly encompassed him. Paul's face gradually lost its outlines in the fringes of the young man's eyelashes. Dimly was seen the expressive hand raised in a familiar gesture; the keenly cleft words became a gentle smear of sound. The face was gone, the hand was gone, the voice was gone.

Eutychus, who probably had worked all day and listened half the night, was soundly asleep. The worshiper packed next to him must have seen the young man's shoulders relax and slump into the attitude of deeper sleep, and (if he was half as human as any of us!) a flicker of amusement must have started across his face. But it turned to stark horror when he noted the wide-open window.

Frantic hands tried to grab Eutychus, but too late: an inert, sodden bundle of sleep, he dropped like a stone to the pavement three stories below. For a split second the window was framed in light and surrounded by silence as Paul's words froze on his tongue. Then a muffled wail, "Eutychus! My son! He will be dead!" And the sound of rushing feet, emptying the huge room, racing down three flights of stairs, and with Luke probably thinking sorrowfully that there would be little left that a doctor could do.

A gray-haired woman screaming, "My son! My son!" as

she tried to lift the inert body from the stones; Luke pushing quietly through the wailing friends, bending over the young man, listening for a heartbeat with his ear against the thin tunic, and then straightening up to speak to those who were holding the body in their arms. "Our friend Eutychus has gone from us to be with our Lord."

Paul, still in the grip of the Holy Spirit, came through the door and approached the stricken group. "Give me the child," he said quietly.

Wondering, perhaps, how he could hold a body whose weight was greater than his own, they nonetheless obeyed him.

Paul felt his soul clothed again with the mantle of ecstasy it had worn to leave a body crushed by stones and left dead on a junk heap. He was remembering again "Paradise . . . and words which it is not lawful for a man to utter." He hardly even heard the wails of mourning as he placed the body gently on the pavement and covered it with his own. His lips moved, but with only a whisper of sound. "Thou mighty One whose power sent back my spirit to its broken clay, restore, I beseech Thee, by that same power the soul that death has plucked from Thy child, Eutychus. O Thou great and mighty God . . . O Thou great and mighty God . . ."

"O Thou great and mighty God," Eutychus heard the words, faint at first, then swelling into glorious sound like the sweep of wind through tree tops. "Strange!" the young man thought, "That wasn't what he was saying when I drifted off to sleep. Oh, I hope I didn't miss many of his words!" Then he was vastly puzzled to find his own lips touched and moving as if manipulated by those of another.

"O Thou great and mighty God!" Two pairs of lips spoke together, but only Paul and God and Eutychus heard the sound.

The young man's bewilderment grew as he heard the sound of sobbing all around him, and then the apostle saying gently, "Be comforted, beloved; weep not, for his life is in him."

They whose mourning had been replaced by the oil of joy went back to the upper room to eat the feast of the Lord, and to listen again to the beloved Paul who **talked a long while, even till break of day.** And then he left them.

The ship that was to take Paul and his companions on the first leg of their journey to Jerusalem was ready to get under way on Monday morning. Paul did not go directly to his stateroom to rest for twelve hours after preaching all night and performing a miracle. In the first place, ships of that time were hardly the floating palaces to which we are accustomed, and they probably had nothing closer to a stateroom than bare boards where the passenger made himself comfortable with whatever bedding he himself had brought along. And in the second place, Paul didn't even go aboard! He decided to hike the twenty miles across the promontory to Assos, their first stop. Why did he decide to walk? Probably because he needed solitude: Time to meditate; time to be completely alone and completely quiet; time to commune in joyous quietude with his Lord as he walked along and drank in the beauty of God's creation in the spring. (This was shortly after Easter, remember?) These things he found as he went afoot to Assos.

Paul made it to Assos and boarded the ship whose next stop was Mitylene. The ships he used were comparable to our "tramp steamers," so they stopped at all the little ports along the way to discharge freight and passengers, and take on more of both.

Luke's recording of the ports of call sounds somehow like the report of a man in a hurry. And he probably was in a hurry because Paul was. Why? He wanted to get to Jerusalem by Pentecost. Again, why? Because, for one reason, Jews from every part of the world converged on Jerusalem for the celebration of Pentecost, and Paul loved his own people. He was commissioned to preach the gospel first to the Jews, and here they would be again as on that memorable day when the Spirit came down: **Jews, devout men, out of every nation under heaven.** Again, Pentecost was the "day of the first fruits when the first loaves made from the new grain were offered on the altar." What more fitting time to bring the great offering from the Gentiles to the poverty-stricken saints in Jerusalem? Was not this indeed "first fruits from the new grain"?

Luke ticks off the days and islands and ports: **And came to Mitylene, and we sailed thence, and came the next day over against Chios; and the next day we arrived at Samos, and tarried at Trogyllium** ["Tarried at Trogyllium"—that sounds like music!] **and the next day we came to Miletus.**

The ship apparently was not to touch at Ephesus. Paul was not willing to risk finding another vessel in time, so he reluctantly abandoned the idea of visiting the Ephesian church. However, it appeared that they would be docked in Miletus long enough for the Ephesian elders to contact the apostle there, and he sent word to them.

The summons from Miletus must have been a joyful surprise for the men of Ephesus. We can well imagine that they dropped whatever they were doing, and hurried to be with the beloved teacher whom they had not seen for nearly a year. How was his health now? (He had been ill when he left them.) Had he faced worse dangers and hardships, fiercer persecutions? They would soon find out from Paul himself. There was not too much time left. They hurried down to the harbor where they could watch for the ship.

An expectant hush settled over the little group as Paul lifted his hand and began to speak the words he had called them to hear: solemn exhortation and a poignant valedictory. He calls on them to remember the years he spent with them, his conduct, his attitude, his labor, his sorrows, his trials, the dangers risked by constant plottings of the Jews, his stubborn persistence in teaching them both in public assembly and privately in their homes, his quiet laboring with his own hands to support himself and those who ministered with him.

Paul is telling them quite matter-of-factly and without a trace of vanity that they are to follow his example. They will not see his face again, for he is going to Jerusalem into unknown peril, possibly even to death. But they are to carry on. They are to feed and minister to the blood-bought church of God which the Holy Spirit has given into their keeping. They are to beware of the "grievous wolves" who will come after Paul's departure to destroy the flock from without. They are also to beware of men who will arise from among their own number to pervert the Truth to make followers for themselves. (Paul probably knows that the busy troublemakers who had tried to work havoc in Corinth and Galatia will eventually get to Ephesus also.)

Finally, he commends them to God who is able, and they all kneel upon the ground and pray. They cling to Paul and kiss him and weep, overwhelmed with grief because they will not see him again.

From the ship came the sound of summons—it was about to sail. His friends from Ephesus clung frantically to Paul and moved with him to the very water's edge, finally tearing themselves away and watching through a curtain of tears as he and his companions went aboard.

Paul and Timothy and Luke and Sopater and Aristarchus and Secundus and Gaius and Tychicus and Trophimus clustered in a knot on the deck and watched and waved as long as they could see the forlorn little group standing by the water's edge.

Chapter Twenty-one

Paul's determination to return to Jerusalem seems almost an obsession. Even without the warnings from the Holy Spirit spoken through disciples all along the way, he would have known that he was walking into danger. The Jews there hated him and had tried at least once to kill him. He was not popular with a great many of the Christian Jews in Jerusalem because they sincerely believed that he was trying to destroy the Law. Representatives of this group were the ones who had originally gone into Antioch to tell the Gentile Christians that they must be circumcised to be saved. They were utterly repudiated by the Jerusalem church, but they did not cease from their activities, and they would not have been unhappy to see Paul in trouble.

A few years ago I heard a brilliant theologian say that Paul's journey to Jerusalem was directly contrary to the will of God! Despite this man's magnificent mind (and it was that) he had evidently overlooked the fact of Paul's absolute obedience to the directives of the Holy Spirit. Paul was warned by the Spirit that "bonds and afflictions" awaited him in Jerusalem, but I have never seen any place in the Bible where the Holy Spirit *forbade* the journey. In fact, I had always taken for granted that Paul's journey to Rome had been mapped out in the mind of God—*through Jerusalem!*

It was a good time of year for sea voyages which threaded the little islands and jutting tongues of land along the west coast of Asia Minor. The ship put out from the harbor at

Miletus, and heading due south with a favorable wind behind her made short work of the forty miles to Coos. The next day they were in Rhodes, and from there they headed a little south but mostly east and made it to Patara which was about as far south as you could go in Asia Minor.

Evidently, Patara was the destination of the ship they were on, but there was another vessel about ready to weigh anchor and head across the Mediterranean toward Phoenicia. We can almost see the nine men hurrying to get their baggage assembled, scurrying off of one ship and on to another. Traveling schedules in those days were not something that a bureau arranged for you with hotel accommodations, meals, and even tips neatly taken care of. Maybe you'd catch a boat, and then again, maybe you wouldn't.

Scholars who have checked the records with remarkable care have reached the conclusion that this part of the voyage was long enough after the Passover season for the full moon to be in evidence again, and that since the run from Patara to Tyre was across open sea (without the danger inherent in creeping in and out among little islands, and such) the ship could travel at night also. Continuous sailing plus a favorable wind would have made the voyage possible in about forty-eight hours. Three hundred and forty miles—if Paul and his companions had been using jet aircraft, the distance could have been handled in an hour with ease! But they wouldn't have seen moonlight on the water nor sails billowing in the wind.

They **discovered** Cyprus looming with sudden beauty from the blue Mediterranean. Did Paul, looking toward the island, recount for his hearers his experience at Paphos with Sergius Paulus and the wicked Elymas? Was this, perhaps, the first time Luke the reporter had heard that story? (Luke had not yet written his book, remember.) The ship was not to touch Cyprus at all, for they **left it on the left hand and sailed into Syria.**

Tyre was the ship's first port of call in Phoenicia, and there she was to discharge her cargo. Paul and his company disembarked and went to seek out disciples who lived there. Some of these believers probably had not seen the apostle since he and Barnabas went through "Phenice and Samaria" on their way from Antioch to Jerusalem to the first great council of the church.

With what gladness the news must have spread from family to family that Paul was in the city, and would be there a whole week. The children must have sat, quiet and wide-eyed, listening to the marvelous adventures of the missionaries. Some of their elders listened with great foreboding, and by the authority of the Holy Spirit warned Paul against going to Jerusalem. Nevertheless, when the week was up, all nine of the men made their way back through the city to the harbor. All the disciples whom they had visited, together with wives and children, went back to the ship with them and knelt on the shore and prayed, as the Ephesian elders had done at Miletus. There is little doubt that the great burden of their prayer was for the safety of the Apostle to the Gentiles when he should reach the great and hostile city of Jerusalem.

Again the nine tore themselves from the tearful embrace of their brothers in Christ who turned sadly away and went back to their homes, recounting over and over again the things which Paul had told them. The ship sailed out of Tyre's harbor and headed south along the coastline to Ptolemais. This was the end of the line for Paul and his friends as far as travel by water was concerned. They got their belongings together, left the ship, and went once more to look for disciples who lived in the vicinity. They spent only one day with these, and left the next morning for Caesarea.

One wonders if Cornelius the centurion was still stationed at Caesarea. Quite probably not, for it had been nearly twenty years since that memorable time when the angelic messenger had instructed him to send for "Simon whose surname is Peter." If Cornelius still lived, we may be sure that wherever he was he was telling the story of the One who had brought salvation to the Gentiles.

But there was in Caesarea one man we have met before: Philip the evangelist, who was one of the seven original deacons. His home was now in Caesarea, and probably had been for a great many years. No mention is made of his wife, but he had four unmarried daughters who had the gift of prophecy. Paul and his party were guests in Philip's hospitable home for "many days" as Luke puts it. They had made much better time than expected, and would not have to be in a hurry now to get to Jerusalem for Pentecost.

While they were in Caesarea, one final warning came to Paul concerning the danger which he faced in Jerusalem. The prophet Agabus, the same man who had gone from Jerusalem to Antioch so many years before to foretell the disastrous famine, now went down from Judea to Caesarea and sought out Paul. While the assembled company watched uneasily, Agabus took Paul's girdle and bound his own hands and feet with it. Then he solemnly pronounced his prophecy: **"Thus saith the Holy Ghost: 'So shall the Jews at Jerusalem bind the man that owneth this girdle, and shall deliver him into the hands of the Gentiles.'"**

This pronouncement brought near-panic to all of them. Frantically they begged Paul to change his mind. Surely, surely it was foolish for him to take so grave a risk when others could deliver the collection sent by the Gentile churches. His work among the Gentiles was far from finished, so why should he risk his life in this gesture of brotherhood which would, in all probability, prove futile? And even if he should not be killed outright, what good purpose could possibly be served by his being in prison? Could he reach the Gentiles from a prison cell? And when would he get to Rome?

Paul was deeply touched, but he shook his head and said gently, "I must go to Jerusalem."

"Why? You'll be killed!"

"Beloved, beloved! I must go to Jerusalem because the Lord sends me there to try to bring peace and understanding. I am His slave. His brand is upon my soul, and upon my flesh in these scars of thong and rod, and if it be His will that I encounter bonds or even death in Jerusalem, I am ready to be bound and I am ready to die. I must go to Jerusalem."

Luke sums up the matter simply: **And when he would not be persuaded, we ceased, saying, "The will of the Lord be done."**

The writer also continues, **And after those days we took up our carriages and went up to Jerusalem.** I used to read that, and feel quite relieved to think that the last lap of the journey was accomplished in comfort—maybe even in style!—

in vehicles that perhaps resembled our poetic "surrey with the fringe on top." It was something of a jolt to discover that the "carriages" were baggage! We don't even know whether they walked or rode.

If they did walk, they probably had to slow their pace for the elderly Mnason who went with them on the trip. Mnason, like Barnabas, was a native of Cyprus. Some commentators think he was converted under the preaching of Barnabas; others think his age was mentioned because he had been—perhaps in middle life—a disciple who followed our Lord during His ministry. At any rate, he had a home in Jerusalem, and he was to be the host of Paul and his companions, and of the friends from Caesarea who accompanied them.

If Mnason was a wealthy man, there were slaves in his house to remove the travelers' sandals and wash their tired feet, as well as to put food before them. And messengers were sent to tell the "brethren" that Paul and his company had arrived. Unless Mnason's house was quite large, it likely was about to burst at the seams that night with all the guests who came to visit with Paul and Timothy and Luke and all the rest. Perhaps there was an "upper chamber" like the one in Troas, and that many lights burned far into the night there also while Jewish and Gentile Christians enjoyed happy fellowship.

That night was one of the few peaceful ones that were left to Paul for a long time.

The next day Paul and his company reported to James, the head of the Jerusalem church, and to all the elders. This undoubtedly was the time when the Gentile offering was laid at the feet of James and the elders, but Luke makes no mention of the matter. He merely says that Paul, **when he had saluted them, declared particularly what things God had wrought among the Gentiles by his ministry.**

Paul's report: Ephesus, Philippi, Corinth, Troas, Thessalonica—citadels of darkness transformed by lamps of God made by the eager hands of the Apostle to the Gentiles. The lamps of God were churches whose sturdy flame would eventually light the whole world; and the storms of Satan could not blow them out. For his Lord, Paul was pushing steadily toward the "uttermost part of the earth."

After hearing Paul's report, James and the elders **glorified the Lord**. They also came up with an idea that was to result in near-disaster for the apostle. They told Paul what he already knew, namely that thousands of Jewish disciples were **zealous of the law**. These still cherished the customs of their fathers. They were true Christians, they knew that their salvation depended upon belief in the Lord Jesus and not upon their keeping of the Commandments, nonetheless they were still Jews and they still revered their ancient traditions. Gentiles did not have to be bound by the burden of the Law, and just as Gentiles did not have to become Jews to become Christians, even so, Jews did not have to *stop being Jews* to become Christians.

These faithful thousands had had their minds poisoned against Paul by the same ones who insisted that Gentiles must be circumcised to be received into Christ's fold. The multitudes had been taught to believe that Paul forbade his Jewish converts among the Gentiles to circumcise their children or keep the other customs of their people.

All of these Jewish Christians—the ones who lived in Palestine and the ones from abroad, on hand for the Feast of Pentecost—would assuredly hear that Paul was in Jerusalem. Therefore this would be a perfect time for him to prove that his accusers were liars. The suspicions in the hearts of the people would be healed, and the Lord's church would be unified. Paul could accomplish all this by the simple act of observing one of the ancient traditions.

Among the members of the church in Jerusalem were four men who were under a Nazarite vow, and if Paul would enter into this ritual with them, that simple act would prove once and for all that he was still a *Jew* in the innermost core of his being.

After the fulfillment of a Nazarite vow, a man was free to make his offering and cut his hair, for a man under such a vow did not cut his hair during the time. It was customary for one person to pay for the offering that another was to bring at the conclusion of this period, provided the person under the vow was too poor to do so. Apparently, all four under the vow were too poor to furnish their own sacrificial animals, and Paul was to buy them.

The chances are that Paul himself did not have that much money—considering the fact that he had to work to support both himself and some of his helpers—but the church officials probably took that amount from the offering from the Gentiles. Truly, if it accomplished its purpose of bringing peace and understanding, it would be well spent. If Paul made this completely Hebrew gesture of **being at charges** with the Nazarites, nobody could believe he repudiated their Law.

Paul went into the temple with the men, was "purified" with them, and was conspiciously with them in the completion of their vows. He was seen by multitudes of the Hebrew Christians who must have rejoiced that the great Apostle to the Gentiles did not scorn to keep their sacred customs.

But Paul was also seen by **Jews which were of Asia,** and they were no end delighted. They hadn't been able to get rid of him in Ephesus, but the sacred temple of their fathers presented a much happier theater of activity! It would be no trick whatever to stir up fatal mob violence here; all they had to do was start screeching a few choice lies, and they'd have it made. Full-throated, they went right into action.

They grabbed Paul and began yelling, "Men of Israel, *help!* This is the man of whom we have been telling you. He has been in far countries teaching all men against the seed of Abraham, tearing down the Law of Moses, and defaming our most holy temple. There is no vileness to which he will not stoop, for he has even polluted this holy place by bringing Gentiles into it!"

The fact that Paul had merely been seen with Trophimus (an Ephesian) in the city, and certainly had *not* brought him beyond the clearly marked boundary of the Court of the Gentiles (in the temple) did not bother these gentlemen in the least. They had a good story and they were going to stick to it.

Multitudes of the faithful converged on the spot in seconds to help their embattled Ephesian brethren, and Paul was pushed, battered, and buffeted through the great temple doors which were closed just as fast as the attendants could manage it. The temple must not be profaned with murder— they'd have to step outside to do it! Like the men who stoned Stephen, this was a law-abiding mob.

That arm of the Roman military service responsible for law and order in Jerusalem was always apprehensive during the great Jewish festivals. The local citizens were hard enough to keep controlled, but when they were increased by several thousand foreigners who had never been reconciled to seeing the holy city of their fathers occupied by the hated Gentiles, a riot was likely to break out at any given hour of the day. So the Fortress of Antonia in one corner of the great temple enclosure was always manned with a force adequate for quelling practically anything that might happen. Stairways ran down from the fortress to the courts of the temple so that the fully armed soldiers could dash down.

The sentry on duty saw the budding riot in the temple court beneath him, and reported laconically to his superior: "They're at it again, sir; and from the look of things, I'd say the whole city could be involved this time."

The report was relayed to the commanding officer, Claudius Lysias, who summoned his centurions and their men and dashed down to the courtyard at top speed. The men of Ephesus were very annoyed, they'd been foiled again. But they had sense enough to respect Caesar's soldiers who sometimes took a very dim view of murder. They stopped beating Paul who by then was bruised and disheveled, with torn clothing and with face beginning to swell from the blows.

Claudius Lysias approached the battered Paul and said curtly, "Chain him—two chains. He's not big enough to put up much of a fight, and he's too old anyway, but for all that, he could be extremely dangerous."

Lysias turned to the now surly crowd. "All right, Jews, [the word on his tongue was an epithet] what's the cause of this unseemly commotion? Who is this man? What has he done?"

"Saul!" somebody yelled, "Traitor to our sacred religion!"

"Paul!" another shouted, "Renegade rabbi!"

"Polluter of our sacred temple!"

"Gentile lover!" somebody snarled, happy to be able to probe with impunity the hated Roman hide.

The commander's lips curled ever so faintly in contempt, or perhaps amusement. "Oh, well, I really didn't expect to get intelligent answers from a mob of Jews. Take the old boy upstairs, and we'll see what we can learn from him. You can't tell, maybe *he* knows what it's all about!"

Paul, half in shock, moved along between his guards, concerned at the moment only with accommodating his steps to their military pace. If he had been able to reason, he might have thought a bit wryly, "Well, they delivered me into the hands of the Gentiles, all right, but they certainly didn't intend to!"

The enraged mob, deprived of its victim, infuriated by the commander's not-too-subtle insults, surged forward among the soldiers and grabbed at Paul again. Claudius Lysias brandished his sword. "Back, you fools!" he thundered, "If you insist on dying, we'll help you. But there won't be enough flunkies in your precious temple to clean these paving stones of your carcasses and your blood."

The centurion commanding the small group closest to Paul issued an order: "Inner guard, litter shields!" The guards chained to the prisoner moved forward two paces while the others lowered their shields and clanked them smartly together, thus forming a long, narrow litter.

Paul found himself lifted like a sack of grain and deposited on the litter. His head began to clear a little. He stiffened his body to maintain an upright position while seated on the shields of the heathen soldiers who had snatched him from death by his own people. As he was borne up the great staircase toward the safety of the fortress, he turned his head and saw other sons of Abraham run howling toward the soldiers, approaching as near as they dared, stopping so suddenly that some were knocked to the pavement by the ones behind them, and all screeching, "Away with him, away with him; stone him, stone him, stone him!"

Paul's soul wept with him, "My people, O my people! O Israel who would not hear! I would surrender my own salvation if it would save you, O Israel, my brother!"

As they neared the heavy doors at the top of the stairs, the prisoner was let down from the shields. He turned to Claudius Lysias and spoke with dignity—and in impeccable Greek. "May I have a word with you?"

In spite of stern military self-discipline, the jaw of Claudius Lysias almost dropped, "Hah! What have we here? *You* speak Greek? Aren't you that crackpot Egyptian who rallied four thousand cutthroats to drive the Romans out a year or so ago?"

Paul answered with a certain quiet pride: "I am a Jew of Tarsus in Cilicia, a citizen of that city which is not without honor and distinction. I beg you, Captain, allow me to speak to these people."

Perhaps the chief captain was intrigued by the very audacity of his prisoner; perhaps he wanted to study the reaction of the still-screaming men below; or perhaps he was affected by that winsomeness which attracted strangers to Paul. At any rate, he figured it was quite safe. He signaled for the chains to be removed, and said, "The prisoner's request is granted."

Chapter Twenty-two

Paul's legs were no longer trembling. He stood erect and gestured toward the howling mob, looking steadily at them with love and pity showing through the battered lineaments of his face while he waited for the beginning of silence. From sheer astonishment, the howls began to fall over the edge of a deep quietness, and when the last ugly sound was gone, Paul opened his mouth and spoke to them—in Hebrew. Greek they would have understood, quite likely, but this man was speaking to them as a devout Jew, forging himself to their souls with the links of language.

"**Men, brethren, and fathers,**" the familiar salutation identified him more closely with them. "**A Jew, . . . born in Tarsus in Cilicia, . . . brought up in** this **city at the feet of Gamaliel** [They remembered Gamaliel.] **. . . perfectly schooled as to the law of the fathers, . . . zealous toward God, as** ye all are **this day.**"

The "great silence" had become breathless. Here was a rabbi from the school of Gamaliel; why had they allowed their hands to touch him in violence?

Paul, because he was a prisoner of the Gentiles, was being allowed to bring his testimony to the Jews: The story of his persecution to the death of "this way" (Was he remembering the holy light on Stephen's face?), of his being struck down on his way to Damascus, of his shattering encounter with Jesus of Nazareth, of his blindness because of "the glory of that light," of his baptism—*by a devout Jew!*

Then comes a facet of the jewel of Paul's experience that Luke had not turned toward the light. **"And it came to pass, that, when I was come again to Jerusalem, even while I prayed in the temple, I was in a trance; and saw him saying unto me, 'Make haste, and get thee quickly out of Jerusalem: for they will not receive thy testimony concerning me.' "**

Paul's answer to the Lord sounds like a plea for tolerance and understanding of his Jewish brethren, an attempt to justify their attitude toward him. **"And I said, 'Lord, they know that I imprisoned and beat in every synagogue them that believed on thee: And when the blood of thy martyr Stephen was shed, I also was standing by, and consenting unto his death, and kept the raiment of them that slew him.' And he said unto me, 'Depart: for I will send thee far hence unto the Gentiles. . . .' "**

We who are bathed in the perspiration of anguish because of *our* civilization's intolerance should look over Luke's shoulder as he writes with matter-of-fact hand, **And they gave him audience unto this word, and then lifted up their voices, and said, "Away with such a fellow from the earth: for it is not fit that he should live." And they cried out, and cast off their clothes, and threw dust into the air.**

What was the one word that transformed a respectful audience into a hysterical mob? The word was "Gentile"! If you had lived in Jerusalem two thousand years ago, you would have needed to be a Jew! We are really rather pale little things in our prejudices when compared to those robust Hebrews.

It is very, very doubtful that Claudius Lysias understood Hebrew any more than you do, and he must have been dumbfounded by the reaction of his prisoner's audience. This wasn't logical behavior, even for Jews! But Lysias didn't have time for small niceties like trying to figure out what made the Hebrews tick, he was going to have a first-class riot on his hands yet. "Take him inside," he ordered, "maybe a little of the torture will get us to the truth of the matter—if there is any such thing as truth!"

By the way, the Roman "examination" of prisoners would also make our "police brutality" look like a small cup of tea at the circle meeting. The theory seems to have been that if anything were left of the prisoner, he'd be delighted to tell all. And, indeed, after a man was stripped of his clothing, bound with leather thongs between two whipping posts so that he stood immobile for the scourging, and was then flogged for the prescribed time, it would not have been too surprising if he had confessed to anything from high treason to strangling his mother-in-law.

Paul was so stripped to be so bound, and as the soldiers were knotting the thongs with expertness born of long practice, the prisoner turned to the centurion in charge and asked a cryptic question: "Is it legal for you to scourge a Roman citizen who has not been condemned?"

The centurion's sunburned face turned pale. "Suspend operation!" he bawled to the soldiers and, turning on his heel, started with all speed commensurate with military dignity to report to his superior. Barely saluting Claudius Lysias, the centurion blurted, "Watch it, sir! Be careful how you handle this man. He's a Roman citizen."

"Oh, woe!" the chief captain muttered, "first I snatch him from stoning by his little brothers; next it turns out he speaks respectable Greek, and so is no ordinary tramp; then he talks to them in some other language and makes them so mad they howl for his blood again; so now, he's a Roman citizen! Tomorrow morning, doubtless, he'll be the emperor's long-lost grandsire. Meanwhile, we'd better be thinking of suitable sacrifices for whatever gods are handy. If it gets reported to the right places that we've bound a Roman citizen for examination by torture, we'll need *all* the gods on our side. And if you think that's funny, lend me your sense of humor—I could use it!"

"Very funny, sir," the centurion answered gloomily, "like being beheaded!"

The prisoner was still standing, bound. The soldiers still stood by like embarrassed stone ghosts. Claudius Lysias approached Paul and asked the question officially. "Are you a Roman citizen? Tell me."

"I am," Paul answered quietly.

The chief captain, almost as if wondering aloud how an obviously impoverished Jew could have managed it, said, "Citizenship cost me an utterly staggering sum!"

"I did not buy my citizenship," Paul answered, "I was free born."

Lysias's order was terse, mechanical, "Release the prisoner."

The soldiers obeyed quickly, and at their commander's gesture, disappeared.

Claudius Lysias went back to his pondering. Tomorrow morning, he'd summon the Jewish council and have the accused man appear before them, and see what could be ascertained. Maybe eventually he'd find out what to put in his report in the space marked "charged with," but he was about to give up hope. But it really did make a Roman officer feel ridiculous to make a report on a prisoner, and not to be able to say what he was charged with.

Twenty-five years earlier, the high priest and the Sanhedrin would have been delighted with the opportunity they now possessed when they were summoned by Claudius Lysias to examine a certain prisoner named Paul. If they could have gotten their hands on Paul then, he would doubtless have followed Stephen into martyrdom.

Paul was escorted into the presence of the council and left before them as Lysias and his men moved a discreet distance away. (The Jews had to be the prescribed number of feet away from a Gentile before they could carry on!)

Paul was about to be examined by a panel of his peers, for he himself had been a member of this religious body. He looked earnestly upon the circle of faces, perhaps looking for a familiar one, or perhaps even a friendly one. Or, it may have been that because of impaired vision, he was merely studying the assemblage. Finally, he spoke—in Greek, in deference to Claudius Lysias. **"Brethren, I have lived in all good conscience before God until this day."**

At least one member of his audience was convinced that he spoke the truth. The words cut like a sharp sword through the mind of that vast blob of hypocrisy, Ananias the high priest, who had been hand-picked for the job by Herod, king of Chalcis. **And the high priest Ananias commanded them that stood by to smite him on the mouth.**

Righteous anger flamed in Paul's words, **"God shall smite** thee, thou whited wall: for sittest thou to judge me after the law, and commandest me to be smitten contrary to the law?"

(God did "smite the whited wall"! Ananias died under the daggers of skulking assassins, after they had set fire to his house to force him out.)

Paul was being tried before a court whose highest member was a thief, a scoundrel, and an oily hypocrite. But his fellow councilmen leaped to his defense by demanding sternly of the prisoner, **"Revilest thou God's high priest?"** Matchless irony, that: *God's* high priest!

Nobody seems actually to know what lay behind Paul's meek answer to that: "I did not know, brethren, that he was the high priest: for it is written, 'Thou shalt not speak evil of the ruler of thy people.' " If the words are taken literally, Paul is saying, "Forgive me. I did not recognize this man as the high priest, and even if he violates the law by having an uncondemned prisoner assaulted, *I* will not break the law by speaking evil of the ruler of my people." Or he could have been saying, "How could this repulsive, obviously evil creature possibly be God's high priest?" Or, if he did recognize the man, he could have been inferring pointedly that Ananias held the position by an unlawful appointment.

Whatever the prisoner meant by his cryptic apology, he had summed up in his own mind the caliber of this court, and he knew he would find no justice here. Left to the mercy of these men, his path would be the path of Stephen. One course was left to him, and he took it. He had observed that part of his judges were Pharisees and part were Sadducees, and knowing that they hated each other even more violently than they hated Christianity, the ghost of an amused smile could have lurked under his beard as he cried out, **"Men and brethren, I am a Pharisee, the son of a Pharisee: of the hope of the resurrection of the dead I am called in question!"**

Little time was ever needed for Pharisees and Sadducees to arise to heated pitch in a doctrinal argument, and they came right through according to form and expectation. Eyes flashing, sleeves billowing, beards waggling wildly, they argued. Claudius Lysias, waiting and listening at a respectful distance, probably wailed to himself, "Here they go *again!*

Well, at least I know now that the whole thing is about their religious gobbledy-gook. Jews!"

In case you have forgotten the main point of contention between the Pharisees and the Sadducees: The Pharisees believed in the resurrection of the body, and in angels, and in spirits; the Sadducees, steeped in cynicism and sophistication, ridiculed all three.

The council was in the wildest sort of an uproar. Scribes (of the Pharisees' party) finally got the floor long enough to deliver their opinion: **"We find no evil in this man: but if a spirit or an angel hath spoken to him, let us not fight against God."** They were evidently referring to Paul's earlier testimony when he had addressed the crowd from the stairway, for in this meeting he had said nothing of his encounters with the Lord.

Fresh howls of derision from the Sadducees greeted this verdict, and the uproar grew even wilder. The Pharisees began to form a tight little ring around Paul, and the opposition began to form a small wedge with the obvious intention of smashing the ring.

The Roman commander's mouth thinned to a tight line of exasperation. "Advance!" he ordered his soldiers, "Rescue the prisoner from this mob. Take him by force and return him to the safety of the fortress."

The opposing forces of the council continued to yell, and punch at each other for some little time before they realized the prisoner was gone. Then they adjourned and went away to figure out a new approach.

Paul was safe in the Roman fortress. Twice now he had been rescued from certain death, but what lay ahead? Had his sermon of the stairway accomplished any good? Had any been swayed by his testimony? Had any man accepted the good news he brought? And what about the church in Jerusalem? Had his brush with death helped to bring peace there? Or were those who would undermine his teaching rejoicing now at the danger he faced from official Jewry? He looked down into the courts of the great temple of his own people, and realized that he was terribly alone. When he lay down to sleep on the crude bedding accommodations of the prison, he gave thanks for deliverance from death; yet his soul was heavy with the burden of melancholy. What lay ahead? How was he to get out of Jerusalem? What of tomorrow?

Paul turned restlessly in his sleep as his pummeled body tried in vain to find a comfortable position. Then, suddenly, the tense body relaxed, and a gentle smile eased anxiety from his face. His lips began to move. "My Lord! Oh, my Lord, I am not forsaken! In mine extremity, gracious Lord, Thou comest unto me."

The shining figure stooped to touch the forehead of His despondent apostle. "My child, my faithful one, thou art utterly mine, and I am with thee. Be of good cheer, Paul: for as thou hast testified of me in Jerusalem, so must thou bear witness also at Rome."

Ah! The testimony in Jerusalem was accepted. (Had it done any good, Paul had wondered drearily. Now he knew: it was accepted!) He had testified in Jerusalem *as a prisoner.* Did the Lord mean that the testimony in Rome would be that of an apostle in chains? That did not matter in the least. The Lord had promised that Paul would testify in Rome, and His apostle was content.

In the mind of Claudius Lysias a great respect had grown for Paul for prisoner. He had watched the man's absolute fearlessness, he must have wondered at his obvious love for those who had been trying to kill him, and he probably felt a certain wry admiration for the way Paul had handled the council which had met to examine him. Add to this his overwhelming gratitude that Paul the Roman citizen had overlooked the capital outrage ordered by Lysias, and it is easy to understand why the prisoner was given as much freedom and privilege as the law allowed. This was probably why his sister's son was able to see and talk to him without any difficulty.

We wish we had more information about Paul's sister's son. The narrative somehow suggests an earnest teenager, but that is not too likely. Paul was near sixty, and unless his sister was much younger than he, it is hardly likely that she had a teenaged son. Whatever the nephew's age, he got around and he heard things. Whether he heard the conspirators discussing their plan, or whether some friend let him in on it, is not known.

It is interesting to note that the **chief priests and elders** were in on the proposed murder. They not only assented, but they were quite willing to play their little part in the drama.

It was such a relief that this Paul matter was to be taken care of at last. Of course, Jewish ecclesiastical officialdom would not be responsible for the death of this Jew who was a Roman citizen. Always and everywhere, the dread Sicarii lurked with ready daggers concealed under their robes, and if they leaped upon a prisoner as he was being brought before the Sanhedrin for further examination—well, Lysias and his Romans simply should have been more careful. Moreover, if anything were said of the matter, it could always be told in the proper Roman high places that the Roman underlings in Judea were not efficient, else they would long since have stamped out this lawlessness.

The Sanhedrin and the forty conspirators had the matter all settled; all they had to do was wait till morning. They who had taken upon themselves a religious vow to neither eat nor drink till they had committed murder, probably were already running over tomorrow's luncheon menu.

Out of breath and badly frightened, Paul's nephew sought out the prisoner in the **castle** (or fortress) and whispered details of the plot: There were forty men who had sworn with a fearful oath that they would neither eat nor drink till they had killed Paul. They had requested the Sanhedrin to ask the Roman commander for another interview with the prisoner that he might be reexamined, and when Paul was brought near, they would kill him.

Paul knew perfectly well that God had arranged an appointment for him in Rome, and that these fanatical men, therefore, were not to be allowed to destroy him. He also knew that God expects His intelligent children to use the intelligence He has given them. He did not tell the young man to relax and leave the matter in the hand of God; instead, he called to a centurion standing a little way off.

"Will you please take this young man to the chief captain? He has something very interesting to tell him."

"I'll be glad to. Come with me, young man." The centurion was thinking that this one looked a little young for a stool pigeon, but one never knew; perhaps he had intelligence of an incipient rebellion.

Claudius Lysias looked keenly at the frightened messenger sent by Paul the prisoner. "Relax, son," a hint of a smile lurked in his eyes, "I'm not going to eat you!" He reached for the young man's hand, "Come along to a place where we can talk in complete privacy."

In his private quarters, the commander asked, "Now, what's this all about? Tell me."

Paul's nephew told his story. The words practically tumbled over each other, and ended with, "Don't believe them, sir. Please don't do as they ask; they only want to get at Paul to kill him!"

Lysias patted his visitor's shaking hand. "Stop being scared; leave everything to me. Nobody is going to kill *my* prisoner, you can be sure of that. You run along home now, and don't tell anybody—and I mean *anybody*—that you've told me these things."

As soon as the informer was out of sight, the commander summoned two of his centurions. "Prepare for a night march to Caesarea. Each of you take his hundred; additionally, you will need seventy cavalry and two hundred spearmen, and mounts for the prisoner, Paul, whom I am sending to Felix for safekeeping. You will leave the fortress at nine this evening. I will send with you a letter of explanation to the governor. That is all."

The centurions saluted and turned on their heels, and as Claudius Lysias reached for his writing materials, he muttered, "Kill *my* prisoner, will they? Pious old goats, I'd like to yank their sanctimonius beards out hair by hair!"

The letter which Luke reports next is, as far as I know, the only thing of its kind in the Bible: the official report of a Roman military commander to a Roman governor.

"Claudius Lysias unto the most excellent governor Felix sendeth greeting." Which, of course, was merely a form of address. Even so, there is a possibility that Lysias murmured, "Most excellent governor, my eye! He *stinks!*" He continued writing, **This man was taken of the Jews, and should have been killed of them: then came I with an army and rescued him, having understood that he was a Roman. And when I**

would have known the cause wherefore they accused him, I brought him forth into their council: whom I perceived to be accused of questions of their law, but to have nothing laid to his charge worthy of death or bonds. And when it was told me how that the Jews laid wait for the man, I sent straightway to thee, and gave commandment to his accusers to say before thee what they had against him. Farewell."

Chapter Twenty-three

At precisely nine in the evening, four hundred foot soldiers and seventy cavalrymen moved briskly from the Fortress Antonia and headed north and west toward Caesarea. There were, however, seventy-one men on horses: the seventy-first was Paul. Darkness had fallen by then, and the few people on the streets, scurrying out of the way or watching sullenly from the darkness, probably paid little attention. They were used to the military comings and goings of their conquerors. The pace was fast, because nearly sixty miles lay between them and the safety of Caesarea, but Roman soldiers were accustomed to forced marches and took the journey in stride.

Before dawn, Paul's military guard had reached Antipatris, about half way on the journey. From this point on to Caesarea, the cavalry would be sufficient protection. The four hundred foot soldiers with one centurion returned to the fortress in Jerusalem where the entire force of a thousand men might be needed any time.

And so it was that on the afternoon of the day when the conspirators had been so sure that he would be dead, Paul the apostle rode into Caesarea and was delivered to Felix the governor along with the Roman commander's letter.

Felix made official inquiry regarding Paul's birthplace, discovered that he was of the province of Cilicia, and ordered him to be kept under guard in Herod's judgment hall until the time for his hearing.

It was five days before the high priest and his minions reestablished their poise sufficiently to descend on Caesarea to try to bring this "Paul matter" to a successful conclusion. Later, Paul was to be kept under a sort of house arrest when he would be allowed to see his friends at will; but for the first five days he probably was held incommunicado. During those five days he must have recovered much of his physical strength and spiritual serenity.

The Jewish council had looked about for the best legal talent to be found before they went to Caesarea to press charges against Paul. They settled on a **certain orator named Tertullus.** Tertullus was also a Roman, and that might have its impact on the Roman governor; no slightest detail must be overlooked.

The prisoner was called in, and the hearing began with a statement by the lawyer for the prosecution. Whatever else he was, Tertullus the orator was a topflight politician, for he began by massaging the proper places with the gentle ointment of flattery. Tertullus would be right at home in high places today.

"Seeing that by thee we enjoy great quietness, and that very worthy deeds are done unto this nation by thy providence, we accept it always and in all places, most noble Felix, with all thankfulness. . . ." I love one of the cross references on that one. It is Psalm 55:21: "The words of his mouth were smoother than butter, but war was in his heart: his words were softer than oil, yet they were drawn swords"!

Tertullus undoubtedly knew that the most noble Felix was a freed slave of the emperor Claudius. He knew that Felix was, among other things, a murderer and a wife stealer. (Drusilla, his wife, had been lured away from her lawful husband with the help of a sorcerer.) He must have known also that his worthy employer, the high priest of the Jews, was not always and in all ways a completely holy character. But then, Tertullus had to eat, even as you and I!

"Notwithstanding, that I be not further tedious unto thee, I pray thee that thou wouldest hear us of thy clemency a few words. For we have found this man a pestilent fellow, and a mover of sedition among all the Jews throughout the world, and a ringleader among the sect of the Nazarenes:

216

Who also hath gone about to profane the temple: whom we took and would have judged according to our law. But the chief captain, Lysias, came upon us, and with great violence took him away out of our hands, commanding his accusers to come unto thee: by examination of whom thyself mayest take knowledge of all these things whereof we accuse him."

And the council assented vehemently. These things were the exact truth!

Felix listened impassively to the flow of flattery, and began mentally cataloging the charges: Mover of sedition among all the Jews throughout the world. (Factious disturbance: offense against Rome, treason against the emperor.) Ringleader in the sect of the Nazarenes. (Heresy against the Law of Moses.) Attempt to profane the temple at Jerusalem. (Offense against Jewish law and also against Roman law which protected Jews in the exercise of their worship.)

Now what was that bit about Lysias again? "Whom we took and would have judged according to our law [as was their right]. But the chief captain, Lysias, came upon us, and with great violence took him away out of our hands." Felix glanced again at Lysias's letter, and there was not the faintest flicker of change in his expression as he said to himself, "Well, well, that isn't *quite* the way Lysias tells it! He says, 'This man was taken of the Jews and should have been killed of them: then came I with an army and rescued him.' H-m-m, now which one of them, do you suppose, could be lying?" He beckoned to the prisoner, signaling that he was free to speak in his own defense.

Paul's words were courteous, sincere, and simple, a startling contrast to the slavering oratory of Tertullus. He said, in effect, that since Felix had been for so many years in his present office as governor and judge of the Jewish people, his knowledge was comprehensive. He understood perfectly their religion and their laws and he, Paul, could present his defense in complete confidence that Felix would render an absolutely just verdict.

These were accusing him of sedition among the Jews. The truth of the matter was—and this could be verified, since there were people in Caesarea who could prove it—that at this very hour it was only twelve days since he had gone up to

Jerusalem (from Caesarea) to worship. He had not created any disturbance of any kind; he had not delivered any sort of public utterance in the temple, in the synagogues, or even in the streets. He had not argued publicly with any man. He had simply gone up to Jerusalem like any other devout Jew to worship at the time of Pentecost. And these who were accusing him could not prove their accusations.

As to their assertions about heresy: That which they called heresy was the *way* in which Paul worshiped the God of his fathers, or, as the Romans would put it, "the hereditary God of the Jews." The Roman law allowed all men to worship the gods of their own nations, and it protected them in that right. Paul had not forsaken the God of his fathers; he believed all things that were written in the law and the prophets. He believed—as indeed did some of his accusers—in the resurrection of the dead, both of the just and the unjust; moreover, he struggled at all times to maintain a conscience void of offense toward God and man.

Felix, acquainted as he was with the sharply divergent viewpoints of the Pharisees and the Sadducees, would understand that Paul's theology was simply another doctrine concerning the "hereditary God of the Jews," and therefore not to be construed as heresy.

Paul continued his testimony. **"Now, after many years, I came to bring alms to my nation, and offerings."**

Felix, as we shall see later, probably attached much significance to that statement. At the moment, his chief reaction must have been that a man occupied with bringing relief to the poor would hardly be stirring up sedition. Incidentally, that is the only official mention in the Book of Acts concerning this great collection for the poor saints in Jerusalem.

The offerings Paul speaks of were undoubtedly the fees he took to the temple to pay for the vows of the four Nazarites he was sponsoring.

He, Paul, the accused, had been in the temple, having undergone purification, and was worshiping quietly, not gathering together a multitude and not causing a tumult, when certain Jews from Asia discovered him there. And it was Paul whose right to worship quietly had been violated; it was the Jews from Asia who had stirred up the mob and caused the uproar which the military had had to quell. And it was these same Jews from Asia who should have appeared before Felix to bring charges against Paul if they had any charges to bring.

As to the present members of the Sanhedrin, let them say what evidence of wrongdoing *they* had found in the prisoner when they examined him officially, except that he stood among them and cried out, **"Touching the resurrection of the dead I am called to question by you this day."**

Felix was convinced of Paul's innocence. Felix was also a seasoned politician. He did not acquit Paul and turn him loose—which, indeed, would probably have proved fatal for the apostle—neither did he wish to antagonize the high priest and the Sanhedrin. So he merely said that he would make a final decision on the matter when Lysias came down and presented his evidence.

The prisoner was, accordingly, remanded to the custody of the centurion, or military custody, which meant that the centurion was responsible—with his own life—for the keeping of the prisoner. In these cases, the prisoner was chained to the soldier, with the chain fastened to the prisoner's right hand and the soldier's left.

Naturally, the soldiers worked in shifts, and Paul must have thus contacted a number of them during his long imprisonment in Caesarea. The governor also gave specific instructions to the centurion that Paul was to have as much liberty as the law allowed under the circumstances, and that his friends should be free to visit with him and minister to his wants and needs at all times.

It would be interesting to speculate on the conversations between Tertullus and the Sanhedrin people on the way back to Jerusalem. I can't help wondering whether Tertullus collected his fee in full!

Luke was free to be with Paul almost at will; so was Philip the evangelist, and any friends from Caesarea or those who had come with Paul from his latest journey. News from all the churches could come to the apostle, and he was free to write to them. Many think that it was at this time also that Luke wrote his Gospel.

For the first time in many years Paul was actually safe.

The Jews who were so vehemently anxious to kill him could not touch him when his wrist was chained to a Roman soldier. The beleaguered apostle relaxed, and in all probability regained his shattered health. He was a prisoner, but he was free. He preached the glad tidings of Christ.

Many people in Caesarea, Jews and Gentiles, humble and highborn, heard of Paul's preaching and wanted to hear him. Among these was Drusilla, wife of Governor Felix.

Felix was a Roman; Drusilla was a Jewess, the daughter, in fact, of the Jewish king Herod Agrippa I. It was her father who had executed James the apostle and imprisoned Peter with the same purpose in mind. Drusilla had been the wife of the king of Emesa, and had been enticed from him to join herself to Felix. She was the sister of King Herod Agrippa II, and of Bernice, whom we shall encounter shortly. This Jewish princess was eager to hear what Paul had to say about the fulfillment of Jewish prophecy, and she was probably curious also to hear more about the "sect of the Nazarenes."

Paul preached the glad tidings of Christ to Felix and Drusilla. The Gentile governor's heart was warmed by the thought of a Savior for all men. The soul of the Jewess Drusilla thrilled at the thought of prophecy fulfilled in the person of the Messiah who would return to restore the kingdom of his father, David.

Then the preacher began to **reason of righteousness, temperance, and judgment to come.** The attributes of a Christian, the marks of citizenship in that coming Kingdom are absolute honesty, absolute justice in all his dealings with his fellowmen, compassion toward the downtrodden of earth, gentleness toward the feebleminded, temperance in all his appetites, and complete purity in his personal life. And any human being, male or female, bond or free, Gentile or Jew, who deliberately rejects the invitation to be born into the kingdom of God will ultimately stand before the throne of God Almighty to be judged. He will long for a place for his shriveled soul to flee from divine justice, but there will not be any place.

Felix caught a glimpse of his soul in all its sordid ugliness. He trembled. He strained with a sort of pathetic yearning toward the ideal man whom Paul described. Peace, he thought wistfully—that man would have peace. Then habit yanked him back to the familiar footpath of avarice. Peace the man would have—and also poverty! This Paul had brought a huge sum of money to be distributed in Jerusalem. Now, wouldn't it be reasonable to suppose that his fellow believers would be most happy to use part of that collection to—well, say, bail their friend out of jail? The bail to be paid to Felix, of course!

"Your words have moved me deeply," Felix said to Paul, "and I want very much to hear more; I must readjust my schedule so that I can find the time. Meanwhile, as you probably have heard already, I have given orders that you are to be allowed all possible privileges, including contact with your friends. It could be that some of your more affluent associates could be of great benefit to you—in a number of ways."

Felix sent for Paul at frequent intervals and talked with him, waiting to see if some of the wealthier Christians might come through with a bribe. None was forthcoming, naturally, and so Paul was held in prison. Of course, Felix might have reasoned that he was doing Paul no actual harm by holding him in jail since he was safe from the high priest there. But he was also mending his own political fortunes and mollifying the temple authorities to some extent by not liberating Paul.

So Felix would just sit tight on the status quo. But the status quo began to be very uncomfortable, for the population was getting dangerously restive. Friction between the Syrian and the Jewish segments of Caesarea went beyond the name-calling stage and blossomed into stone hurling and street fights. Finally, Felix called out the troops to quell the disturbances, and the resultant killing and plundering (by the soldiers) did not endear the governor to the wealthy Jews.

Reports of the outrages were sent to the emperor, and Nero the musician-actor-poet-lover must have been wandering through one of those rare periods when the God Nero was also a just ruler. He summoned Felix before the imperial presence, and sent Porcius Festus out to take his place.

Felix, of course, knew perfectly well that the wealth and political prestige of official Jewry would accuse him before the emperor, and in an effort to parry that thrust of accusation he tried one last favor to mollify his accusers: He left Paul the apostle in prison in Caesarea.

Porcius Festus, seasoned with political acumen plus a dash of religious tolerance, **ascended from Caesarea to Jerusalem** three days after his arrival in the province. The new governor was no dewy-eyed novice about to be taken in by the bland gentlemen of the Jerusalem hierarchy. The chances are that he was very familiar with the general situation before him, and that he had had at least a dozen "aides" scurrying around Rome, Caesarea, and Jerusalem to see that he was briefed on the more acute particulars. Therefore, he probably was not at all surprised when the high priest and all the other influential temple people launched almost instantly into the "Paul matter."

Would His Excellency remedy a sad breach of justice by sending this malefactor to Jerusalem to be tried by the Sanhedrin?

Convenient roadside ambush and attendant assassination were not unknown to Festus. He answered smoothly, politely, that since the prisoner in question was already in Caesarea, and since he himself would be returning there in a matter of days, it would be better if the proper officials from the temple went down with him for the hearing there. And he could assure them that justice would be speedily rendered.

Paul and his friends probably looked forward with anticipation—perhaps tempered with apprehension—to the administration of Festus. At long last, Paul would be freed, or at least his case would be brought up again. Or would Festus, like Felix, refuse to release the prisoner without payment of a bribe?

I think we may take for granted also that the soldiers to whom Paul had been chained during his long imprisonment were deeply interested in his fate. We are told nothing definite about Paul's influence upon his guards, but since all men from governors to slaves responded to the magnetism of his love of God and to them, it is not too presumptuous to assume that many of these guards were converted through the prisoner's preaching. The hard-faced soldier who led Paul into the courtroom where Festus was to rehear his case could very well have been offering silent petitions for his prisoner's welfare.

Paul saw the same familiar faces marked with the same lineaments of vehement hate; he heard the same cultured voices, shrill now with passion, accuse him of the same offenses and demand his death in the name of law and justice.

Porcius Festus listened with judicial calm while the prosecution shrilled and thundered, and eventually got itself slightly fouled up in the folds of its own oratory. Then he signaled the prisoner to speak in his own defense.

Paul answered with simplicity: **"Neither against the law of the Jews, neither against the temple, nor yet against Caesar have I offended any thing at all."** Thus he refuted the charges of heresy, sacrilege, and treason, which had been repeated.

Since the prosecution with all its vehemence had not been able to prove its charges, Festus would have been glad to dismiss the whole matter. But he didn't want to get off on the wrong foot with Jerusalem at the very beginning of his administration, so he sought to please the high priest's people with a proposal which, in his opinion, could do no harm to the prisoner.

Since Paul had a choice in the matter, Festus asked him whether he would be willing to go to Jerusalem for the continuing and conclusion of his trial.

Paul knew perfectly well that even if he reached Jerusalem alive some of these men before him would see to it that, barring a miracle, he would not leave Jerusalem alive, regardless of the court's verdict. His reply must have shocked Festus:

"I stand before Caesar's tribunal, and there ought my trial to be. To the Jews I have done no wrong, as thou knowest full well. If I am guilty, and have done anything worthy of death, I refuse not to die: but if the things whereof these men accuse me are nought, no man can give me up to them. *I appeal unto Caesar.*"

Paul would go to Rome, all right. He would go as the "guest" of the empire—in chains. He was remembering the words of the Lord: **"Be of good cheer, Paul: for as thou hast testified of me in Jerusalem, so must thou bear witness also at Rome."**

"Yea, my Lord," Paul's soul made answer now, "So shall I bear witness also at Rome—in chains. But Thou wilt make the fetters light, and the chains of my humiliation shall be the golden links that bind the world to Thee."

From the depths of shock, Festus began to experience gratitude to this extraordinary prisoner who had taken him off the hook by transferring his trial to the foot of Caesar's throne. Certainly the high priest and his brethren, whom the governor must needs keep "buttered up" could not hold him responsible for this turn of events.

Paul had exercised his prerogative as a Roman citizen to have his case transferred to the emperor's tribunal. Now he need only wait for the governor's hasty consultation with his council to make officially sure that the prisoner making such an appeal was neither a bandit nor a pirate caught red-handed. (Caesar, it seems, wouldn't have such before his throne!) This legal formality taken care of, Festus intoned the words: "**Hast thou appealed unto Caesar? Unto Caesar shalt thou go.**"

For the members of the Sanhedrin, the air had suddenly become clogged with the dust of frustration, and it was difficult for them to breathe.

On their way across the courtyard, as Paul was trying to match his short-legged stride to his guard's military pace, the soldier murmured, "Thank God, thou hast escaped their poisoned fangs, *Paul my brother!*"

Chapter Twenty-four

Porcius Festus was about to have company. Herod Agrippa II, king of Chalcis, was coming with his beautiful sister Bernice for a "state visit."

In case you too get a headache trying to unscramble the Herods: This Herod Agrippa II was the very last king named Herod. He was the son of Herod Agrippa I, who was the son of Aristobulus, the unfortunate prince who was killed by his father, Herod the Great. Thus we see that Agrippa II was the great-grandson of Herod the Great, that monarch who committed murder with magnificent abandon, disposing of wives, sons, or anybody else who happened to incur the suspicion of his twisted mind.

The last Herod grew up in Rome, as indeed did most of the other Herodian offspring. He grew up with Claudius Caesar, who owed his own accession to power in great measure to the young prince's father, Agrippa I. When Agrippa I died, the grateful Claudius had been ready to appoint the son to succeed him, even though Agrippa II was only seventeen years old. The emperor was talked out of that by counselors who pointed out that seventeen wasn't quite the ideal age for a man to become king of anything. So Agrippa Junior had to wait till he was twenty-one, and his Uncle Herod, king of Chalcis obligingly died and left a vacant throne. By that time, all Jewish royalty took for granted that they lived or died, reigned or were banished by the whims of Rome. Claudius Caesar appointed Herod Agrippa II king over Chalcis, and so he was.

Herod's sister Bernice was the widow of the king of Chalcis, who was also her uncle. Those Herodians were a badly mixed-up dynasty in a number of ways, apparently. History still buzzes with rumor about the relationship of Agrippa and Bernice because she left her second husband to return to her brother's home.

We wonder if the state visit of Agrippa and Bernice was as fraught with boredom as such modern tea parties seem to be, and if dignitaries of that day also got around to issuing joint communiques after they had listened to endless pretty speeches and reclined day after day at the banquet table.

Festus, reclining at table with his royal guests, observed a momentary flicker of boredom touch Agrippa's face as a naked dancing girl slithered in and began her sinuous gyrations. But after all, the host reminded himself wryly, what had he expected? Agrippa had been watching nude dancing girls at banquets ever since he was old enough to be invited, and this one wasn't nearly as sensational as the king's own cousin, Salome, whose performance had cost a holy man his head. The governor cast about in his mind for something that might interest his guest. "By the way, I have a prisoner whose case in intriguing. In fact, the man fascinates me."

"Political prisoner?" Agrippa asked.

"Well, yes and no. I thought so, at first. It seems he was unfinished business from Felix's administration; when he was recalled to Rome, he simply left the man in jail.

"Naturally, almost the first thing I did when I arrived was to go up to Jerusalem, and the first thing the temple authorities did when I got there was to begin clamoring for the death of this prisoner, Paul by name. I reminded them—tactfully, I hope!—that it is *not* the Roman way to hand a man over for execution without the formality of trial in a court of law where the accused has the opportunity to defend himself.

"The high priest and his people accompanied me back to Caesarea, so I arranged a hearing for the very next morning, and had the prisoner brought in to face them. I was prepared to hear charges of anything from brigandage through simple murder to insurrection, so you can imagine my astonishment when their accusations boiled down to nothing more heinous than points of difference in their religious superstition! It seems that the high priest insisted that someone named Jesus is dead, and Paul insisted with equal fervor that the same man is alive again.

"I think you can imagine my state of mind at being asked to render impartial judgment over such utter nonsense! So I asked Paul the prisoner whether he would be willing to go up to Jerusalem for a hearing, and—now comes the astounding part!—*he appealed to Caesar!* So now I have no alternative except to hold him here until I can arrange for his passage to Rome. Did you ever hear of such a thing?"

Agrippa applauded absently as the naked dancer finished her act. "For a thing like *that* a prisoner appeals his case to the Caesar? The man sounds delightfully mad; I'd like to meet him and hear him talk!"

Festus began to feel much better. The banquet was saved; in fact, the whole state visit might now turn out to be an exciting success. He applauded the dancer till he nearly blistered his palms while answering, "It shall be so. In fact, that will be tomorrow's order of business."

And so it came about once more that Paul the apostle witnessed to his Lord before people in high places: a king, a princess, a governor of a province, and top military and political figures in an important city.

It is likely that Paul's guard flashed discreet but admiring glances at the gorgeous Bernice as Festus launched into his little speech of explanation for the gathering. He emphasized again that both at Jerusalem and Caesarea the "multitudes" of the Jews had overwhelmed him with clamoring for Paul's death; that he himself had not been able to find anything to justify their demands, and was to send the prisoner to Rome only because he had appealed to Caesar. The problem of Festus was that though he was sending a prisoner to his "lord" to be judged, he couldn't figure out what technical charge to lodge against him. Now, this not only failed to make sense, in a way it was downright ludicrous!

(The audience silently sympathized with Festus in his plight, realizing that if this situation caught the whimsical Nero in a nastier mood than usual, the governor might lose not only his job, but his head as well.)

This was the reason, Festus continued, that he had ordered Paul to be brought out to be heard of them all. In particular he hoped that Agrippa, having heard the prisoner's testimony, could help to frame formal charges against him.

Festus bowed to his royal guests and sat down.

With a gesture of his jeweled hand, the last King Herod spoke to Paul the apostle. "You are permitted to speak for yourself."

Luke says, **Then Paul stretched forth the hand, and answered for himself.** By now, the soldier chained to Paul must have become so familiar with that sudden, eloquent "stretching forth of the hand" that he raised his own left hand automatically in unison.

Paul began his defense by courteously expressing pleasure at being allowed to present his case before one who was **"expert in all Jewish customs and questions."**

For all his Roman training, for all his Romanisms, Herod Agrippa II somewhere along the line had absorbed the traditions of his people. He knew the fierce hopes, the pathetic dreams of the Jews concerning the Hope of Israel, the Messiah, the Deliverer. The half-pagan Roman politician Agrippa smiled cynically at the idea of political freedom for Israel. The Jew Agrippa remembered the hidden hopes and dreams, and his soul warmed and surged in spite of itself as he listened to the words of the man Paul.

"After the most straitest sect of our religion, I lived a Pharisee...." Pharisee ... absolute, meticulous keeping of the Law. The Law ... God's thunder from the mountain, made articulate by the man Moses, carved on stone, written on parchment, etched on the heart of Israel.

"I AM THE LORD THY GOD.... THOU SHALT HAVE NO OTHER GODS BEFORE ME." The First Commandment. Agrippa winced; his mind fled through the Ten, seeking vainly for one he had *not* violated. He passed on through the lesser decrees till he approached the one forbidding incest. His mind tried to turn and flee without so much as looking, but was caught and chained and made to look. He stole a glance at his sister. Her face was very pale, and she seemed to be having a little difficulty in breathing.

"Alas!" Agrippa thought, "Could I bring again every

beast that has ever burned on Israel's altars, my soul would still be unclean."

The man with the shackled wrist continued, "**And now I stand and am judged for the hope of the promise made of God unto our fathers: Unto which promise our twelve tribes, instantly serving God day and night, hope to come. For which hope's sake, king Agrippa, I am accused of the Jews.**"

"Hope of the promise made of God unto our fathers. . . ." Unto *our* fathers. Agrippa was suddenly all Jew, his soul straining mightily against Caesar's leash. Back through the centuries he went, searching, searching furiously for the hand of prophecy stabbing the blackness with the promise of Hope. Moses, David, Isaiah who promised, "And there shall come forth a rod out of the stem of Jesse, and a Branch shall grow out of his roots." And Jeremiah, and Ezekiel. "But where are their prophecies now?" Agrippa thought bitterly, "For to us is left only the blackness of utter desolation, and the voice of Rachel wailing in the wilderness because her sons are dead!"

Again, the voice of Paul. "**Why should it be thought a thing incredible with you that God should raise the dead?**"

"Why is he wandering?" Agrippa asked himself petulantly, "What has the raising of the dead to do with Israel's lost Hope?"

The prisoner continued his story, telling of his enmity toward Jesus of Nazareth, and his frenzied persecution of the saints in Jerusalem. His zeal for persecuting and helping to kill Christians had reached beyond that city to others, even pointing toward Damascus. Armed with authority from the chief priests, he had started to Damascus to arrest and bring back—in chains—any followers of Jesus in the Syrian city.

Agrippa listened intently, his eyes wandering from the speaker's face to the eloquently gesturing hands, particularly the right hand. "Chains!" thought the king, "He went out to bind others with chains; now, he himself is bound, and when he lifts holy hands to God he also raises, perforce, the hand of a Gentile soldier. H-m-m, could that be the summation of the man's life?"

Paul's voice was saying, "**And I said, 'Who art thou, Lord?' and he said, 'I am Jesus whom thou persecutest. But** rise and stand upon thy feet: for I have appeared unto thee for this purpose, to make thee a minister and a witness both of these things which thou hast seen, and of those things in the which I will appear unto thee; delivering thee from the people, and from the Gentiles, unto whom I now send thee, to open their eyes, and to turn them from darkness to light, and from the power of Satan unto God, that they may receive forgiveness of sins, and inheritance among them which are sanctified by faith that is in me.' "

"Face down in the scorching sand, Saul, you have called Me Lord, and so I am. On your face you have worshiped, now stand and be ready for *work,* for that is why I have revealed Myself to you. From this hour forth, Saul, you are *My minister!*"

"Whereupon, O king Agrippa, I was not disobedient unto the heavenly vision, but . . . " Paul sketched his career . . . witnessing, preaching, reasoning, exhorting . . . first to the Jew, and then to the Gentile; laboring to the end that they should repent and turn to God, and then exhibit works that were proof of repentance.

Agrippa, listening to the man, noting his eloquence, his brilliance of mind, found himself suddenly wondering, "What would he have been if he *had* been disobedient to the heavenly vision? H-m-m, high priest, perhaps," then in a burst of cynical honesty, "Yes, indeed! A glittering worm—like *me!*"

Because he was a faithful and effective minister of the Lord Jesus, he said, the Jews (of the hierarchy) made one final, frenzied effort to kill him when they found him worshiping in the temple, but through God's help he had been snatched from their hands. He was still witnessing to the humble and the mighty, carrying the message of Moses and the prophets, namely that Christ should suffer and die, and that He would be the first to rise from the dead to bring immortal light to Israel His people, and to the Gentiles.

This almost casual statement that a dead man had come back to life was too much for the logical Roman mind of Festus. Torn between pity and amusement, he shouted, "Paul! You're completely out of your mind! You've read too much, you've studied too much, and you've done too much thinking during these long months in prison. It's been too much for your mind."

Paul bowed toward the governor, and answered, "No, your Excellency, I am not insane. I am giving a simple account of a historical fact which I am sure the king has heard of many times before, because all of these things were done in the open—none of it was hidden." He turned again to the king, and asked a searching question. "King Agrippa, do you believe the prophets?"

The answer of Agrippa the Jew was written in the tragic yearning in his eyes. Paul spoke the answer to his own question. "Yes. You do believe. I know it."

Abruptly, the puppet king stopped straining against Caesar's string. Once more, he was the suave politician, wondering with a certain uneasiness if he had made a fool of himself before Festus. He shrugged his shoulders and answered enigmatically, "You've nearly talked me into being a Christian!"

With that answer, Paul knew that this one was lost. He said sadly, "I would to God that not only you, O king Agrippa, but everyone else within the sound of my voice this day might be exactly as I am, except for this chain."

Agrippa rose, signifying that the hearing was ended. The governor and the princess, and all the other dignitaries followed him. And as they talked among themselves later they all agreed that this man to whom they had listened was certainly no criminal. In fact, the king went so far as to tell the governor that it was a shame that Paul had appealed to Caesar, because otherwise he could have been freed immediately.

Chapter Twenty-five

Paul and Aristarchus and Luke were about to take ship for the long, long journey to Rome. Paul went, of course, as a prisoner of the state, as, quite likely, did Aristarchus; but Luke simply paid his fare on the small merchant ship from Adramyttium, and went along.

With comfortable smugness we regard our jet aircraft and our gilded ocean liners, and it frightens us just a little even to look at pictures of the elongated tubs equipped with sails which the ancients used for sea travel. Of course, nineteen centuries from now people may wonder shudderingly how we brave pioneers of the twentieth century managed to get anywhere in our crude conveyances! But the hardy ancients got around, and probably were not particularly conscious of their deprivations—it merely took them longer than it does us, and they were less comfortable en route.

Festus delivered his Rome-bound prisoners into the custody of a centurion named Julius who was a part of the Augustan cohort stationed in Caesarea. The men of this cohort were Roman, as against the main body of troops which were Syrian. Julius might or might not have heard anything about the prisoner, Paul, whom he was to deliver into imperial custody, but it is certain he had no inkling that his life would be saved because of this man.

But as the little ship left the harbor at Caesarea and headed north along the coast to Sidon, the commander must have become very well acquainted with the apostle, because the very next day when they **touched at Sidon** he graciously allowed Paul shore leave to visit with friends who lived there. It is also possible, of course, that Festus had given orders to the centurion to show Paul every possible courtesy because this extraordinary prisoner was certainly no criminal.

When the ship left Sidon to set sail for **the coasts of Asia** (at whose ports she would call to discharge or pick up passengers and cargo as she made the run north to her home port of Adramyttium for the winter) the first contrary winds struck. They forced her to sail **under** [the lee of] **Cyprus**, passing that island on the east and north instead of sailing south and west of it as would have been normal procedure to reach the **coasts of Asia**.

The sailors, naturally familiar with the seas they navigated, took advantage of the current which runs in a north-westerly direction along the southern coast of Asia Minor and **sailed over the sea** [near the coasts] **of Cilicia and Pamphylia**. Thus they came to Myra, a seaport on the south coast of the province of Lycia. From Myra the master of the small vessel would shortly turn his craft northward to travel up the coasts of the province of Asia, so passengers wishing to reach Rome would have to find themselves another ship.

(By the way, all these comings and goings will make a great deal more sense if you will follow them on a map of "The Missionary Journeys of Saint Paul." You probably have one in the back of your Bible.)

In Myra's harbor, Julius found another and much larger ship from Alexandria in Egypt, heading for Rome with a cargo of wheat. Rome with its teeming population of slaves, politicians, and just plain loafers would have starved to death in short order had it not been for bread made from Egyptian grain; so these relatively large merchant vessels which sailed the Mediterranean between Alexandria and Rome were a very vital part of Roman life.

Since Myra is approximately due north of Alexandria, and Rome is very far west and north, the grain ship must have been forced off her course by the same contrary winds which forced the smaller coast-trading vessel to sail on the wrong side of Cyprus. Whatever the reason for her presence, she was there, and the captain must have been getting impatient to get going toward Rome with his precious cargo. It was fast getting on to that time of the year when sea voyages were hazardous in the extreme.

Either the ship already had a good-sized passenger list, or Julius had quite a collection of prisoners, because we find a little later that there were 276 people altogether on board.

The vessel put out from Myra for the run to Cnidus which was only 130 miles distant. They were either becalmed, or the winds were contrary, or both, for Luke says they **sailed slowly many days**. Again, the wind forced them south and a little west toward the island of Crete. Everybody on the ship must have been getting a little worried by that time. Many precious days had already been lost because of nonexistent or capricious winds, and their prospects of reaching Rome before winter were becoming very dim indeed. They worked their way gingerly around the promontory of Salmone at the east edge of the island and, thus protected from the hindering wind, sailed along the south coast of Crete till they came to the place called Fair Havens. In that safe harbor they anchored to wait for better sailing weather.

But the better sailing weather did not come, and the days were ticking off relentlessly. Luke says, **when sailing was now dangerous, because the fast was already now past, Paul admonished them** . . .

Naturally, the "fast" as such had nothing to do with the safety of an ocean voyage. This fast was observed on the tenth of the month Tisri, and corresponded to the end of September and the beginning of October, and this period marked the end of safe sea travel for the year. So, among the Jews it was proverbial that a sea voyage undertaken "after the fast" was fraught with danger.

"Paul admonished them." Paul was by this time a familiar figure to everyone aboard the ship. The fact that he, a prisoner, was allowed to give advice about the progress of the voyage indicates that he was respected by the ship's authorities, that is, the owner, the master, and the centurion. Paul's advice came partly from divine intimation and partly from rugged experience. This was *after* he had written those remarkable lines to his Corinthian converts: " . . . thrice I suffered shipwreck, a night and a day I have been in the deep . . . in perils of waters . . . in perils in the sea. . . ."

Paul told them that to continue the voyage would mean danger to the cargo, to the ship, and even to their very lives.

But the centurion, representing Roman military authority, seems to have had the final say in the matter, and he figured that the ship's owner and her master were in a position to know more about this problem than a man who dealt with religion and philosophy.

However, the ship's authorities did agree completely with Paul in one respect: They didn't figure it was safe to try to make it all the way to Rome, but they did want to try for a better harbor to winter in. Phoenix was such a place, and it was only about forty miles away to the north and west.

They would wait for better sailing weather, and then they would try for that larger and more comfortable harbor and there wait out the winter. Since their plan seemed so completely feasible—after all, when the weather turned decent they could make that forty miles in a few hours—it would seem that Paul's warning must have been more from divine revelation than from his hazardous experiences.

Eventually, **the south wind blew softly,** as Luke puts it, and if they traveled about five miles west they would head north, and that long-awaited wind would propel them into Phoenix. So they loosed from their moorings and put out to sea.

Things went beautifully—for the first five miles! Then, shortly after they left the protecting lee of the island and turned north, disaster struck.

If you have ever lived through a tornado, you will probably shudder as you read Luke's account of what happened next. If you have had the misfortune to be at sea when a hurricane struck, the next few verses may make you a little seasick. The gentle south wind was routed, flung back against its source by a typhonic northeast blast swooping down across the island of Crete. The sailors had a name for that wind—Euroclydon—and they knew it could spell disaster and death in short order.

Did they try frantically to head the vessel in again toward the shore of Crete, hoping for even scant shelter from the wind's fury? Perhaps so; Luke says, **And when the ship was caught and could not bear up into the wind** (literally, to look at, or "eye" the wind: an eye being painted on either side of the prow) the sailors abandoned their effort and let her drive before the blast.

A vessel with 276 humans aboard flipped around like a match stick as it was lifted to the crest of a house-high wave and then dropped into a trough just as deep. The prisoners of Julius, probably unaccustomed to sea travel, must have huddled in absolute terror in whatever shelter they could find while they screamed supplication to their gods, and wished that they had died on the solid ground of Judea or Galilee.

The wild wind drove the ship across the open water and under the lee of a small island called Clauda, some twenty-three miles from the point where the storm struck. The sailors took advantage of the comparatively sheltered area to brace themselves as best they could against disaster. First, they brought up the small boat (tender) which had been towing from the stern. This was no small accomplishment since the boat must have been heavy with water, and even in this sheltered spot the sea was far from calm. Next, they used **helps** to undergird the ship.

This procedure seems very strange to people accustomed to the mighty strength of modern vessels, but it was routine to the ancients. Their ships carried cables or chains that could be passed around the hull—at right angles to the ship's length—and drawn tight by means of pulleys or levers. This provided extra strength that helped to keep the timbers from pulling apart under the terrible stress of a storm.

Clauda was a very small island with no safe place for anchorage. They couldn't stop; they were still being blown by the wind, and they must have worked with frantic haste to do what must be done before they were blown beyond the scant shelter.

Unless they could do something to change their course, they would be blown pell-mell southwest toward Africa and would find themselves in the quicksands (Syrtis) in the bay off the northwest coast of Libya. Luke says they **strake sail,** that is, they lowered the heavy, cumbersome main sail with its accompanying gear, a feat that could hardly have been accomplished in the full fury of "Euroclydon." The small storm sail was run up, and the vessel was maneuvered into a position (called "lying to") for weathering a gale. This way they would drift, but not toward the African quicksands.

The storm still raged. The next day they began to lighten the ship by throwing unnecessary things overboard. The day after that even the passengers helped to throw out the heavy tackling. By this time the ship's owner was quite likely cursing himself for not having listened to the Jewish prisoner who had turned out to be a most excellent prophet. It seemed most unlikely now that his precious cargo of grain would ever reach the port of Rome; in fact, there seemed little in the way of a future for cargo, ship, or even people.

And when neither sun nor stars in many days appeared, Luke writes. Why was that significant? To us that would seem a dreary but otherwise unimportant aspect of the stormy weather. *A compass was unknown to the ships of that day*—they steered by sun and stars—so if "neither sun nor stars appeared" they had no idea where they were nor which way they were going! (If you should want to take time out at this juncture to preach yourself a sermon: Our world is in precisely the same predicament as that ship!) And still the storm was on them. So they abandoned hope—all but Paul.

Paul stood forth in the midst of them. . . . He would have had to cling to something solid to maintain his footing as the ship rolled and pitched. He raised his voice to be heard above the roar of the wind, and said, **"Sirs, ye should have hearkened unto me, and not have loosed from Crete, and to have gained this harm and loss. . . ."** Was he saying in effect, "See, *I told you so!*"? He was not. He was saying, "Since you see now that what I told you then has indeed come to pass, you may be more inclined to heed my words this time."

The forthcoming message of hope must have been very powerful indeed to penetrate—as it must—the numbness of despair and cold and fatigue, and the lesser but nagging misery of clothing saturated with salt water.

"Be of good cheer. . . ." Cheer up; stop worrying. Everything is going to come out all right. **"For there shall be no loss of any man's life among you, but of the ship."**

What must have been the reaction of the heathen sailors

to that one! "Hah! This screwball little Jew stands there, and when he opens his mouth wide enough to talk, the storm nearly blows his teeth down his throat. So he tells us to stop worrying because nobody is going to be lost. So he *did* foretell this trouble. So what? Who does he think he is, anyway?"

Paul's powerful voice still comes to them above the roar of the wind, **"For there stood by me this night the angel of God, whose I am, and whom I serve, saying, 'Fear not, Paul; thou must be brought before Caesar: and lo, God hath given thee all them that sail with thee.' Wherefore, sirs, be of good cheer: for I believe God that it shall be even as it was told me. Howbeit, we must be cast upon a certain island."** That was quite likely the first and only time that Paul preached a sermon on the deck of a storm-battered ship!

Who believed him? Luke and Aristarchus, without a doubt; the centurion and some of the soldiers, quite possibly. The rest must have been deeply impressed. The man had seen a vision from his God; and since he had foretold what was going to happen, maybe he *did* actually have something. It was fortunate that there was no modern psychiatrist aboard to explain that this unfortunate man was the victim of hallucinations induced by the horror of what he had experienced!

As far as anybody could see, there was not one shred of evidence to back up Paul's hopeful prophecy: The storm still raged, the ship was still battered, her timbers threatening to give way in spite of the "undergirding." Some writers who have gone into the matter most thoroughly are of the opinion that the ship had long since sprung a leak, and was in imminent danger of sinking.

How long it was between Paul's prophecy and the **fourteenth night** we are not told, but it cannot have been very long. Three days of the storm were accounted for before Luke notes, **And when neither sun nor stars in many days appeared** . . .

But on that fourteenth night about midnight, the sailors thought they detected signs of land. How? Certainly, they couldn't see! In all probability their sea-trained ears could detect the sound of waves pounding against a rocky shore. They **sounded** and found twenty-fathoms; a little later they sounded again, and it was fifteen. Pitch black; breakers roaring off a rocky coast, and they were drifting closer to it!

Orders were given to drop four anchors from the stern. The wind was from that direction, and if anchors had been dropped from the front part, the vessel might have been whipped around with such force that the anchor cables would have snapped and she would have been blown against the rocks. **They cast four anchors out of the stern, and wished for the day.** Land was so near, but it was a threatening land; would their anchors hold till daybreak?

It was at this juncture that the ship's crew decided to let down the boat (tender) over the side under pretense of letting anchors out of the forepart of the vessel. This was perfectly legitimate, inasmuch as it would have helped to further steady the ship. But that was not their intention: they were about to abandon ship and leave the hapless passengers to their fate. Paul knew what was in their minds. Whether he had heard them talking, or whether it was God-given intimation does not matter particularly; the important thing was that he knew. He turned to the centurion and the group of soldiers, and pointing to the sailors about to go over the side, said succinctly, **"Except these abide in the ship, ye cannot be saved."**

Julius did not waste time reminding the apostle of his promise from the angel. "Sever the ropes!" he ordered instantly, and it is doubtful that his men ever obeyed faster as they cut the ropes with their short, sharp swords and let the boat fall off into the sea.

Why didn't Paul keep quiet, confidently expecting God to keep His promises regardless of circumstances? For the same reason that he didn't sit quietly on the lap of God when he learned that the high priest's thugs were about to kill him. Certainly God would have kept His promise; but Paul knew that God's children are not to be presumptuous like a capricious child who decides to have his mother spoon-feed him because he knows she won't see him starve.

Along about that point, Roman military respect and admiration for Paul the prisoner must have changed to absolute awe: He not only had visions, he was also gifted with horse sense! (If the Romans ever used that term.) They were pretty much willing to turn things over to Paul.

The thoughts, reactions, or conversations of the crew members are not recorded for us, but one thing is quite completely evident: the only way to save their own skins now was to save everybody else's—by doing their work on the ship so long as she remained under them.

Their long ordeal was about over. When the new day arrived, they would know more clearly just what was before them. In the face of prolonged and overwhelming emotion, one does not notice the pangs of hunger, and so it must have been with all the people on board the ill-fated ship. While they waited for daybreak, Paul urged them to eat. He reminded them that this was the fourteenth day since they had taken food. He assured them again that all would be saved, and even without any injury whatever, **"For there shall not an hair fall from the head of any of you."** And they would need a good meal to strengthen them against whatever strenuous activity the new day might demand, **"For this is for your health."**

Heeding his own advice, Paul took bread, and after giving thanks to God, he broke the bread and began to eat.

The horror began to lift. A measure of cheerfulness returned to the others; they discovered that they also were hungry and they, too, began to eat. Perhaps some of them, besides Luke and Aristarchus, even gave thanks to Paul's God.

After they had eaten, they threw the cargo of wheat overboard. Certainly they knew by now that the ship would be lost, and so, naturally, would the wheat. The grain was water-soaked by then, and had settled to one side of the vessel because the fury of the storm had caused her to run practically on her side. With the holds emptied, the ship would come closer to being on even keel, and could be maneuvered more easily.

When daylight was fully upon them, the people on the ship looked long and earnestly at the coast before them, but there were no landmarks familiar even to the sailors.

But there was a **certain creek with a shore** as Luke puts it, describing a bay with a smooth beach. The seamen decided to maneuver their vessel into the opening of the bay and, aided by the violent thrust of the wind behind, beach her. So they—simultaneously no doubt—cut the anchor cables (since the ship would have no further need of anchors), loosed the paddle rudders, and hoisted the foresail. Thus, with the thrust of the wind, they **made toward the shore**.

But the **creek with a shore** (as they had thought it) proved to be a spot at the mouth of a tiny strait separating an islet (Salmonetta) from the mainland, hence the **falling into a place where two seas met** where they ran aground. The fore-part stuck fast and remained unmovable; the hinderpart, battered by the lashing waves, began breaking up.

The soldiers with visions of their prisoners swimming ashore and escaping, advised the centurion to settle the matter by killing them. Roman justice would not be served by killing a man who had saved the lives of all on board (by foiling the plans of the seamen for abandoning ship), Julius answered them; and if they killed any of the prisoners, they would have to kill all of them, even Paul. Then he gave the order that the prisoners who could swim should go first. Then, the ones who couldn't swim were to grab themselves boards, or broken pieces of the ship, and, clinging to these, make for the beach.

And so it was that every man of the 276 made it to safety.

Chapter Twenty-six

There must have been people back of the beach watching the death throes of the doomed ship and the frantic descent into the water of the men on board. Some of them quite likely waded as far out into the surf as they dared, to be ready to grab an exhausted swimmer or a terrified man whose fingers were frozen in shock to the edges of his board. Others scurried about to find enough dry wood to make a roaring bonfire, which must have been a little difficult because rain was falling.

The soaked and shivering refugees gathered around the fire, held out their hands to its comforting warmth, and began to realize that they were actually safe. Somebody asked a kindly native the name of his island (Paul had told them that they must be cast upon a certain *island,* remember?) and was told that it was Malta.

When Luke refers to the islanders as "barbarians," he is casting no aspersions whatever. People who were neither Greek nor Roman were classified as "barbarians," and these people were of Phoenician descent.

The islanders were still bringing wood for the fire. Paul, who was accustomed to doing practical things for others as well as for himself, promptly set about helping. He brought his **bundle of sticks** and placed them on the fire, and it was at that moment that a poisonous snake was aroused from its torpid state by the heat and struck at its ancient enemy, the hand of a man.

The watching natives, superstitious as all heathen are, looked at each other and wagged their heads as they saw the viper hang by its fangs in Paul's hand. Here, they told each other, undoubtedly was a murderer who thought he had escaped just punishment when the sea failed to kill him. But the viper was the tool of the gods to execute justice: This criminal would be dead in a matter of minutes.

Paul, with a jerk of his hand, shook the creature off into the fire. He smiled reassuringly at Luke the physician—whose medicines had all been lost, quite likely—and said, "Be of good cheer, my brother; no harm shall come of this, but rather good. Let us be grateful that this evil thing struck me instead of one of these gracious ones who are befriending us."

The men of the island continued to watch Paul closely. The poison was in his veins, it had to be, for with their own eyes they had seen the fangs embedded in his flesh. Why wasn't his arm beginning to swell? Paul continued to warm himself by the bright fire, and to talk with the people around him.

Grudgingly, the natives began to change their minds. But then, on the other hand, one argued, this stranger might be a little tougher than most humans, but he'd probably fall dead within a few minutes just the same. So they continued watching the apostle. Eventually they were convinced. This stranger was utterly impervious to the venom of a poisonous snake; therefore it was evident that he was *not* human, and the only logical conclusion was that he must be one of the gods. In great haste, a deputation set forth to inform Publius (who seems to have been the legate of the praetor of Sicily, to whom the province of Malta belonged) that they were being honored by the presence of a god.

Publius received the refugees with gracious hospitality and entertained them for three days. Paul undoubtedly lost little time in setting the islanders right concerning his status as a mere human being like themselves. He must, however, have told them about the power of God to perform miracles for His servants and through His servants. If Paul's God worked miracles for His own, would He also help an outsider? Publius's father was very ill with fever and dysentery in its severest form; would Paul help him? Paul went into the room where the elderly man lay, sick, weak, and with life and remaining strength being dissipated by the disease. The apostle prayed, and laid his hands on the sick man, and healed him.

Throughout the island the word spread fast: A shipwrecked stranger had been stranded on their island, and through his God he had a mysterious power to cure sickness. He had cured the father of Publius who would have died otherwise. He had shaken off a poisonous snake that struck him, paying little more attention to it than if it had been a gnat. First a trickle, then a stream of sick people came to Paul, and he healed them. For three months he brought the good news of God to a heathen people, and he demonstrated the love and the compassion of that God toward all people by healing the sick in His name.

How those people must have thanked God for the storm that had sent the luckless ship to their coast! They heaped love and honors upon Paul and Luke and Aristarchus, and when the time came for the beloved strangers to resume their voyage, they eagerly "loaded them down" with gifts of things which would be needed.

When the three months were past and good sailing weather had once again been ushered in, Julius the centurion found another ship of Alexandria which had wintered in the island. Luke with his curious habit of including seemingly unimportant details now and again, mentions that the ship's sign was Castor and Pollux. These twin deities, sons of Jupiter, were favorite gods with the ancient sailors, and must have been carved at the prow of many a ship.

If all the people from the wrecked ship took passage on this one, and if she had any passenger list of her own, she must have been a bit crowded. And we can well imagine that Publius and his father and many more of Paul's new friends and converts must have gathered at the dock to bid him Godspeed on his renewed journey to Rome.

The first port of call was Syracuse, east and north about eighty miles, and the most important city in the province of Sicily. They docked at Syracuse for three days, possibly unloading some cargo and passengers, and taking on more. Then they headed north toward Rhegium, swinging east to make a somewhat circuitous route (**fetching a compass**) in order to take advantage of better sailing conditions.

At Rhegium they waited over another day, hoping for better sailing weather, and when it came—a brisk south wind—it propelled them into Puteoli in good time—180 miles in about twenty-six hours. Puteoli was the port of Rome, so from there on in to the great metropolis the journey would be by land—and on foot. But the final leg of the journey was not quite yet, for Luke says, . . . **Puteoli, where we found brethren, and were desired to tarry with them seven days.**

The "brethren" of Puteoli, rejoicing in the fellowship of the Apostle to the Gentiles, hastily sent messengers to Rome to tell the believers there that Paul was on his way to them.

If Aquila and Priscilla were still living in Rome—and they probably were—the messengers sought them out and left the details with them. The word sped from home to home among the believers: At long last, the beloved apostle was coming to them. His visit would not be, as he had hoped, a long pause on his journey to Spain. It would be in Caesar's prison, and no man could tell what the time or what the outcome of that visit would be. Those who could get away from their work began making plans to start south on the way to meet Paul before he reached the city.

After the seven days' stopover in Puteoli, Julius with his prisoners and Luke and Aristarchus resumed their journey toward Rome. Their route was, for the most part, along the famous Appian Way, a road so well built that it shrugged off the centuries in a way that would be terribly distressing to our modern road builders who love to replace or relocate a highway before its concrete has time to harden.

At regular intervals the Appian Way was dotted with post stations which were for changing to fresh horses, and for travelers to refresh and rest themselves. There is nothing in modern life even vaguely corresponding to one of these post stations, unless it might be a huge motel complete with swimming pools, restaurants for every taste from hot dogs to caviar, and beautiful, beautiful bars where the traveler can find everything from beer to beautiful girls.

It was at one of these post stations, the Appi Forum,

forty-three miles out of Rome, that Paul was met by the first group of Christians from the city. Ten miles farther along at a station with the intriguing name of the Three Taverns the second group of believers met the party, and Paul's heart overflowed with love and gratitude. Here were people who had left their work to trudge the weary miles along the highway to welcome him, Christ's storm-battered, shipwrecked apostle chained to a Gentile soldier. They were not "ashamed of his chain," they loved him, and they dared to demonstrate that love publicly by going forth to meet Caesar's prisoner. Their presence told Paul that they were waiting and eager to join him in that battle for the conquest of Rome which would bring the matchless city and her empire to its knees at the foot of the Messiah's cross. Paul's war in Rome would not be a one-man war; he **thanked God, and took courage.**

Walking along the great highway, accommodating their footsteps to the soldiers' military stride, what joy there must have been, what talk to fill them in on the wild scenes in Jerusalem and his escape to Caesarea, of his long (and unjust) stay in prison, of the sea voyage and the storm and shipwreck, of the strange way God had worked to bring him to Rome. And there must have been singing, "in psalms and hymns and spiritual songs . . . making melody in their hearts to the Lord."

Romans traveling the Appian Way must have marveled. Here was a Jewish prisoner surrounded by a retinue suggestive of the followers of a conquering general, and yet there was certainly nothing of the military in the songs this group was singing. There was a haunting beauty about the music. The words they did not understand, of course, for these, being Jews, would sing in Hebrew; and what self-respecting Roman would stoop to learning Hebrew? And even though there was unbelievable joy on the face of the prisoner and of his followers, their music bespoke whispered sorrow. How were the bemused Romans to know that the cadence of Hebrew music was the sound of a river of sorrow cutting its path across the sands of time, a crimson river flowing with the blood of God's oppressed people—and God's only Son?

If the Romans passing by were wealthy aristocrats riding in their richly appointed litters borne by slaves, or if they happened to be politically important in the empire, they had much more serious matters to occupy the mind than dwelling upon the conduct of unknown Jews meeting a friend in chains. At the back of their minds was always dread of the dark caprice of an emperor who had already murdered his mother (whose intrigues had gotten him the job in the first place!) and who might demand a man's fortune, or his wife, or his life, according to the mood of the moment.

Into such a Rome came Paul the apostle and was, with other prisoners, delivered by the centurion Julius into the custody of Burrus, the Praetorian prefect, whose official duty it was to keep in custody all accused persons who were to be tried before the emperor.

It is quite likely that Julius had a very interesting private conversation with Burrus about one of the prisoners, a man named Paul, because Paul was not confined in the prison proper. With his ever-present soldier-guard, he was allowed to stay first in the home of a friend (some writers think it was the home of Aquila) and then in his own dwelling, rented for him no doubt by the generosity of his friends. This was **his own hired house,** as Luke expresses it. It does not take too much imagination to picture Luke and Aristarchus and possibly Aquila scurrying around the city to find a suitable place to rent for Paul.

In a new city Paul always preached first to the Jews, and Rome was no exception. But, being a prisoner he could hardly appear in their synagogue, so he sent for the **chief of the Jews,** that is, the most prominent members of the Jewish community in Rome. These did not reject Paul without a hearing. They listened courteously to his explanation of his presence among them as a prisoner of Caesar; they assured him that they had heard nothing unfavorable about him out of Judea (which was most extraordinary, considering the hatred of the temple hierarchy) but that on every side this "sect" was spoken against. They wanted to hear his opinion of it, so they made an appointment with him, and on the day indicated many of the Jews of Rome came to hear him.

Paul talked all day (**from morning till evening**) and the burden of his discourse was the same as it had been the very first time he preached after his conversion: Jesus of Nazareth is the Messiah. And as always, he used as his authority their Scriptures, "Moses and the prophets." And again as always, some believed but many did not.

This last account in the history of the Acts of the Apostles, of the gospel being preached to the sons of Israel only, ends with the foreboding, tragic words of Isaiah: "Go unto this people, and say, 'Hearing ye shall hear, and shall not understand; and seeing ye shall see, and not perceive: for the heart of this people is waxed gross, and their ears are dull of hearing, and their eyes have they closed; lest they should see with their eyes, and hear with their ears, and understand with their hearts, and should be converted, and I should heal them.' "

And this final rejection of Christ by His own brings this solemn and final pronouncement by His apostle: **"Be it known therefore unto you that the salvation of God is sent unto the Gentiles, and they will hear it!"**

Apparently his majesty, the emperor Nero was remarkably busy with murder and rape and writing poetry, as well as his responsibility for improving his singing voice, for two whole years were required for him to get around to reviewing the case of one, Paul, sent to him by Festus from Caesarea. It is interesting to speculate on Nero's reaction had he realized that this two years' dawdling across the stage of time was being strictly regulated by the God of the Jews in order that an inspired historian might write:

And Paul dwelt two whole years in his own hired house, and received all that came in unto him, preaching the kingdom of God, and teaching those things which concern the Lord Jesus Christ, with all confidence, no man forbidding him.

"But ye shall receive power after that the Holy Ghost is come upon you: and ye shall be witnesses unto me both in Jerusalem, and in all Judaea, and in Samaria, and unto the uttermost part of the earth."

Energized by the power of the Holy Spirit, they thrust their feet into dusty sandals and strode forth, out and out and ever out, carrying the glad tidings of Jesus Christ to the outside rim of the world.

What are *your* sandals doing on the top shelf of the closet?